Amiga
Machine Language

Dittrich

A Data Becker Book

Sixth Printing, 1991
Printed in U.S.A.
Copyright © 1988, 1989, 1990   Abacus Software, Inc.
1991   5370 52nd Street SE
                                      Grand Rapids, MI 49512

Copyright © 1987, 1988, 1989, 1990   Data Becker, GmbH
1991   Merowingerstraße 30
                                      4000 Deusseldorf, Germany

Every effort has been made to ensure complete and accurate information concerning the material presented in this book. However, Abacus Software can neither guarantee nor be held legally responsible for any mistakes in printing or faulty instructions contained in this book. The authors always appreciate receiving notice of any errors or misprints.

AmigaBASIC and MS-DOS are trademarks or registered trademarks of Microsoft Corporation. Amiga 500, Amiga 1000, Amiga 2000, Amiga, Graphicraft, Musicraft, Sidecar and Textcraft are trademarks or registered trademarks of Commodore-Amiga Inc. Seka assembler is a registered trademark of Kuma Corporation.

Dittrich, Stefan. 1959-
    Amiga Machine Language / Dittrich.
        p. cm.
    "A Data Becker book."
    ISBN 1-55755-025-5 : $19.95
        1. Amiga (Computer)--Programming.   2. Assembler language (Computer
program language)   3. Motorola 68000 (Microprocessor)--Programming.
I Title.
QA76.8.A177D58 1989   89-18497
005.265--dc20   CIP

Table of Contents

Preface

Machine language is the native language of the Amiga and allows the programmer to take complete advantage of the Amiga's capabilities and speed.

Programming the Amiga in machine language requires knowledge of the MC68000 processor and the internal characteristics of the Amiga. The large number of functions offered by the Amiga's operating system should be accessible and usable by the machine language programmer.

Accessing the Amiga's operating system has been difficult for the machine language programmer. The Amiga's documentation is written for the C-programmer, and is not much help to the machine language programmer. In this book we will introduce you to the Amiga's processor, the operating system and how to access them using machine language.

First we'll take a look at memory organization and the basic operations of the computer. Next we'll take a more detailed look inside the Amiga and its 68000 processor. Sample programs will allow you to program the Amiga's 68000 processor while learning about it.

After the tour of the 68000 processor we'll show you how you can create windows and menus. The sample programs will allow you to build a library of machine language routines. You can use these routines to create fast, user friendly, professional programs.

We hope you'll enjoy applying the knowledge you will soon gain from this book in your own programs and experiments.

Stefan Dittrich   Gummersbach April 1987

Chapter 1

Introduction

1. Introduction

Before you tackle machine language, you should take a closer look at several things that are vital to machine language programming.

1.1 Why machine language?

Machine language is actually the only language the MC68000 processor understands. All other languages, such as BASIC, Pascal or C, must first be translated (interpreted or compiled) into machine code. This process can take place either when the program is executed (the BASIC interpreter), or before program execution (the Pascal and C compilers).

Advantages   The great advantage of machine language over an interpreted and compiled program is machine language programs are faster. With an interpreter like BASIC, each line must first be interpreted before it is executed, which requires a great deal of time. A Pascal or C compiler translates the source code into machine language. This translation procedure does not produce programs that are as fast as a pure machine language program.

Another advantage machine language has over BASIC is that an interpreter is not needed for the execution of a machine language program.

Machine language can access all the capabilities of the computer since it is the language native to the computer. It is possible that machine language subroutines are required by a higher level language to access functions that aren't directly accessible by that language.

1.2 A look into the Amiga's memory

Before a machine language program can be written, you must know exactly what the program is required to do. You must also be aware of what resources are needed and available to achieve those goals. The most important of these resources is the memory in the Amiga.

1.2.1   RAM, ROM, hardware register

Random Access Memory, referred to as RAM, allows information to be placed in it and then withdrawn at a later time. This memory consists of electronic components that retain data only while the computer is turned on (or until a power-failure).

So that the computer is able to do something when it is first turned on, such as prompting for the WorkBench or Kickstart disk, a program has to remain in memory when the power is off. A memory type which can retain data without power is needed. This second memory type is known as ROM.

ROM

ROM stands for Read Only Memory, indicating that data can only be read from this memory, not written to it. The Amiga contains a ROM, that loads the Workbench or Kickstart disk into RAM. The first version of the Amiga did not contain the Kickstart in ROM.

PROM

One variation of ROM is the PROM, or Programmable Read Only Memory. This special type of ROM can actually be programmed once. Since it cannot be erased once programmed, it isn't encountered very often. More often you'll see EPROM's, or Erasable Programmable ROM's. These special chips, which can be erased with ultraviolet light, have a little window on the surface of the chip usually covered by tape.

EEROM

Although not available on the consumer market and much more expensive than RAM, the EEROM (Electrically Erasable ROM) offers another alternative to programmable ROM. These chips function like RAM, except that information is not lost when the power is turned off.

WOM   With the birth of the Amiga, another type of memory, WOM, was
                 created. This particular type of memory is Write Once Memory. The
                 Kickstart disk is read into this memory when the computer is first booted.
                 After this, no more data can be read into that memory. Actually this isn't
                 a completely new component, but simply RAM that is locked once data
                 has been read into it, after which the data can only be read from that
                 memory.

Registers   In addition to RAM and these variations of ROM there is another type of
                 memory situated between those two groups. This memory is connected to
                 the processor through a group of peripheral controllers. Thus it is com-
                 monly referred to as the hardware register, since the computer's hardware
                 is managed by this system. We'll go into greater detail on how to use
                 these hardware registers later in this book.

                 Let's take a closer look at the structure and use of the memory most
                 familiar to us all, RAM.

1.2.2   Bits, bytes, and words

Kilobyte   The standard size in which memory is measured is a kilobyte (Kbyte).
                 One kilobyte consists of 1024 bytes, not 1000 as you might expect. This
                 unusual system stems from the computer's binary mode of operation,
                 where numbers are given as powers of 2, including kilobytes.

                 To access a memory block of one kilobyte, the processor requires 10
                 connections which carry either one volt or zero volts. Thus $2^{10}=1024$
                 combinations or 1024 bytes of memory, are possible.

Byte   A byte, in turn, consists of yes/no, on/off information as well. A byte
                 can be one of 2^8 different values, and thus it can represent any one of
                 256 numbers. The individual numerical values that make up a byte,
                 which also are the smallest and most basic unit encountered in any com-
                 puter, are called bits (short for binary coded digit).

                 A 512 Kbyte memory, such as the Amiga's, contains $2^{19}=524288$ bytes
                 and 4194304 bits. It may seem unimaginable, but a memory of that size
                 has $2^{4194300}$ different combinations.

Word

Back to the basics...bits and bytes are sufficient to program an eight bit processor like the 6500, since it can work only with bytes. To program a 16/32 bit processor like the Amiga's MC68000, you'll need to know two new data forms: words, consisting of 16 bits (the equivalent of two bytes), and long words, which are 32 bits (the equivalent of 4 bytes or 2 words).

A word can be any number between 0 and 65536, a long word can be 0 to 4294967295. The MC68000 processor can process these gigantic numbers with a single operation.

Once in a while you need to use negative numbers as well as positive ones. Since a bit can only be 1 or 0 and not -1, an alternate system has been adopted. If a word is to have a specific sign, the highest value digit or 15th bit in the word (positions are always counted from zero) determines the sign of the word. With this method words can carry values from -32768 to +32768. One byte can range from -127 to +127. In a byte, the value -1 is given by $FF; in a word it's $FFFF, -2 is $FE ($FFFE), etc.

Let's stick with positive values for the time being, to aid in the visualization of a bit in relation to its bit-pattern. Machine language does not use the familiar decimal system. Instead, it commonly employs the binary as well as the octal and hexadecimal number systems.

1.2.3   Number systems

Let's take a look at the decimal system: its base number is 10. This means that every digit represents a power of 10. This means that the 246 represents $2*10^2+4*10^1+6*10^0$. The decimal system offers a selection of 10 characters, namely 0 to 9.

Binary

This procedure is different for the binary system. The binary system offers only two different characters: 1 and 0. Thus the system's base number is two. The decimal value of 1010 would therefore be:

```
1*2^3+0*2^2+1*2^1+0*2^0=2^3+2^1=8+2=10 (in the decimal system)
```

Generally binary numbers are identified by having a percentage symbol as a prefix. See if you can determine the decimal value of this number: %110010...

Well, did you get 50? That's the right answer. The most simple method to arrive at this result is to simply add up the values of the digits that contained a 1. The values of the first eight digits are as follows:

```
digit       8    7    6    5    4    3    2    1
value     128   64   32   16    8    4    2    1
```

Octal

The octal system, whose base is eight, is similar. The character set consists of the numbers 0 to 7. The decimal equivalent of the octal number 31 is: $3*8^\wedge1+1*8^\wedge0=25$. However, the octal system isn't nearly as important as the next one...

The base number of the hexadecimal system is 16, and its character set ranges from 0 to F. Thus, A would be the equivalent of a decimal 10, and F would be 15. The dollar sign ($) indicates a hexadecimal number. The binary and hexadecimal systems are the most important numerical systems for assembly language programming.

Hex

The hexadecimal representation of a byte ranging from 0 to 256 always has two digits: $00 to $FF. A word ranges from $0000 to $FFFF and a long word from $00000000 to $FFFFFFFF.

It is quite easy to convert binary numbers into hexadecimal: simply split up the binary number into groups of four digits. Each of these groups of four digits then corresponds to one hexadecimal digit. Here's an example:

```
binary number   %110011101111
split up         %1100 %1110 %1111
result           $C   $E   $F
thus:            %110011101111 = $CEF
```

The opposite operation is just as easy...

```
hexadecimal      $E30D
split up         $E    $3    $0    $D
result           %1110 %0011 %0000 %1101
thus:            $E30D=%1110001100001101
```

This method can also be used to convert binary into octal and vice versa, except that groups of three digits are used in that case.

```
octal number    7531
split up        7      5      3      1
result          %111   %100   %011   %001
thus:           octal 7531=%111101011001
```

This binary number can then be converted into hexadecimal, as well:

```
binary number    %111101011001
split up         %1111 0101 1001
result           $F      $5       $9
thus:            octal 7531 = $F59
```

The following calculation can then be used to convert the number into the familiar decimal system:

```
hexadecimal      $F59
split up         $F      $5       $9
result           15*16^2 +5*16 +9
thus:            $F59 = 3929 decimal
```

Although these conversions are quite simple, they can get to be rather annoying. Many assemblers can ease this task somewhat: they allow you to enter a value with '?' upon which it returns the value in decimal and hexadecimal forms. There are even calculators that perform number base conversions.

Often this conversion has to be performed in a program, for instance when a number is entered by the user and then processed by the computer. In this case the number entered, being simply a combination of graphic symbols, is evaluated and then usually converted into a binary number, in effect, a word or a long word.

This process is often required in reverse order, as well. If the computer is to display a calculated value in a specific number system, it must first convert that number into a series of characters. In a later chapter you will develop machine language routines to solve these problems. You can then use these routines in your own programs. First you still have to cover some things that are fundamental to machine language programming on the Amiga.

1.3 Inside the Amiga

In order to program machine language, it is not sufficient to know only the commands of the particular processor, one must also have extensive knowledge of the computer being programmed. Let's take a good look inside the Amiga.

1.3.1   Components and libraries

The Amiga is a very capable machine, due to the fact that there are components that do a large part of the workload, freeing up the 68000 processor. These are referred to as the "custom" chips, which perform various tasks independently of the 68000 processor.

Custom chips   This task force is comprised of three chips, whose poetic names are Agnus, Denise and Paula. The main task of Agnus, alias blitter, is the shifting of memory blocks, which is helpful for operations such as quick screen changes. Denise is responsible for transferring the computer's thoughts onto the screen. Paula's tasks consist of input/output jobs, such as disk operation or sound.

These chips are accessed by the processor through several addresses starting at $DFF000, which are also known as the hardware registers (you'll find more detailed information about the registers in the corresponding chapter). To simplify the otherwise rather complicated procedure of utilizing these chips, several programs have been included in the Kickstart and Workbench libraries. These programs can be called by simple routines and then take over the operation of the respective chips.

If only these library functions are used to program the Amiga, the parameters are the same, regardless of the language used. Only the parameter notation differs from language to language. BASIC is an exception in this respect, since its interpreter translates the program calls, which is why you don't need to know how the Amiga executes these functions in order to use them.

The library functions are written in machine language and are thus closely related with your own machine language programs. Actually you could do without the library programs and write all of the functions yourself.

However, the incredible workload of this task is so discouraging, that you'd rather stick with the library functions.

1.3.2   Memory

First let's look at the RAM of the Amiga 1000. The standard version of this computer has over 512 Kbytes of RAM, ranging from the address $00000 to $7FFFF, or 0 to 524287. If the memory is expanded to one megabyte, the first 512K still starts at address $000000 however the start of anything greater than 512K can go anywhere in the address space between $200000 to $9FFFFF. With the release of AmigaDOS 1.2, the Amiga figures out where to put memory expansion by using a special 'Autoconfig' scheme. This allows you to add memory and I/O without worrying about addresses and dip switches.

Chip RAM

The chips that support the Amiga's processor access RAM almost totally independently and thus ease the workload of the processor. However, there is a drawback: these chips can only access the first 512K bytes of RAM. Thus, graphics and sound data handled by these chips <u>must</u> be stored in this memory range. Because of this, that memory range is referred to as *chip* RAM.

Fast RAM

The counterpart to chip RAM is the remaining RAM which, if the computer is equipped with it, begins at $200000. Since only the processor itself has access to this part of memory it is known as *fast* RAM.

Here's an overview of the Amiga's memory :

```
$000000-$07FFFF        chip RAM
$080000-$1FFFFF        reserved
$200000-$9FFFFF        potential fast-RAM
$A00000-$BEFFFF        reserved
$BFD000-$BFDF00        PIA B (even addresses)
$BFE001-$BFEF00        PIA C (odd addresses)
$C00000-$DFEFFF        reserved for expansion
$DFF000-$DFFFFF        custom chip registers
$E00000-$E7FFFF        reserved
$E80000-$EFFFFF        expansion ports
$F00000-$F7FFFF        reserved
$F80000-$FFFFFF        system ROM
```

Since the Amiga is multi-tasking, when a program is loaded into memory, it is simply loaded into any memory location. The memory range thus occupied is added to a list of occupied memory and the memory range is then considered barred from other uses. If another program is loaded, which is quite possible with the Amiga, it is read into another memory location which is then marked on the occupied list. If the first program should require additional memory, to use a text buffer for example, that memory first has to be reserved. Otherwise another program could accidentally be loaded into the memory needed for this task.

What's interesting about this procedure is that when the first program loaded has ended, the memory occupied by it is freed for further use. As a result, RAM is then chopped up into occupied and free parts, which are no longer related to each other. The Amiga can still utilize these chunks of memory as if they were one continuous chunk. After all, parts is parts. An example of this is the dynamic RAM disk which is always available under the name RAM:.

This RAM disk is actually quite a phenomenon, since it is always completely filled. If a program is erased from RAM disk, the memory allocated to that program, regardless of its location and structure, is given back to the system. Thus, if you reserve and fill 100 Kbytes of memory, it would be quite possible that the 100 Kbytes actually consist of various pieces of memory independent of one another. You never notice this since the Amiga automatically corrects the difference between apparent and actual memory.

1.3.3   Multi-tasking

The Amiga is truly an amazing machine, being capable of doing several things at one time. A red and white ball might be bouncing around in one window while you're working on text in another window and watching a clock tick away in a third.

At least that's the impression most people get when they receive their first Amiga demonstration. However, there is a catch to this: even the Amiga has only one processor, which can really only do one thing at a time.

The tricky part is when more than one program is running, each program is executed part by part, and the Amiga is constantly switching from one program back to the other program. In the example above, the ball would first be moved by one pixel, then the processor would check for a text entry and if necessary display it, after which it would move the clock's second hand. This procedure would be repeated over and over, as the three programs are executed together. The problem is, that the greater the workload on the processor, the slower things happen. Thus, programs run slower during heavy multi-tasking.

Tasks

Each of these jobs that the Amiga has to execute are commonly referred to as tasks...thus, multi-tasking. During multi-tasking, each task is assigned a special time segment during which that particular task is executed. These time segments can be controlled, so that more time-consuming programs can be allotted somewhat more processing time.

The programmer actually doesn't need to know how this time slicing works. You can write a program without paying any attention to multi-tasking and then run it simultaneously with another program running in the background. The only restriction is that you'll have to start the program either from the CLI with 'run', or from the Workbench. If you execute the program from the CLI by simply typing its name, the processor allots all the time it can get from the CLI to that program, until the execution is complete. Starting the program with 'run' frees the CLI for other uses while the program is being executed.

There is another restriction regarding multi-tasking that applies to assembler programmers. Aside from the use of extra memory, which must first be reserved, the hardware registers should not be directly accessed. Instead, the library functions should be used. The reason for this is quite simple:

Should you, for instance, specify the printer port as the input line and are reading data in, another task might suddenly think it's supposed to be printing. The line would thus be switched to output and data would be written out. After this, your program would try to read more data in, which would not be possible.

This is an oversimplified example, but it points out the problem nevertheless. In real programming situations the effects of multiple direct programming of the hardware registers can be much more catastrophic. If your program still needs to access the hardware registers directly (which can have some advantages), then make sure that the program always runs by itself.

Chapter 2

The MC68000 processor

2. The MC68000 processor

The Amiga's MC68000 processor is a 16/32 bit processor, which means that while it can process data of 32 bits, it "only" has a 16 bit data bus and a 24 bit address bus. Thus, it can access 2^24=16777216 bytes (or 16 Mbytes) of memory directly.

7.1 megaherz   The Amiga 68000 processor, running at 7.1 megaherz, is quite fast, which is required for a computer with a workload as heavy as the Amiga's. The Amiga also possesses a number of custom chips that greatly ease the workload of the processor. These custom chips manage sound, in/output, graphics and animation, thus freeing the processor for calculations.

2.1 Registers

In addition to the standard RAM, the processor contains internal memory called *registers* There are eight data registers (D0-D7), eight address registers (A0-A7), a status register (SR), two stack pointers, a user stack pointer, a system stack pointer (USP and SSP) and the program counter (PC).

Register Sizes   The data registers, the address registers, and the program counter are all 32 bits, while the status register is 16 bits. These registers are located directly in the processor so they aren't accessed the same way memory would be accessed. There are special instructions for accessing these registers.

Data Registers   The data registers are used for all kinds of data. They can handle operations with bytes (8 bits), words (16 bits) and long words (32 bits).

Address Registers   The address registers are used for storing and processing addresses. This way they can be used as pointers to tables, in which case only word and long word operations are possible.

Stack pointer   The address register A7 plays a special role: this register is utilized as the Stack Pointer (SP) by the processor, and thus is not recommended for normal use by the programmer. Which of the two possible stacks is being pointed to depends on the present mode of the processor, but more about that later.

This stack, to whose actual position the stack pointer is pointing, is used to store temporary internal data. The stack works similar to a stack of notes on your desk: the note that was added to the stack last is the first one to come off of the stack. This type of stack is known as LIFO (Last In, First Out). There is another type of stack, the FIFO (First In, First Out) which is not used by the processor itself.

How these registers and the SP can be manipulated, or how to work with the stack, is presented in the next chapter. Let's continue with the registers for now.

Status Register   The Status Register (SR) plays an important role in machine language programming. This 16-bit quanity (word) contains important information about the processor status in 10 of its bits. The word is divided into two bytes, the lower byte (the user byte) and the upper byte (the system byte). The bits that signify that certain conditions are referred to as flags. This means that when a certain condition is present, a particular bit is set.

The user byte contains five flags, which have the following meanings:

Bit	Name	Meaning
0	(C, Carry)	Carry bit, modified by math calculations, and shift instructions.
1	(V, Overflow)	Similar to carry, indicates a change of sign, in other words, a carry from bit six to bit seven.
2	(Z, Zero)	Bit is set when the result of an operation is zero.
3	(N, Negative)	Is set when the result of an operation is negative.
4	(X, Extended)	Like carry, is set for arithmetic operations,
5-7		not used

The system byte contains five significant bits:

Bit	Name	Meaning
8	I0	Interrupt mask. Activates interrupt levels
9	I1	0 to 7, where 0 is the lowest and 7 is the
10	I2	highest priority.
11		not used
12		not used
13	(S, Supervisor)	This bit indicates the actual processor mode (0=User, 1=Supervisor mode).
14		not used
15	(T, Trace)	If this bit is set, the processor isin single step mode.

Here's an overview of the status word:

```
bit :  15 14 13 12 11 10  9  8  7  6  5  4  3  2  1  0
name:   T  -  S  -  - I2 I1 I0  -  -  -  X  N  Z  V  C
```

Don't let the new terms, like mode and interrupt confuse you. We'll talk about these in greater detail in the chapter dealing with the operating conditions of the processor.

2.2 Addressing memory

In the standard Amiga 500's and 1000's the processor has over 512 Kbytes of RAM available. The Amiga 2000 has one megabyte of RAM that can be accessed by the processor. How does the processor access all this memory?

If you're programming in BASIC you don't have to worry about memory management. You can simply enter MARKER%=1, and the value is stored in memory by the BASIC interpreter.

In assembler, there are two ways of accomplishing this task:

1)   Store the value in one of the data or address registers, or

2)   Write it directly into a memory location.

To demonstrate these two methods let's get a little ahead and introduce a machine language instruction, which is probably the most common: MOVE. As its name states, this instruction moves values. Two parameters are required with the instruction: source and destination.

Let's see what the example from above would look like if you utilize the MOVE instruction...

```
1)  MOVE #1,D0
```

This instruction moves the value 1 into data register D0. As you can see, the source value is always entered before the destination. Thus, the instruction MOVE D0,#1 is not possible.

```
2)  MOVE #1,$1000
```

deposits the value 1 in the memory location at $1000. This address was arbitrarily chosen. Usually addresses of this form won't be used at all in assembler programs, since labels that point to a certain address are used instead. Thus, the more common way of writing this would be:

```
...
MOVE #1,MARKER

...
MARKER:DC.W 1
```

These are actually two pieces of a program: the first part executes the normal MOVE instruction whose destination is 'MARKER'. This label is usually defined at the end of the program and specifies the address at which the value is stored.

The parameter DC.W 1 is a pseudo-op, a pseudo operation. This means that this isn't an instruction for the processor, but an instruction for the assembler. The letters DC stand for 'DeClare' and the suffix .W indicates that the data is a Word. The other two suffix alternatives would be .B for a Byte (8 bits) and .L for a Long word (32 bits).

This suffix (.B .W or .L) is used with most machine language instructions. If the suffix is omitted, the assembler uses .W (word) as the default parameter. If you wanted to use a long word, you'd use an instruction that looks something like this: MOVE.L #$12345678,D0 whereas an instruction like MOVE.B #$12,D0 would be used for a byte of data. However, with this instruction there's one thing you must be aware of...

Caution: If the memory is accessed by words or long words, the address must be even (end digit must be 0,2,4,6,8,A,C,E)!

Assemblers usually have a pseudo-op, 'EVEN' or 'ALIGN', depending on the assembler, that aligns data to an even address. This becomes necessary in situations similar to this:

```
    ...
VALUE1:     DC.B 1
VALUE2:     DC.W 1
```

If the VALUE1 is located at an even address, VALUE2 is automatically located at an odd one. If an ALIGN (EVEN) is inserted here, a fill byte (0) is inserted by the assembler, thus making the second address even.

```
    ...
VALUE1:     DC.B 1
ALIGN
VALUE2:     DC.W 1
```

Back to the different ways of addressing. The variations listed above are equivalent to the BASIC instruction MARKER%=1 where the % symbol indicates an integer value.

Let's go a step further and translate the BASIC instruction MARKER%=VALUE% into assembler. You've probably already guessed the answer, right?

```
            MOVE VALUE,MARKER
            ...
            ...
MARKER:         DC.W 1
VALUE:          DC.W 1
```

In this case, the contents in the address at VALUE are moved into the address at MARKER.

With the help of these simple examples, you've already become familiar with four different ways of addressing, in other words, ways that the processor can access memory. The first is characterized by the number sign (#) and represents a direct value. Thus, this method is also known as *direct addressing*, and is legal only for the source parameter!

A further method in which a direct address (in our case, 'MARKER' and 'VALUE') can be specified, is known as *absolute addressing*. This method is legal for the source parameter as well as for the destination parameter.

This method can be divided into two different types, between which the programmer usually doesn't notice a difference. Depending on whether the absolute address is smaller or larger than $FFFF, in other words if it requires a long word, it is called *absolute long addressing* (for addresses above $FFFF) or otherwise *absolute short addressing*. The assembler generally makes the distinction between these two types, and thus only general knowledge of absolute addressing is required.

The fourth method of addressing that you've encountered so far is known as *data register direct*. It was the first one introduced (MOVE #1,D0) in conjunction with direct addressing, the only difference being that this type accesses a data register (such as D0).

These four methods aren't the only ones available to the 68000 processor, in fact there are a total of 12. One other variation called *address register direct*, is almost identical to data register direct, except that it accesses the address register instead of the data register. Thus, you can use MOVE.L #MARKER,A0 to access address register A0 directly.

You now know of five ways to address memory with which quite a bit can be accomplished. Now, let's tackle something more complicated and more interesting.

Let's take another example from BASIC:

```
10      A=1000
20      POKE A,1
```

In this example the first line assigns the value 1000 to the variable A. This can be done in assembler as well: MOVE.L #1000,A0. In the assembler version the absolute value of 1000 is stored in the address register A0.

Line 20 doesn't assign a value to the variable A itself, but rather to the memory location at the address stored in A. This is an indirect access, which is quite easy to duplicate in assembler:

```
MOVE.L  #1000,A0      ;bring address in A0
MOVE    #1,(A0)       ;write 1 into this address
```

The parentheses indicate an addressing method known as *address register indirect*. This method works only with address registers, since a 'data register indirect' does not exist.

There are several variations of this method. For instance, a distance value can be specified, which is added to the address presently located in the address register before the register is actually accessed. The instruction MOVE #1,4(A0), if applied to the example above, writes the value 1 into the memory cell at 1000+4=1004. This distance value can be 16 bits long and can be positive or negative. Thus, values from -32768 to +32768 are accepted. This specific variation of addressing is called *address register indirect with a 16 bit displacement* value.

There is another very similar variation: *address register indirect with an 8 bit index* value. While this variation is limited to 8 bits, it also brings another register into play. This second register is also a distance value, except that it is a variable, as well.

We'll try to clarify this with an example. Let's assume that a program includes a data list that is structured like this:

```
          ...
RECORD:       DC.W 2    ;number of entries-1
        DC.W 1,2,3      ;elements of list
```

We'll use MOVE.L #RECORD,A0 to load the list into the address register A0. Then you can use MOVE (A0),D0 to pull the number of elements in the list into the data register. To access the last element of the list only one instruction is needed. The whole thing looks something like this:

```
        CLR.L   D0              ;erase D0 completely
        MOVE.L  #RECORD,A0      ;address of list in A0
        MOVE    (A0),D0         ;number of elements-1 in D0
        MOVE    1(A0,D0),D1     ;last element in D1
        ...
RECORD: DC.W 2                  ;number of entries-1
        DC.W 1,2,3              ;elements of list
```

This last instruction accesses the byte that is located at 1+A0+D0, in other words, the record +1 where the data begins plus the contents of D0 (in this case 2).

This method of accessing is very useful. It works exquisitely for the processing of tables and lists, as the example demonstrates. If no distance value is needed, simply use a distance value of zero, which some assemblers automatically insert as the default value if, for instance, only MOVE (A0,D0) is entered.

The latter two methods have a third variation, which has its own characteristic trait. It doesn't utilize an address register, but uses the Program Counter (PC) instead. The *program counter with displacement* method proves useful when a program must function without any changes in all address ranges. The following two statements (in the 15 bit limits) have the same effect:

```
MOVE    MARKER,D0
```

and

```
MOVE    MARKER(PC),D0
```

This method is actually rather imprecise, since the first instruction specifies the actual address of the marker with MARKER, while the second line specifies the distance between the instruction and the marker. However, since it would be quite cumbersome to constantly calculate the distance, the assembler takes this task off our hands and calculates the actual value automatically.

Let's examine the difference between the two instructions. In a program they'll accomplish the same thing, although they are interpreted as two completely different things by the assembler. You'll assume a program begins at the address $1000 and the marker is located at $1100. The generated program code then looks something like this:

```
$001000        30 39 00 00 11 00       MOVE    MARKER,D1
```

or

```
$001000        30 3A 00 FE             MOVE    MARKER(PC),D1
```

As you can see, the generated code of the second line is two bytes shorter than the first line. In addition, if you were to shift this code to the address $2000, the first version still accesses memory at $1100, while the second line using the PC indirect addressing accesses memory at $2100 correctly. Thus, the program can be transferred to almost any location.

This, then, is *program counter with 16 bit diplacement* value. As we mentioned, there is also *program counter with an 8 bit index* value, which permits a second register as a distance value, also known as an offset.

There are two more addressing modes left. These two are based on indirect addressing. They offer the capability of automatically raising or lowering the address register by one when memory is accessed with address register indirect.

To automatically increase the register, you'd use *address register indirect with post-increment*. The address register raises this by the number of bytes used AFTER accessing memory. Thus, if you write

```
MOVE.L #1000,A0
MOVE.B #1,(A0)+
```

the 1 is written in the address 1000 and then A0 is raised by one. Instructions like this are very helpful when a memory range is to be filled with a specific value (for instance when the screen is cleared). For such purposes the instruction can be placed in a loop...which we'll get to later.

The counterpart to post-increment is *address register indirect with pre-decrement*. In this case the specified address register is lowered by one BEFORE the access to memory. The instructions

```
MOVE.L #1000,A0
MOVE.B #1,-(A0)
```

writes 1 in the address 999, since the content of A0 is first decremented and the 1 is written afterwards.

These two methods of addressing are used to manage the Stack Pointer (SP). Since the stack is filled from top to bottom, the following is written to place a word (s.a. D0) on the stack:

```
MOVE.B D0,-(SP)
```

and to remove it from the stack, again in D0:

```
MOVE.B (SP)+,D0
```

This way the stack pointer always points to the byte last deposited on the stack. Here, again, you'll have to be careful that an access to the stack with a word or a long word is always on an even address. Thus, if you're going to deposit a byte on the stack, either use a whole word or make sure that the byte is not followed by a JSR or BSR. The JSR or BSR instructions deposit the addresses from which they stem on the stack in the form of a long word.

In the code above, the SP is generally replaced by the address register A7 in the program code, since this register is always used as the SP. Thus, you can write A7 as well as SP, the resulting program is the same. However, we recommend the use of SP, since this makes the code somewhat easier to read. After all, quite often you'll want to employ your own stacks, in which case the difference between the processor stack and your own stacks become very important.

These are the 12 ways of addressing the MC68000 processor. Here's a summary:

No.	Name	Format
1	data register direct	Dn
2	address register direct	An
3	address register indirect	(An)
4	address register indirect with post-increment	(An)+
5	address register indirect with pre-decrement	-(An)
6	address register indirect with 16 bit displacement	d16(An)
7	address register indirect with 8 bit index value	8(An,Rn)
8	absolute short	xxxx.W
9	absolute long	xxxxxxxx.L
10	direct	#'data'
11	program counter indirect with 16 bit displacement	d16(PC)
12	program counter indirect with 8 bit index value	d8(PC,Rn)

The abbreviations used above have the following meanings:

An	address registers A0-A7
Dn	data registers D0-D7
d16	16 bit value
d8	8 bit value
Rn	register D0-D7, A0-A7
'data'	up to a 32 bit value, (either .B .W or .L)

These are the addressing modes used by the 68000 processor. The bigger brother of this processor, the 32 bit MC68020, has six more methods which we won't discuss here.

Next, you're going to see under what conditions the processor can operate.

2.3 Operating modes

In the previous section about registers you encountered the Status
Register (SR). The individual bits of this register reflect the present
operating condition of the processor. You differentiated between the
system byte (bits 8-15) and the user byte (bits 0-7). Now, let's take a
closer look at the system byte and its effects upon the operation of the
processor.

2.3.1   User and supervisor modes

Isn't is rather strange that the processor classifies you either as a 'user' or
a 'supervisor'? Both of these operating modes are possible, the user mode
being the more common mode. In this mode it is impossible to issue
some instructions, and that in your own computer!

Don't worry, though, you can get around that, as well. The Amiga's
operating system contains a function that allows us to switch the
processor from one mode to the other.

The mode is determined by bit 13 of the status register. Usually this bit
is cleared (0), indicating that the processor is in user mode. It is possible
to write directly into the status register, although this is a privileged
instruction that can only be executed from the supervisor mode. Thus,
this instruction could only be used to switch from the supervisor mode
into the user mode, by using AND #$DFFF,SR to clear the supervisor
bit. However, it is quite preferable to let the operating system perform the
switch between these two modes.

Now what differentiates these two modes in terms of their application?

Well, we already mentioned the first difference: some instructions, such as
MOVE xx,SR, are privileged and can only be executed from the supervisor
mode. An attempt to do this in the user mode would result in an exception and interruption of the program. Exceptions are the only way of
switching to the supervisor mode, but more about that later.

A further difference is in the stack range used. Although A7 is still used
as the stack pointer, another memory range is used for the stack itself.
Thus, the SP is changed each time you switch from one mode to the

other. Because of this you differentiate between the User SP (USP) and the Supervisor SP (SSP).

Accessing memory can also depend on these two modes. During such accessing, the processor sends signals to the peripheral components informing them of the current processor mode. This way a 68000 computer can protect (privilege) certain memory ranges so they cannot be accessed by the user.

In the supervisor mode it is possible to execute all instructions and access all areas of memory. Because of this, operating systems usually run in the supervisor mode. This is accomplished through the use of exceptions.

2.3.2   Exceptions

Exceptions are similar to interrupts on 6500 computers. This allows stopping a program, running a sub-program, and then restarting the stopped program. When an exception occurs the following steps are taken:

1)   The status register is saved
2)   The S bit in the SR is set (supervisor mode) and the T bit is cleared (no trace)
3)   The program counter and the user SP are saved
4)   The exception vector, which points to the needed exception routine, is retrieved
5)   The routine is executed

The vectors mentioned, which contain the starting addresses for the various routines, are located at the very beginning of the memory. Here's an overview of the vectors and their respective addresses:

Number	Address	Used for
0	$000	RESET: starting SSP
1	$004	RESET: starting PC
2	$008	bus error
3	$00C	address error
4	$010	illegal instruction
5	$014	division by zero
6	$018	CHK instruction
7	$01C	TRAPV instruction
8	$020	privilege violation
9	$024	trace
10	$028	Axxx-instruction emulation
11	$02C	Fxxx-instruction emulation
	$030-$038	reserved
15	$03C	uninitialized interrupt
	$040-$05F	reserved
24	$060	unjustified interrupt
25-31	$064-$083	level 1-7 interrupt
32-47	$080-$0BF	TRAP instructions
	$0C0-$0FF	reserved
64-255	$100-$3FF	user interrupt vectors

The individual entries in the table above need detailed explanation. So let's go through them one by one...

RESET: starting SSP

At reset, the long word stored at this location is used as the stack pointer for the supervisor mode (SSP). This way you can specify the stack for the RESET routine.

RESET: starting PC

Again at reset, the value at this location is used as the program counter. In other words, the RESET routine is started at the address stored here.

Bus error   This exception is activated by a co-processor when, for instance, a reserved or non-existent memory range is accessed.

Address error   This error occurs when a word or long word access is attempted at an odd address.

Illegal instruction

Since all MC68000 instructions consist of one word, a total of 65536 different instructions are possible. However, since the processor doesn't know that many instructions, there are a number of words that are invalid instructions. Should such a word occur, this exception is prompted.

Division by zero

Since the processor has a division function, and the division of anything by zero is mathematically undefined and thus illegal, this exception occurs when such an operation is attempted.

CHK instruction

This exception occurs only with the CHK instruction. This instruction tests that a data register's contents are within a certain limit. If this is not the case, the exception is activated.

TRAPV instruction

If the TRAPV instruction is executed and the V bit (bit 1) in the status word is set, this exception is prompted.

Privilege violation

If a privileged instruction is called from the user mode, this exception is activated.

Trace   If the trace bit (bit 15) in the status word is set, this exception is activated after each instruction that is executed. This method allows you to employ a step by step execution of machine programs.

Axxx-instruction emulation
Fxxx-instruction emulation

These two vectors can be used for a quite interesting trick. If an instruction beginning with $A or $F (such as $A010 or $F200) is called, the routine to which the corresponding vector is pointing is accessed. In these routines you can create chains of other instructions, in effect expanding the processor's instruction vocabulary!

Reserved   These vectors are not used.

Uninitialized interrupt

This exception is activated when a peripheral component that was not initialized sends an interrupt.

Unassigned interrupt

Is activated when a BUS error occurs during the interrupt verification of the activating component. However, the interrupt is usually activated only by some type of disturbance.

Level 1-7 interrupt

These seven vectors point to the interrupt routines of the corresponding priority levels. If the level indicated in the status word is higher than the level of the occurring interrupt, the interrupt is simply ignored.

TRAP instructions

These 16 vectors are used when a corresponding TRAP instruction occurs. Thus, TRAP instructions from TRAP #0 to TRAP #15 are possible.

User interrupt vectors

These vectors are used for interrupts which are activated by several peripheral components that generate their own vector number.

At this point you don't want to delve any deeper into the secrets of exceptions, since we'd be expanding this book beyond its framework. However, there's one last thing to say about exceptions: the exception routines are ended with the RTE (ReTurn from Exception) instruction, with which the original status is restored and the user program is continued.

2.3.3   Interrupts

Interrupts are processed similarly to exceptions. They are breaks (or interruptions) in the program which are activated through hardware (such as a peripheral component or an external trigger).

The interrupt level is stored in bits 8-10 of the status register. A value between 0 and 7 indicates the interrupt level. There are eight different possible interrupts, each of which has a different priority. If the level of this interrupt happens to be higher than the value in the status register, the interrupt is executed, or otherwise ignored.

When a valid interrupt occurs, the computer branches to the corresponding routine whose address is indicated in the exception vector table above.

The interrupts are very important if you're trying to synchronize a program with connected hardware. In this manner, a trigger (s.a. the keyboard) which is to feed the computer data, can signal the request for a legal value using an interrupt. The interrupt routine then simply takes the value directly. This method is also employed for the operation of the serial interface (RS232).

We'll talk more about the use of interrupts at a later time. The last thing we want to mention about interrupts at this time is that, like exceptions, interrupt routines are terminated with the RTE instruction.

2.3.4   Condition codes

When you write a program in any language, the need for a conditional operation arises quite often. For instance, in a BASIC program

```
IF D1=2 THEN D2=0
```

represents a conditional operation. To write the equivalent in machine language, you first need to make the comparison:

```
CMP #2,D1
```

CMP stands for compare and compares two operands, in this case D1 and D2. How is this operation evaluated?

For this purpose you have condition codes (CC's), which exist in the branch instructions of machine language. Because of this, you must specify when and where the program is to branch.

The simplest variation of the branch instructions is an unconditional branch. The corresponding instruction is 'BRA address', although this won't help you here. After all, you need a conditional branch.

To retain the result of an operation, in this case a comparison (CMP), several bits are reserved in the status word. Let's look at bit 2 first, which is the zero flag. This flag is set when the result of the previous operation was zero.

To explain the relationship between CMP and the Z flag, you must first clarify the function of the CMP instruction. Actually this instruction performs the subtraction of the source operand from the destination operand. In the example above, the number 2 is subtracted from the content of the memory cell at D1. Before the result of this subtraction is discarded, the corresponding flags are set.

If the content of D1 in our example above happened to be 2, the result of the subtraction would be 0. Thus, the Z flag would be set, which can then be evaluated through a corresponding branch instruction. Our example would then look like this:

```
        ...
        CMP     #2,D1       ;comparison, or subtraction
        BNE     UNEQUAL     ;branch, if not equal (Z flag not set)
        MOVE    #0,D2       ;otherwise execute D2=0
UNEQUAL:
        ...                 ;program branches to here
```

BNE stands for Branch if Not Equal. This means, that if the Z flag was cleared (=0) by the previous CMP, the program branches to the address specified by BNE (here represented by UNEQUAL). The counterpart to the BNE instruction is the BEQ (Branch if EQual) instruction, which is executed if Z=1.

Here's a list of all condition codes, which allow you to form conditional branches using the Bcc (cc=condition code) format:

cc	Condition	Bits
T	true, corresponds to BRA	
F	false, never branches	
HI	higher than	$C' * Z'$
LS	lower or same	$C + Z$
CC, HS	carry clear, higher or same	C'
CS, LO	carry set, lower	C
NE	not equal	Z'
EQ	equal	Z
VC	Overflow clear	V'
VS	Overflow set	V
PL	plus, positive	
MI	minus, negative	
GE	greater or equal	$N*V + N'*V'$
LT	less than	$N*V' + N'*V$
GT	greater than	$N*V*Z'+N'*V'*Z'$
LE	less or equal	$Z + N*V' + N'*V$

*=logic AND, +=logic OR, '=logic NOT

Here are a few examples to demonstrate how these numerous conditions can be utilized:

```
        CMP #2,D1
        BLS SMALLER_EQUAL
```

This branches if the content of D1 <= 2, whether D1 is 0, 1 or 2. In this example, the BLE instruction would allow the program to branch even if D1 is negative. You can tell this by the fact that the V bit is used in the evaluation of this expression (see chart above). When the sign is changed during the operation, this V bit is compared with the N bit. Should both bits be cleared (N bit=0 and V bit=0) after the CMP subtraction (D1-2), the result has remained positive: the condition has not been met.

The conditions EQ and NE are quite important for other uses, as well. For instance, they can be used to determine if particular bits in a data word are set, by writing the following sequence...

```
        ...
        AND #%00001111,D1        ;masks bits out
        BEQ SMALLER              ;branches when none of the four
;                                ;lower bits is set
        CMP #%00001111,D1
        BEQ ALL                  ;branches when all four bits set
```

The AND instruction causes all bits of D1 to be compared with the bits of the parameter (in this case #%00001111). If the same bits are set in both bytes, the corresponding bits are also set in the result. If one bit of a pair is cleared, the resulting bit is zero as well. Thus, in the result, the only bits that are set are those bits of the lowest four that were set in D1.

This technique is known as masking. In the example above, only the lowest four bits were masked out, which means that in the resulting byte, only the lowest four appear in their original condition. All other bits are cleared with the AND operand. Of course you can use any bit combination with this method.

If no bit at all is set in the result, the zero flag is set, thus fulfilling the BEQ condition and branching the program. Otherwise, the next instruction is processed, in which D1 is compared with %00001111. When both are equal, at least all of the four lowest bits of the original byte have been set, in which case the following BEQ instruction branches.

Aside from CMP, the CC and CS conditions can also be used to determine whether a HI bit was pushed out of the data word during data rotation with the ROL and ROR instructions.

Before you move on the instruction vocabulary of the MC68000, we'd like to give you another tip:

The AssemPro assembler makes it quite easy to try every command in all possible situations. Take the CMP command which we've been talking about, for example. To test this command with various values and to receive the results of the comparisons directly via the flags, try the following.

Type the following into the editor.

```
        run:
        cmp $10,d1
        bra run
        end
```

Assemble it, save the resulting code and enter the debugger. After re-loading the code you can then single step through the program observing the results the program has on the flags. Try changing the values in register D1 and see how higher and lower values affect the flags.

By the way, using the start command as this time causes it to run forever. Well, at least until reset is hit, which isn't exactly desirable, either....

This procedure isn't limited to just the CMP instruction. You can use it to try any other instruction you're interested in.

2.4 The 68000 Instructions

It's about time to explain the MC68000 instructions. You don't have room for an in-depth discussion of each instruction in this book; for that purpose we recommend *Programming the 68000* from Sybex by Steve Williams.

The following tables show the required parameters and arguments for each instruction. AssemPro owners have access to built in help tables covering effective addressing modes and many of the Amiga Intuition calls. The following notation is used for arguments:

Label	a label or address
Reg	register
An	address register n
Dn	data register n
Source	source operand
Dest	destination operand
<ea>	address or register
#n	direct value

Here is a short list of the instructions for the MC68000 processor, AssemPro owners can simply place the cursor at the beginning of the instruction and press the help key to see the addressing modes allowed:

Mnemonic		Meaning
Bcc	Label	conditional branch, depends on condition
BRA	Label	unconditional branch (similar to JMP)
BSR	Label	branch to subprogram. Return address is deposited on stack, RTS causes return to that address.
CHK	<ea>,Dx	check data register for limits, activate the CHK instruction exception
DBcc	Reg,Label	check condition, decrement and branch.
JMP	Label	jump to address (similar to BRA)
JSR	Label	jump to a subroutine. Return address is deposited on stack, RTS causes return to that address.
NOP		no operation
RESET		reset peripherals (Caution!)
RTE		return from exception
RTR		return with loading of flags
RTS		return from subroutine (after BSR or JSR)
Scc	<ea>	set a byte to -1 when condition is met
STOP		stop processing (Caution!)
TRAP #n		jump to an exception
TRAPV		check overflow flag, then TRAPV exception

Here are a few important notes...

When a program jumps (JSR) or branches (BSR) to a subroutine, the return address to which the program is to return is placed on the stack. At the RTS instruction, the address is pulled back off the stack, and the program jumps to that point.

Let's experiment a little with this procedure. Please enter the following short program:

```
run:
        pea     subprogram      ; address on the stack
        jsr     subprogram      ; subprogram call
        move.l  (sp)+,d1        ; get long word from stack
;       illegal                 ; for assemblers without
                                ; debuggers

subprogram:
        move.l  (sp),d0         ; return address in D0
        rts                     ; and return
        end
```

The first instruction, PEA, places the address of the subprogram on the stack. Next, the JSR instruction jumps to the subprogram. The return address, or the address at which the main program is to continue after the completion of the subprogram, is also deposited on the stack at this point.

In the subprogram, the long word pointed to by the stack pointer is now loaded into the data register D0. After that, the RTS instruction pulls the return address from the stack, and the program jumps to that address.

Back in the main program, the long word which is on the top of the stack, is pulled from the stack and written into D1. Assemblers that do not have the debugging features of AssemPro may need the ILLEGAL instruction so they can break the program and allow you to view the register contents.

Assemble the program and load the resulting code into the debugger. Single step thru the program and examine the register contents.

Here you can see that D0 contains the address at which the program is to continue after the RTS command. Also, D1 contains the address of the subprogram which you can verify by comparing the debugger listing.

The STOP and RESET instructions are so powerful that they can only be used in the supervisor mode. Even if you do switch to the supervisor mode, you should not use these instructions if there is any data in memory that has not been saved and you wish to retain.

The TRAP instruction receives a number between 0 and $F, which determines the particular TRAP vector (addresses $0080-$00BF) and thus the corresponding exception routine. Several operating systems for the 68000 utilize this instruction to call operating system functions. You'll deal more with this instruction later.

In the short sample program that compared two numbers, the CMP instruction performed an arithmetic function, namely a subtraction. This subtraction could be performed with an actual result as well using the SUB instruction. The counterpart to this is in addition, for which the ADD instruction is used. In eight bit processors, like the 6502, these two arithmetic functions are the only mathematical operations. The MC68000, can also multiply, divide, and perform these operations with a variety of data sizes.

Most of the functions require two parameters. For instance the ADD instruction...

```
ADD source,destination
```

where source and destination can be registers or memory addresses. Source can also be a direct value (#n). The result of the operation is placed in the destination register or the destination address. This is the same for all operations of this type. These instructions can be tried out with the Assempro assembler. In this case we recommend the use of a register as the destination.

Here's an overview of the arithmetic operations with whole numbers:

Mnemonic		Meaning
ADD	source,dest	binary addition
ADDA	source,An	binary addition to an address register
ADDI	#n,<ea>	addition with a constant
ADDQ	#n,<ea>	fast addition of a constant which can be only from 1 to 8
ADDX	source,dest	addition with transfer in X flag
CLR	<ea>	clear an operand
CMP	source,dest	comparison of two operands
CMPA	<ea>,An	comparison with an address register
CMPI	#n,<ea>	comparison with a constant
CMPM	source,dest	comparison of two memory operands

Mnemonic		Meaning
DIVS	source,dest	sign-true division of a 32 bit destination by a 16 bit source operand. The result of the division is stored in the LO word of the destination, the remainder in the HI word.
DIVU	source,dest	division without regard to sign, similar to DIVS
EXT	Dn	sign-true expansion to twice original size (width) data unit
MULS	source,dest	sign-true multiplication of two words into one long word
MULU	source,dest	multiplication without regard to sign, similar to MULS
NEG	<ea>	negation of an operand (twos complement)
NEGX	<ea>	negation of an operand with transfer
SUB	source,dest	binary subtraction
SUBA	<ea>,An	binary subtraction from an address register
SUBI	#n,<ea>	subtraction of a constant
SUBQ	#n,<ea>	fast subtraction of a 3 bit constant
SUBX	source,dest	subtraction with transfer in X-Flag
TST	<ea>	test an operand and set N and Z flag

For the processing of whole numbers, the processor can operate with
BCD numbers. These are Binary Coded Decimal numbers, which means
that the processor is working with decimals. In this method, each halfbyte
contains only numbers from 0 to 9, so that these numbers can be easily
processed. For this method, the following instructions are available:

Mnemonic		Meaning
ABCD	source,dest	addition of two BCD numbers
NBCD	source,dest	negation of a BCD number (nine complement)
SBCD	source,dest	subtraction of two BCD numbers

Again, we recommend that you try this out yourself. Although handling
the BCD numbers is relatively easy, it can be rather awkward at first. Be
sure that you enter only BCD numbers for source and destination, since
the results are not correct otherwise.

Next are the logical operations, which you might know from BASIC.
With these functions, you can operate on binary numbers bit for bit.

Mnemonic		Meaning
AND	source,dest	logic AND
ANDI	#n,<ea>	logic AND with a constant
EOR	source,dest	exclusive OR
EORI	#n,<ea>	exclusive OR with a constant
NOT	<ea>	inversion of an operand
OR	source,dest	logic OR
ORI	#n,<ea>	logic OR with a constant
TAS	<ea>	check a byte and set bit 7

Single bits can also be manipulated by the following set of instructions:

Mnemonic		Meaning
BCHG	#n,<ea>	change bit n (0 is changed to 1 and vice versa)
BCLR	#n,<ea>	clear bit n
BSET	#n,<ea>	set bit n
BTST	#n,<ea>	test bit n, result is displayed in Z flag

These instructions are particularly important from the manipulation and evaluation of data from peripherals. After all, in this type of data, single bits are often very significant. You'll come across this more in later chapters.

The processor can also shift and rotate an operand within itself ('n' indicates a register, '#' indicates a direct value which specifies the number of shiftings)...

Mnemonic		Meaning
AS	n,<ea>	arithmetic shift to the left (*2^n)
ASR	n,<ea>	arithmetic shift to the right (/2^n)
LSL	n,<ea>	logic shift to the left
LSR	n,<ea>	logic shift to the right
ROL	n,<ea>	rotation left
ROR	n,<ea>	rotation right
ROXL	n,<ea>	rotation left with transfer in X flag
ROXR	n,<ea>	rotation right with transfer in X flag

All these instructions allow you to shift a byte, a word or a long word to the left or right. It's not too surprising that this is the equivalent of multiplying (dividing) the number by a power of 2. Here's a little example to demonstrate why.

Let's take a byte containing the value 16 as an example. In binary, it looks like this:

```
%00010000 = 16
```

Now, if you shift the byte to the left by inserting a 0 at the right, you'll get the following result...

```
%00010000 shifted to the left equals
%00100000 = 32, in effect 16*2
```

Repeated shifting results in repeated doubling of the number. Thus, if you shift the number n times, the number is multiplied by 2^n.

The same goes for shifting to the right. However, this operation has a slight quirk: here's a sample byte with the value 5:

```
%00000101 = 5, shifted once to the right equals
%00000010 = 2
```

The answer in this case is not 2.5 as you might expect. The result of such a division is always a whole number, since any decimal places are discarded. If you use the DIV instruction instead of shifting, you'll retain the digits to the right of the decimal point. However, shifting is some-what faster, and shifting can also receive long words as results.

After explaining the principle of shifting, you still need to know why more than two instructions are required for the procedure. Well, this is because there are several different types of shifting.

First, you must differentiate between shifting and rotating. In shifting, the bit that is added to the left or the right side is always a zero. In rotating, it is always a specific value that is inserted. This means that with the ROR or the ROL instruction, the bit that is taken out on one side is the one that is inserted on the other. With the ROXR and the ROXL instructions this bit takes a slight detour to the X flag. Thus, the content of the flag is inserted into the new bit, while the old bit is loaded into the flag.

Shifting, as well, has two variations: arithmetic and logical shifting. You've already dealt with logical shifting. In this variation, the inserted bit is always a zero, and the extracted bit is deposited in the C flag and in the X flag.

Although the highest bit, which always represents the sign, is shifted in arithmetic shifting, the sign is still retained by ASR. This has the advan-tage that when these instructions are used for division, the operation retains the correct sign (-10/2 equals -5). However, should an overflow or underflow cause the sign to change, this change is noted in the V flag, which always indicates a change in sign. With logical shifting this flag is always cleared.

Now to the instructions that allow you to move data. These are actually the most important instructions for any processor, for how else could you process data?

Mnemonic		Meaning
EXG	Rn,Rn	exchange of two register contents (don't confuse with SWAP!)
LEA	<ea>,An	load an effective address in address register An
LINK	An,#n	build stack range
MOVE	source,dest	carry value over from source to destination
MOVE	SR,<ea>	transfer the status register contents
MOVE	<ea>,SR	transfer the status register contents
MOVE	<ea>,CCR	load flags
MOVE	USP,<ea>	transfer the user stack pointer
MOVE	<ea>,USP	transfer the user stack pointer
MOVEA	<ea>,An	transfer a value to the address register An
MOVEM	Regs,<ea>	transfer several registers at once
MOVEM	<ea>,Regs	transfer several registers at once
MOVEP	source,dest	transfer data to peripherals
MOVEQ	#n,Dn	quickly transfer an 8 bit constant to the data register Dn
PEA	<ea>	deposit an address on the stack
SWAP	Dn	swap the halves of the register (the upper 16 bits with the lower)
UNLK	An	unlink the stack

The LEA or PEA instructions are often used to deposit addresses in an address register or on the stack. The instruction

```
LEA label,A0
```

loads the address of the label 'label' into the address register A0. In practice, this corresponds to

```
MOVE.L #label,A0
```

which is equivalent to

```
PEA label
```

All these instructions deposit the address of 'label' on the stack. The following instruction also does this:

```
MOVE.L #label,-(SP)
```

The LEA instruction becomes much more interesting when the label is replaced by indirect addressing. Here's an example:

```
LEA 1(A0,D0),A1
```

The address that's produced by the addition of 1 (direct value-offset) +A0+D0 is located in A1. To duplicate this instruction with MOVE would be quite cumbersome. Take a look:

```
MOVE.L A0,A1
ADD.L  D0,A1
ADDQ.L #1,A1
```

As you can see, the LEA instruction offers you quite some interesting possibilities.

Those are all the instructions of the MC68000. Through their combination using the diverse methods of addressing, you can create a great number of different instructions, in order to make a program as efficient as possible.

The following table is an overview of all MC68000 instructions along with their possible addressing types and the influence of flags. The following abbreviations are used:

x=legal s=source only   d=destination only
-=not affected   0=cleared   *=modified accordingly
1=set   u=undetermined   P=privileged

Mnemonic	1	2	3	4	5	6	7	8	9	10	11	12	XNZVC	P
ABCD	x				x									
ADD	s	s	x	x	x	x	x	x	x	s	s	s	*****	
ADDA	x	x	x	x	x	x	x	x	x	x	x	x	-----	
ADDI	x		x	x	x	x	x	x	x				*****	
ADDQ	x	x	x	x	x	x	x	x	x				*****	
ADDX	x				x								*****	
AND	s		x	x	x	x	x	x	x	s	s	s	-**00	
ANDI	x		x	x	x	x	x	x	x				-**00	
ASL, ASR	x		x	x	x	x	x	x	x				*****	
Bcc													-----	
BCHG	x		x	x	x	x	x	x	x				--*--	
BCLR	x		x	x	x	x	x	x	x				--*--	
BRA													-----	
BSET	x		x	x	x	x	x	x	x				--*--	
BSR													-----	
BTST	x		x	x	x	x	x	x	x	z	x	x	--*--	
CHK	x		x	x	x	x	x	x	x	x	x	x	-*uuu	
CLR	x		x	x	x	x	x	x	x				-0100	
CMP	x	x	x	x	x	x	x	x	x	x	x	x	-****	
CMPA	x	x	x	x	x	x	x	x	x	x	x	x	-****	
CMPI	x		x	x	x	x	x	x	x				-****	
CMPM			x			x	x	x	x		x	x	-***	
cpGEN													-----	
DBcc													-----	
DIVS	x		x	x	x	x	x	x	x	x	x	x	-***0	
DIVU	x		x	x	x	x	x	x	x	x	x	x	-***0	
EOR	x		x	x	x	x	x	x	x				-**00	
EORI	x		x	x	x	x	x	x	x				-**00	
EORI CCR													*****	
EORI SR													*****	
EXG													-----	
EXT													-**00	
EXTB													-**00	
ILLEGAL													-----	
JMP			x			x	x	x	x		x	x	-----	
JSR			x			x	x	x	x		x	x	-----	
LEA			x			x	x	x	x		x	x	-----	
LINK		x											-----	
LSL, LSR			x	x	x	x	x	x	x				***0*	
MOVE	x	s	x	x	x	x	x	x	x	s	s	s	-**00	
MOVEA	x	x	x	x	x	x	x	x	x	x	x	x	-----	
MOVE to CCR	x		x	x	x	x	x	x	x	x	x	x	*****	
MOVE from SR	x		x	x	x	x	x	x	x				-----	P
MOVE to SR	x		x	x	x	x	x	x	x	x	x	x	*****	P

Mnemonic	1	2	3	4	5	6	7	8	9	10	11	12	XNZVC	P
MOVE USP		x											-----	P
MOVEM			x	s	d	x	x	x	x		s	s	-----	
MOVEP	s	d											-----	
MOVEQ	d												-**00	
MULS	x		x	x	x	x	x	x	x	x	x	x	-**00	
MULU	x		x	x	x	x	x	x	x	x	x	x	-**00	
NBCD	x		x	x	x	x	x	x					*u*u*	
NEG	x		x	x	x	x	x	x					*****	
NEGX	x		x	x	x	x	x	x					*****	
NOP													-----	
NOT	x		x	x	x	x	x	x					-**00	
OR	s		x	x	x	x	x	x	x	s	s	s	-**00	
ORI	x		x	x	x	x	x	x					-**00	
PEA			x			x	x	x	x		x	x	-----	
RESET													-----	P
ROL, ROR			x	x	x	x	x	x	x				-**0*	
ROXL, ROXR			x	x	x	x	x	x	x				-**0*	
RTE													-----	P
RTR													*****	
RTS													-----	
SBCD	x				x								*u*u*	
Scc	x		x	x	x	x	x	x					-----	
STOP										x			-----	
SUB	s	s	x	x	x	x	x	x	x	s	s	s	*****	
SUBA	x	x	x	x	x	x	x	x	x	x	x	x	-----	
SUBI	x		x	x	x	x	x	x					*****	
SUBQ	x	x	x	x	x	x	x	x					*****	
SUBX	x				x								*****	
SWAP	x												-**00	
TAS	x		x	x	x	x	x	x					-**00	
TRAP										x			-----	
TRAPV													-----	
TST	x		x	x	x	x	x	x					-**00	
UNLK		x											-----	

Chapter 3

Working with Assemblers

3. Working with Assemblers

The instructions that you've learned so far are incomprehensible to the MC68000 processor. The letters MOVE mean absolutely nothing to the processor—it needs the instructions in binary form. Every instruction must be coded in a word—which normally takes a lot of work.

An assembler does this work for you. An assembler is a program that translates the instructions from text into the corresponding binary instructions. The text that is translated is called mnenomic or memcode. It's a lot easier working with text instructions—or does $4280 mean more to you than CLR.L D0?

This chapter is about working with assemblers. We'll describe the following three:

ASSEM   This is the assembler from the Amiga's development package. This assembler is quite powerful, but it is clearly inferior to it's two fellow compilers in some areas.

AssemPro   This is the Abacus assembler. It has a debugger in addition to the assembler. This lets you test and correct programs. In our opinion, it is the best one to use for writing and testing practice programs. For this reason, we wrote the programs in this book with this assembler.

KUMA-SEKA   This is a popular assembler that also has a debugger.

All assemblers perform a similar task—they translate memcode, so that you can write a runnable program to disk. To test the program directly, you need a debugger which is something ASSEM doesn't have.

3.1 The Development Assembler

This assembler is a plain disk assembler. That means that it can only assemble text files that are on disk and write the results back to disk. You can't make direct input or test run the new program.

You can call ASSEM from the CLI by typing ASSEM followed by parameters that specify what you wish the assemble to do.

In the simplest case, you call it like this:

```
ASSEM Source -O Destination
```

Source is the filename of the file containing the program text. Destination is the name of the file that contains the results of assembling after the process is over. The "-O" means that the following name is used for the object file.

There are several other parameters that can be passed. These are written with their option (ie. -O), so that the assembler knows what to do with the file that you've told it to use. The following possible options must be followed by a filename:

-O   Object file

-V   Error messages that occur during assembling are written to a file. If this isn't given, the error messages appear in the CLI window.

-L   The output of the assembled program lines are sent to this file. You can also use "PRT:" to have it printed.

-H   This file is read in at the beginning of the assembled file and assembled along with it.

-E   A file is created that contains lines which have EQU instructions.

-C   This option isn't followed by a filename but by another option. You can also use OPT to do this. The following options are available:

           OPT S   A symbol table is created which contains all the labels and their values.

           OPT X   A cross-reference list is created (where labels are used)

           OPT W   A number must follow this option. It sets the amount of work space to be reserved.

The assembler creates an object file. This is not runnable. To make it runnable, you need to call the linker, ALINK. This program can link several assembled or compiled object files together to make a runnable program. In the simplest case, you enter the following instruction in the CLI:

```
ALINK Source TO Destination
```

Source is the object file produced by the assembler. Destination is the name of the program. It can be started directly.

3.2 AssemPro

Abacus's AssemPro is a package which combines editor, assembler and debugger in an easy to use package.

The AssemPro program is divided into several windows—one for the assembler, the editor, the debugger and several help functions. Producing a program is very easy:

1)   Write the program with the editor and then store it to disk.
2)   Start the assembler, so that the program is translated.
3)   If desired, start the debugger, load the program and test it.

Within the debugger you can work through parts of the program or even through single commands. As after each one of these steps the debugger shows you the state of registers and flags in its status register, you can easily try the programs presented in this book.

You need to load Assempro only once when working with machine language programs. Thus you don't need to save back and to between editor, assembler, linker and debugger.

Assempro has an especially interesting function: the reassembler. With this debugger function you are able to convert runable programs into the source text of the program. Once you have made the source text, you can edit the program using the editor and assemble it again. Assempro is equipped with functions other assemblers miss. There are however, some differences you should know about. As many programs you see were written for the K-SEKA, be aware of one difference: the EVEN command. AssemPro uses the ALIGN instruction.

Note, that when entering and assembling one of the programs in Assempro you must make sure that you place an END directive at the end of the source text.

The following is an introduction into working with Assempro and the programs in this book.

Start AssemPro normally, next click on the editor window and start typing in your program. If the program is on disk already, load it by selecting the appropriate menu or by using the key combination right

<AMIGA> key and <o>. To do this you only need to click on the file-name in the displayed requestor and click the OK gadget.

Once you have typed in or loaded the program into the editor, you can assemble it. It is best to save your source before you start assembling. You assemble your program by clicking on the assembler window displayed above the editor window and pressing <AMIGA> and <a>. You can then chose how to locate your program in the memory. Remember that data used by the co-processors must be located in CHIP RAM.

By clicking OK you start the assembler process. If you additionally select "breakable", you can cancel the process by pressing both shift keys. If any error occurs during assembling, Assempro uses a window to tell you this. Use this window to correct the error and continue with "Save and try again".

Now the runable program is located in the Amiga's memory. Use the menu item "Save as" to save it on disk. If you want to store it on RAM disk, click the given filename and enter RAM: in front of this name. In addition you can click on the menu item "ICON" and chose if you only want the program itself on disk but the icon too. Use this icon to start the program at a later time from the Workbench.

To test-run the program, you move the debugger window to the fore-ground of the screen (for instance by clicking on the back gadget). Use "Load" in the debugger menu or <AMIGA> <o> to call the select-file window, where you select the saved program. The program is then loaded into the memory and its shown disassembled.

The highlighted line (orange) represents the current state of the program counter. This is the line where the processor reads its next instruction, provided you tell the processor so. There are three ways to do so.

The first one is to start the program with "Start". This alternative does not enable you to stop the program if anything goes wrong.

The second possibility, "Start breakable" is better in this respect. After the program starts, it continuously displays the register's contents on the left side of the window. In addition to that you can cancel the process by pressing <Esc>. Note that this only works if your program doesn't use the <Esc> key itself.

The third possibility enables you to only partly run your program. You can do this by stepping through the program or by placing breakpoints throughout the program. You place these by clicking on the desired address and then pressing <AMIGA> <b>. "BREAKPOINT" is displayed

where the command was displayed before. If you start the program now, it
stops whenever it comes across one of the breakpoints.

You can start a small part of the program by moving the mouse pointer
to the orange line, clicking the left button and holding it down while you
drag the mouse pointer downward. If you release the button, the processor
works through this part of the program, stopping at the line, where you
positioned the mouse pointer. This is a very useful method to step by
step test a program.

AssemPro has another helpful window: the Table. This window lists the
valid address methods for instructions and the parameters of Amiga functions. This is extremely helpful whenever you are not sure about one of
the instructions.

3.3 The K-SEKA Assembler

The SEKA assembler, from KUMA, has a simple text editor and a
debugger in addition to the assembler. This program is controlled by
simple instructions and is easy to use. It is also multi-functional and
quick, so it is great for small test and example programs. You can use it
to write bigger programs once you've gotten use to the editor. Now let's
look at the editor.

To load a program as source code (text) into the editor, enter "r" (read).
The program asks you for the name of the file with the "FILENAME>"
prompt. You then enter the name of the text file. If you created the file
with SEKA, the file is stored on disk with ".S" on the end of its name.
You don't need to include the ".S" when you load the file. That's taken
care of automatically. ("S" stands for source.)

You can store the programs you've just written or modified by using the
"w" instruction. The program asks you for the name. If you enter "Test",
the file is written to disk with "Test.S" as its name. This is a normal text
file in ASCII format.

There are two ways to enter or change programs: using the line editor or
using the screen editor. You can enter the second by hitting the <Esc>
key. The upper screen section is then reserved for the editor. You can
move with the cursor keys and change the text easily. The lines that you
enter are inserted into the existing text and automatically numbered. By
hitting the <Esc> key again, you leave the screen editor.

There's really not much to say about this editor. It's really just for simple
insertions and changes. Other functions are called in normal instruction
mode, the mode in which ">" is the input prompt.

The following instructions are available to you for text editing (<n>
stands for a number. The meaning of the instructions is in parenthesis.)

Instruction	Function
t (Target)	Puts the cursor on the highest line in the text.
t <n>	Puts the cursor on line n.
b (Bottom)	Puts the cursor on the last line of the text.
u (Up)	Go up one line.
u <n>	Go up n lines.
d (Down)	Go down one line.
d <n>	Go down n lines.
z (Zap)	Deletes the current line.
z <n>	Deletes n lines starting at the cursor line.
e (Edit)	Let's you edit the current line (and only that line).
e <n>	Edit from line n.
ftext (Find)	Searches for the text entered starting at the current line. The case of a letter makes a difference, so make sure to enter it correctly. Blanks that appear after the f are looked for as well!
f	Continues searching beyond the text that was previously given.
i (Insert)	Starts the line editor. Now you can enter a program line by line. However, you can't use the cursor to move into another line. Line numbers are generated automatically. The lines that follow are moved down, not erased.
ks (Kill Source)	The source text is deleted if you answer "y" when the program asks if you're sure. Otherwise nothing happens.
o (Old)	Cancels the "ks" function and saves the old text.
p (Print)	Prints the current line.
p <n>	Prints n lines starting at the cursor line.

Those are K-SEKA's editor functions. In combination with the screen editor, they allow for simple text editting. You can, for example, delete the current line (and other lines) while working in the screen editor by hitting <Esc> to get into instruction mode and then entering "z" (or "z <n>").

If you'd like to edit all the lines that contain "trap", for example, you can do the following:

- Jump to the beginning of the text using "t".
- Search for a "trap" instruction by entering "ftrap" in the first line.
- Press <Esc> and edit the line.
- Press <Esc> again to get into instruction mode.
- Search using "f", <Esc>, etc. until you get to the end of the text.

This sounds very clumsy, but in practice it works quite well and goes quickly. Experiment with the editor a bit, so that you can get use to it.

Now here are the instructions for working with disks:

Instruction	Function
v (View Files)	Look at the disk's directory. You can also include the disk drive or subdirectory that interests you. For example, "vc" causes the "c" subdirectory to be listed and makes it the current directory.
kf (Kill File)	The program asks for the name of a file. The file is deleted (and you aren't asked if you are sure either—so be careful).
r (Read)	After inputting this instruction, you'll be asked which file to load (FILENAME>). The file that you specify is then loaded. If only "r" is entered, a text file is loaded in the editor.
ri (Read Image)	Loads a file into memory. After you've entered the filename, SEKA asks for the address the file should begin at in memory (BEGIN>) and the highest address that should be used for the file (END>).
rx (Read from Auxillary)	This works just like the "ri" function except that it reads from the serial port instead of from the disk. (You don't need a filename).
rl (Read Link file)	This instruction reads in a SEKA created link file. First you'll be asked if you're sure, because the text buffer is erased when the link file is loaded.
w (Write)	After entering this instruction, you'll be asked for the name of the file the text should be written to. A ".S" is automatically appended to the name, so that it can be recognized as a SEKA file.
wi (Write Image)	Stores a block of memory to disk after the name, beginning and end are entered.
wx (Write to Auxillary)	This is similar to "wi"; the only difference is that the output is to the serial intrface.
wl (Write Link file)	Asks for the name and then stores a link file that was assembled with the "I" option to disk. If this isn't available, the message "** Link option not specified" appears.

Once you've typed in or loaded a program, you can call the assembler and have the program translated. Just enter "a" to do so. You'll then be asked which options you want to use. If you enter a <Return>, the program is assembled normally—ie the results of translating a program in memory is stored in memory. Then the program can be executed right a way.

You can enter one or more of the following options however:

v   The output of the results goes to the screen

p   or

e   goes to the printer with a title line.

h   The output stops after every page and waits for a key stroke. This is useful for controlling output to the screen or for putting new sheets of paper in the printer.

o   This option allows the assembler to optimize all possible branch instructions. When possible, a .S is appended to the branch instructions. This allows the program code to be shorter than it would otherwise be. Several messages appear, but you can ignore them.

l   This option caused linkable code to be produced. You can save it with the "wl" instruction and read it with the "rl" instruction.

A symbol table is included at the end of the listing if desired. The table contains all labels and their values. It also contains macro names. A macro allows several instructions to be combined into a single instruction.

For example, suppose you wrote a routine that outputs the text that register A0 points to. Every time you need to use the routine, you must type:

```
lea text,a0     ;Pointer to text in A0
bsr pline       ;Output text
```

You can simplify this by defining a macro for this function. To do this, put the following at the beginning of the program:

```
print: macro    ;Macro with the name "print"
  lea ?1,a0     ;Parameter in A0
  bsr pmsg      ;Output text
  endm          ;end of macro
```

Now, you can simply write the following in your program:

```
print text      ;Output text
```

This line is replaced using the macro during assembly. The parameter "text" is inserted where "?1" appears in the macro. You can have several parameters in a macro. You give them names like "?2", "?3", etc...

You can also decide whether you'd like to see the macros in the output listing of the assembler. This is one of the pseudo-operators (Pseudo-ops) that are available in the assembler. The SEKA assembler has the following pseudo-ops:

dc   Defines one or more data items that should appear in this location in the program. The word length can be specified with .B, .W, or .L—and if this is left off, .B is used. Text can be entered in quotation marks or apostrophes.
For example: dc.b "Hello",10,13,0

blk   Reserves a number of bytes, words or long words, depending on whether .B, .W or .L is chosen. The first parameter specifies the number of words to be reserved. The second (which is optional) is used to fill the memory area.
For example: blk.w 10,0

org   The parameter that follows the org instruction is the address from which the (absolute) program should be assembled.
For example: org $40000

code   Causes the program to be assembled in relative mode, the mode in which a program is assembled starting at address 0. The Amiga takes care of the new addressing after the program is loaded.

data   This means that from here on only data appear. This can be left out.

even   Makes the current address even by sometimes inserting a fill byte.

odd   The opposite of "even"—it makes the address odd.

end   Assembling ends here.

equ or Used for establishing the value of a label.

=   For example: Value = 123 or Value: equ 123

list   Turns the output on again (aften nlist). You can use the following parameters to influence the output:

           c   Macro calls
           d   Macro definitions
           e   Macro expansion of the program
           x   Code expansions

           For example: list e

nlist   Turns off output. You can use the same parameters here as with "list".

page   Causes the printer to executed a page feed, so that you'll start a new page.

if   The following parameter decides whether you should continue assembling. If it is zero, you won't continue assembling.

else   If the "if" parameter is zero, you'll begin assembling here.

endif   End of conditional assembling

macro   Start of a macro definition

endm   End of a macro definition

?n   The text in the macro that is replaced by the nth parameter in the calling line.

?0   Generates a new three digit number for each macro call—this is very useful for local labels.

For example: x?0: bsr pmsg

illegal   Produces an illegal machine language instruction.

globl   Defines the following label as global when the "I" option of the assembler is chosen.

Once you've assembled your program, the program code is in memory. Using the "h" instruction, you can find out how large the program is and where it is located in memory. The beginning and end address is given in hex and the length is given in decimal (according to the last executed operations):

Work	The memory area defined in the beginning
Src	Text in memory
RelC	Relocation table of the program
RelD	Relocation table of the memory area
Code	Program code produced
Data	The program's memory area

You'll find your program in memory at the location given by Code. It's a pain to have to enter this address whenever you want to start the program. It makes good sense to mark the beginning of the program with a label (for example, "run:"). You can use the "g" instruction to run the program as follows:

       g run

The "g" (Go) instruction is one of SEKA's debugger instructions. Here's an overview:

x	Output all registers
xr	Output and change of registers (ie xd0)
gn	Jump to address n. You'll be asked for break points, addresses at which the program should terminate.
jn	This is similar to the one above—a JSR is used to jump into the program. The program must end with a RTS instruction.
qn	Output the memory starting at address n. You can also specify the word length.
	For example: q.w $10000
nn	Disassembled output starting at address n
an	Direct assembling starting at address n. Direct program instructions are entered.
mn	Modify the contents of memory starting at address n. Here too, the word length can be given. You can terminate input with the <Esc> key.
sn	Executes the program instruction that the PC points to. After you enter this instruction, n program steps are executed.

f	Fill a memory area. You can choose the word width. All the needed parameters are asked for individually.
c	Copies one memory area to another. All the needed parameters are asked for individually.
?	Outputs the value of an expression or a label For example: ? run+$1000-256
a	Sets an instruction sequence that is passed to the program when it starts as if it was started from CLI with this sequence
!	Leave the SEKA assembler after being asked if you are sure.

You saw some of the calculations like SEKA can make in the "?" example. You can also use them in programming. The following operations work in SEKA:

+	Addition
-	Subtraction
*	Multiplication
/	Division
&	Logical AND
!	Logical OR
~	EXclusive OR (XOR)

These operations can also be combined. You can choose the counting system. A "$" stands for hexadecimal, "@" for octal, and "%" for binary. If these symbols aren't used, the number is interpreted as a decimal number.

Let's go back to the debugger. As mentioned, after entering "g Address", you'll be asked for break points. You can enter up to 16 addresses at which the program halts. If you don't enter break points, but instead hit <Return>, the program must end with an ILLEGAL instruction. If it ends instead with a RTS, the next return address from the stack is retrieved and jumped to. This is usually address 4 which causes SEKA to come back with "** Illegal Instruction at $000004", but there's no guarantee that it will. You're computer can end up so confused that it can't function.

The SEKA program puts an ILLEGAL instruction in the place specified as break points after saving the contents of these locations. If the processor hits an illegal instruction, it jumps back to the debugger by using the illegal instruction vector that SEKA set up earlier. Then SEKA repairs the modified memory locations and then displays the status line. Here you can find out where the program terminated.

Using break points is a good technique for finding errors in the program. You can, for example, put a break point in front of a routine that you're not sure about and start the program. When the program aborts at this spot, you can go through the routine step by step using the "s" option. Then you can watch what happens to the status line after each instruction and find the mistake.

Program errors are called bugs. That's why the program which finds them is called a debugger.

Chapter 4

Our First Programs

4. Our First Programs

You're getting pretty far along in your knowledge of machine language programming. In fact, you're to the point where you can write programs, and not just programs for demonstration purposes, but ones which serve a real function. We're assuming that you have the AssemPro assembler and have loaded it.

If you're using a different assembler, a few things must be done differently. We covered those differences already in the chapter on the different assemblers.

We've written the example programs as subroutines so they can be tried out directly and used later. After assembling the program, you can put the desired values in the register. Then you can either single-step thru the programs or run the larger programs and observe the results in the registers directly. (Using the SEKA assembler you can type "j Program_name" to start the program. Then you can read the results from the register directly, or use "q Address" to read it from memory.)

Let's start with an easy example, adding numbers in a table.

4.1 Adding tables

Imagine that you have numbers in memory that you'd like to add. Let's assume that you have five numbers whose length is one word each. You want their sum to be written in register D0. The easiest way to do this is:

```
;(4.1A)
adding1:
        clr.l   D0              ;Erase D0 (=0)
        move    table,d0        ;First entry in D0
        add     table+2,d0      ;Add second entry
        add     table+4,d0      ;Add third entry
        add     table+6,d0      ;Add fourth entry
        add     table+8,d0      ;Add fifth entry
        rts                     ;Return to main program
table:  dc.w 2,4,6,8,10
        end
```

Try out the program using the debugger by single stepping thru the program until you get to the RTS instruction (left Amiga T). (SEKA owners use "j adding1"). You see that data register D0 really contains the sum of the values.

The method above only reads and adds numbers from a particular set of addresses. The Amiga's processor has lots of different sorts of addressing modes that give us a shorter and more elegant solution. Let's add a variable to the address of the table, so that the program can add different tables.

Let's put the address of the table in an address register (for example, A0) instead. This register can be used as a pointer to the table. You must use move.l since only long words are relocatable. By using a pointer to a table you can use indirect addressing. You can change the expression "table+x" to "x(a0)".

```
;(4.1B)
adding1:
        clr.l   D0              ;Erase D0 (=0)
        move.l  #table, a0      ;Put table address in A0
        move    0(a0),d0        ;Put first entry in D0
        add     2(a0),d0        ;add second entry
        add     4(a0),d0        ;add third entry
        add     6(a0),d0        ;Add fourth entry
        add     8(a0),d0        ;Add fifth entry
        rts                     ;Return to main program
table:  dc.w 2,4,6,8,10

        end
```

Assemble this program, load it into the debugger. Then single step (left-Amiga T) thru this program and you'll see that this program adds five numbers in order just like the last one. The reason you used a step size of two for the offset is that words are two bytes long. AssemPro also defaults to relocatable code so that you must move #table as a long word.

Let's improve the program more by using "(a0)+" instead of "x(a)". This way, every time you access elements of the table, the address register A0 is automatically incremented by the number of bytes that are read (in this case two). The difference between this and the last example is that here the register's contents are modified. The pointer is to the next unused byte or word in memory.

Let's make it even better. Let's make the number of words to be added to a variable. You'll pass the number in register D1. Now you need to do a different sort of programming, since you can't do it with the old methods.

Let's use a loop. You need to add D1 words. You can use (a0)+ as the addressing method (Address register indirect with post increment), since this automatically gets you to the next word.

Now for the loop. You'll have D1 decremented by one every time the contents of the pointer are added. If D1 is zero, then you're done. Otherwise, you need another addition. The program looks like this:

```
;(4.1C)
adding2:
        clr.l   d0              ;Erase D0
        move.l  #table, a0      ;Put table address in A0
        move    #$5, d1         ;Put number of entries in d1

loop:                           ;Label for loop beginning
        add     (a0) +,d0       ;Add a word
        subq    #1,d1           ;Decrement counter
        bne     loop            ;Continue if non-zero
        rts                     ;Else done

table:  dc.w 2,4,6,8,10
        end
```

Let's take a close look at this program. Load the pointer A0 with the address of the data and the counter D1 with the number of elements. Then you can single step thru the program and watch the results. Make sure not to run the final command, the RTS command, because otherwise a return address is popped from the stack, and the results of this are unpredictable. (SEKA owners can use "x pc" to point the program counter to "adding2". You can then step through the program using the "s" command and watch the results.)

To finish up this example, you're assigning a little homework. Write the program so that it adds single bytes or long words. Try to write a program that takes the first value in a table and subtracts the following values. For example, the table

```
        table: dc.w 50,8,4,6
```

should return the value 50-8-4-6, ie 32 ($20).

4.2 Sorting a table

Let's keep working with tables. You don't want to just read data from one this time. You want to change it. You'll sort the table in ascending order.

You need to decide how to do the sorting. The simplest method is to do the following.

Compare the first and the second value. If the second value is larger than the first one, things are OK so far. Do the next step, compare the second and third values, and so on. If you come to the final pair and in each case the preceding value was smaller than the following value, then the sorting is done (it was unnecessary).

If you find a pair where the second value is smaller than the first, the two values are exchanged. You then set a flag (here let's use a register) that is checked once you're done going through the table. If it is set, the table probably isn't completely sorted. You then erase the flag and start again from the beginning. If the flag is still zero at the end, the sorting is complete.

Now let's write a program to do this. First let's figure out the variables you need. You'll use registers for the variables. You need a pointer to the table you're sorting (A0), a counter (D0) and a flag (D1). While the program is running, change these values, so you'll need two more registers to store the starting values (address and the number of table entries). You'll use A1 and D2.

Let's start writing the program, each section will be written and then explained. Then the complete program will be given. You put the table's address in A1 and the number of entries in D2.

```
;(4.2A) part of sort routine
sort:                          ;Start address of the program
        move.l  #table,a1      ;Load pointer with address
        move.l  a1,a0          ;Copy pointer to working register
        move.l  #5,d2          ;Number in the counter
        move.l  d2,d0          ;Copy number of elements
        subq    #2,d0          ;Correct counter value
        clr     d1             ;Erase flag

table: dc.w 3,6,8,9,5

        end
```

Now the preparations are complete. The pointer and the counter are ready and the flag is cleared. The counter is decremented by two because you want to use the DBRA command (take off one) and only X-1 comparisons are needed for X numbers (take off one more).

Next let's write the loop that compares the values. You compare one word with another. It looks like this:

```
loop:
        move    2(a0),d3        ;Next value in Register D3
        cmp     (a0),d3         ;Compare values
```

You need to use register D3 because CMP (A0),2(A0) isn't a legal choice. If the second value is greater than or equal to the first value, you can skip an exchange.

```
        bcc     noswap          ;Branch if greater than or equal
                                ;to
```

Now you need to do the exchanging (unfortunately you can't use exc 2(a0),(a0) since this form of addressing doesn't exist).

```
doswap:
        move    (a0),d1         ;Save first value
        move    2(a0),(a0)      ;Copy second into first word
        move    d1,2(a0)        ;Move first into second
        moveq   #1,d1           ;Set flag
noswap:
```

Now increment the counter and continue with the next pair. You do this until the counter is negative.

```
        addq.l  #2,a0           ;Pointer+2
        dbra    d0,loop         ;Continue looping until the end
```

Now you'll see if the flag is set. You start again at the beginning if it is.

```
        tst     d1              ;Test flag
        bne     sort            ;Not finished sorting yet!
        rts                     ;Otherwise done. Return.
```

If the flag is zero, you're done, and the subroutine ends. You jump back to the main program using the RTS command.

Now a quick overview of the complete program.

```
(4.2B)
sort:                                   ;Start address of the program
        move.l  #table,a1               ;Load pointer with address
        move.l  a1,a0                   ;Copy pointer to working
                                        ;register
        move.l  #5,d2                   ;Number in the counter
        move.l  d2,d0                   ;Copy number of elements
        subq    #2,d0                   ;Correct counter value
        clr     d1                      ;Erase flag

loop:
        move    2(a0),d3                ;Next value in Register D3
        cmp     (a0),d3                 ;Compare values
        bcc     noswap                  ;Branch if greater than or equal
                                        ;to

doswap:
        move    (a0),d1                 ;Save first value
        move    2(a0),(a0)              ;Copy second into first word
        move    d1,2(a0)                ;Move first into second
        moveq   #1,d1                   ;Set flag

noswap:
        addq.l  #2,a0                   ;Pointer+2
        dbra    d0,loop                 ;Continue looping until the end
        tst     d1                      ;Test flag
        bne     sort                    ;Not finished sorting yet!
        rts                             ;Otherwise done. Return.

table:  dc.w    10,8,6,4,2              ;When finished, acceding

        end
```

To test this subroutine, assemble the routine with AssemPro, save it and then load it into the debugger. The table is directly after the RTS, notice its order. Set a breakpoint at the RTS, select the address with the mouse and press left-Amiga-B sets a breakpoint in AssemPro. Start the program then redisplay the screen by selecting "Parameter-Display-Dissassem-bled" and examine the order of the numbers in the table, they should now be in ascending order.

You use several registers in this example for storing values. Usually in machine language programming your subroutines cannot change any registers or can only change certain registers. For this reason, there is a machine language command to push several registers onto the stack at the same time. This is the MOVEM ("MOVE Multiple") command. If you insert this command twice into your program, then you can have the registers return to the main program with the values they had when the subroutine was called. To do this, you need one more label. Let's call it "start"; the subroutine is started from here.

```
start:
        movem.l d0-d7/a0-a6,-(sp)      ;Save registers
sort:
        etc...
        ...
        ...
        bne     sort                  ;Not finished sorting yet!

        movem.l (sp)+,d0-d7/a0-a6      ;Retrieve registers
        rts                           ;Finished!
```

This powerful command moves several registers at the same time. You can specify which registers should be moved. If you want to move the D1, D2, D3, D7, A2 and A3 registers, just write

```
        movem.l d1-d3/d7/a2-a3,-(sp)
```

Before you quit sorting, do one little homework assignment. Modify the program, so that it sorts the elements in descending order.

4.3 Converting number systems

As we mentioned in the chapter on number systems, converting numbers from one base to another can be rather difficult. There is another form of numeric representation—as a string that can be entered via the keyboard or output on the screen.

You want to look at some of the many conversions possible and write programs to handle the task. You'll start by converting a hex number into a string using binary numbers and then print the number value in hex.

4.3.1   Converting hex to ASCII

First you need to set the start and finish conditions. In this example, let's assume that data register D1 contains a long word that should be converted into an 8-digit long string of ASCII characters. You'll write it to a particular memory location so that you can output it later.

The advantage of using hex instead of decimal is pretty clear in this example. To find out the hexadecimal digit for a particular spot in the number, you just need to take the corresponding 4 bits (half byte) and do some work on it. A half byte (also called a nibble) contains one hex digit.

You'll work on a half byte in D2. To convert this to a printable character, you need to use the correct ASCII code. The codes for the 16 characters that are used as hex digits are the following:

```
0    1    2    3    4    5    6    7    8    9    A    B    C    D    E    F

$30  $31  $32  $33  $34  $35  $36  $37  $38  $39  $41  $42  $43  $44  $45  $46
```

To convert the digits 0-9, you just need to add $30. For the letters A-F that correspond to the values 10-15, you need to add $37. The program to evaluate a half byte must make a distinction between values between 0 and 9 and those between A and F and add either $30 or $37.

Now let's write a machine language subroutine that you'll call for each digit in the long words hex representation.

```
nibble:
        and     #$0f,d2         ;Just keep low byte
        add     #$30,d2         ;Add $30
        cmp     #$3a,d2         ;Was it a digit?
        bcs     ok              ;Yes: done
        add     #7,d2           ;Else add 7
ok:
        rts                     ;Done
```

This routine converts the nibble in D2 to an ASCII character that corresponds to the hex value of the nibble. To convert an entire byte, you need to call the routine twice. Here is a program to do this. The program assumes that A0 contains the address of the buffer that the characters are to be put in and that D1 contains the byte that is converted.

```
;(4.3.1a) bin-hex
;                               ;your program
        lea     buffer,a0       ;Pointer to buffer
        move    #$4a,d1         ;Byte to be converted (Example)
        bsr     byte            ;and convert
        rts
;       ...                     ;more of your program
byte:
        move    d1,d2           ;Move value into D2
        lsr     #4,d2           ;Move upper nibble into lower
                                ;nibble
        bsr     nibble          ;Convert D2
        move.b  d2,(a0)+        ;Put character in buffer
        move    d1,d2           ;Value in D2
        bsr     nibble          ;Convert lower nibble
        move.b  d2,(a0)+        ;and put it in buffer
        rts                     ;Done
nibble:
        and     #$0f,d2         ;Just keep low byte
        add     #$30,d2         ;Add $30
        cmp     #$3a,d2         ;Was it a digit?
        bcs     ok              ;Yes: done
        add     #7,d2           ;Else add 7
ok:
        rts                     ;Done

buffer:
        blk.b 9,0               ;Space for long word data

        end
```

To test this subroutine, use AssemPro to assemble the routine, save the program and load it into the debugger. Next set a breakpoint at the first RTS, to set the breakpoint in AssemPro select the correct address with the mouse and press the right-Amiga-B keys. Start the program and watch the contents of D2, it is first $34 (ASCII 4) and finally $41 (ASCII A). Select "Parameter-Display-HEX-Dump" and you'll see that 4A has been moved into the buffer.

This is how the routine operates. First, you move the value that you wish to convert into D2. Then you shift the register four times to the right to move the upper nibble into the lower four bits. After the subroutine call, you use "move.b d2,(a0)+" to put the HI nibble in the buffer. Then the original byte is put in D2 again. It is converted. This gives us the LO nibble as an ASCII character in D2. You put this in the next byte of the buffer.

The buffer is long enough to hold a long word in characters and closing the null byte. The null byte is usually required by screen output routines. Screen output will be discussed in a later chapter. Now let's worry about converting a long word.

When converting a long word, you need to be sure to deal with the nibbles in the right order. Before calling the "nibble" routine for the first time, you need to move the upper nibble into the lower four bits of the long word. You need to do this without losing anything.

The LSR command isn't very good for this application. If you use it, you'll lose bits. It's better to use the rotation commands like ROR or ROL, since they move the bits that are shifted out, back in on the other side.

If you shift the original long word in D1 four times to the left, the upper four bits are shifted into the lower four bits. Now you can use our "nibble" routine to evaluate it and then put the resulting ASCII character in the buffer. You repeat this eight times and the whole long word has been converted. You even have D1 looking exactly the way it did before the conversion process began!

```
;(4.3.1B) bin-hex-2
hexlong:
        lea     buffer,a0       ;Pointer to the buffer
        move.l  #$12345678,d1   ;Data to convert
        move    #7,d3           ;Counter for the nibbles: 8-1

loop:
        rol     #4,d1           ;Move upper nibble into lower
        move    d1,d2           ;Write in D2
        bsr     nibble          ;And convert it
        move.b  d2,(a0)+        ;Character in buffer
        dbra    d3,loop         ;Repeat 8 times
        rts                     ;Finished!

nibble:
        and     #$0f,d2         ;Just keep low byte
        add     #$30,d2         ;Add $30
        cmp     #$3a,d2         ;Was it a digit?
        bcs     ok              ;Yes: done
        add     #7,d2           ;Else add 7
```

```
ok:
        rts                     ;Done

buffer:
        blk.b 9,0               ;Space for long word, null byte

        end
```

To test this subroutine, use AssemPro to assemble the routine, save the
program and load it into the debugger. Next set a breakpoint at the first
RTS, to set the breakpoint in AssemPro select the correct address with
the mouse and press the right-Amiga-B keys. Start the program and when
it is finished redisplay the output by selecting "Parameter-Display-HEX-
dump" so you can examine the new buffer contents.

You'll find that there's an error in the program—the buffer contains the
digits "56785678" instead of "12345678". Try to find the error!

Have you found it? This is the sort of error that causes you to start
pulling your hair out. This sort is hard to find. The assembler assumes
that the rotation operation should be done on a word, because the ".l" was
left off. As a result, only the lower word of D1 was rotated—so you get
the same value twice. If you change it to "rol.l", things work just right.

This error shows how easy it is to convert the program above into one
that converts four digit hex numbers into ASCII characters. Just leave off
the ".l" on the "rol" command and change the counter from seven to three.
The program is done.

Now for a little homework: change the program so that it can handle six
digit hex numbers (D1 doesn't necessarily have to stay the same ...)!

Now let's look at a different conversion problem: converting a four digit
decimal number.

4.3.2   Converting Decimal to ASCII

It's not quite as easy to convert to decimal as hex. You can't group the
bits to form individual digits. You need to use another method.

Let's look at how a decimal number is constructed. In a four digit number, the highest place is the thousand's place, the next is the hundred's
place, etc...

If you have the value in a register and divide by 1000, you'll get the value that goes in the highest place in the decimal number. Since the machine language command DIV not only gives us the result of division but also gives us the remainder, you can work with the remainder quite easily. You divide the remainder by 100 to find the hundred's place, divide the remainder of this by ten and get the ten's place, and the final remainder is the one's place.

This isn't so hard after all! Here's the program that follows the steps above to fill the buffer with D1's ASCII value.

```
main:
        lea     buffer,a0       ;Pointer to the buffer
        move    #1234,d1        ;Number to convert
        jsr     deci_4          ;test subroutine
        illegal                 ;room for break point

deci_4:                         ;Subroutine - four digit numbers

        divu    #1000,d1        ;Divide by 1000
        bsr     digit           ;Evaluate result-move remainder

        divu    #100,d1         ;Divide by 100
        bsr     digit           ;Evaluate result and move
                                remainder
        divu    #10,d1          ;Divide by 10
        bsr     digit           ;Evaluate result-move remainder

                                ;Evaluate the remainder directly

digit:
        add     #$30,d1         ;Convert result into ASCII
        move.b  d1,(a0)+        ;Move it into buffer
        clr     d1              ;Erase lower word
        swap    d1              ;Move the remainder down
        rts                     ;Return

buffer:blk.b 5,0                ;Reserve bytes for result

        end
```

To test this subroutine, use AssemPro to assemble the routine, save the program and load it into the debugger. Next set a breakpoint at the illegal instruction. To set the breakpoint in AssemPro select the correct address with the mouse and press the right-Amiga-B keys. This break point stops the program. Start the program and when it is finished redisplay the output by selecting "Parameter-Display-HEX-dump" so you can examine the ASCII values now in the buffer.

You use a little trick in this program that is typical for machine language programming. After calling "digit" three times from the subroutine "deci_4", you go right into the "digit" subroutine. You don't use a BSR or JSR command. Once the processor hits the RTS command, it returns to the main program, not the "deci_4" subroutine. Doing this, you save a fourth "bsr digit" command and an "rts" command for the "deci_4" routine.

Try the program out. Make sure that you use values that are smaller than 9999, because otherwise strange things can happen.

Now let's reverse what you've been doing and convert strings into binary numbers.

4.3.3   Converting ASCII to hex

In a string, each hex digit represents a half byte. You just need to write a program that exactly reverses what the hex conversion program did.

You have two choices

1.   The number of hex digits is known in advance
2.   The number is unknown

The first is easier to program, but has the disadvantage that if, you assume the strings are four digits in length and want to enter the value 1, you must enter 0001. That is rather awkward, so you'll use the second method.

Let's convert a single digit first. You'll pass a pointer to this digit in address register A0. You want the binary value to come back in data register D0.

The program looks like this:

```
          move.l   #string,a0     ;this example
          jsr      nibblein       ;test routine
          nop                     ; set breakpoint here

nibblein:                         ;* Convert the nibble from (A0)
          clr.l    d0             ;Erase D0
          move.b   (a0)+,d0       ;Get digit, increment A0
          sub      #'A',d0        ;Subtract $41
          bcc      ischar         ;No problem: In the range A-F

          add      #7,d0          ;Else correct value
ischar:
          add      #10,d0         ;Correct value
```

```
          rts

string: dc.b 'B',0                    ;character to convert

          end
```

To test this subroutine, use AssemPro to assemble the routine, save the program and load it into the debugger. Next set a breakpoint at the first NOP, to set the breakpoint in AssemPro select the correct address with the mouse and press the right-Amiga-B keys. Start the program and watch the contents of D0.

Let's see how the program works. A0 points to a memory location that contains the character "B" that is represented by the ASCII value $42. This number is loaded into D0 right after this register is erased.

After subtracting $41, you end up with the value $1. Now you're almost done. Before returning to the main program, you add 10 to get the correct value 11, $B.

If the buffer has a digit in it, the subtraction causes the register to become negative. The C flag is set. Let's take the digit 5 as an example.

The ASCII value of 5 is $35. After subtracting $41, you end up with -12 and the C flag is set. In this case, you won't branch with the BCC command. Instead you'll add 7 to get -5. Then 10 is added, and you end up with five. Done!

This routine has a disadvantage. If an illegal character is given, one that doesn't represent a hex digit, you'll get some nonsense result. Let's ignore error checking for the moment though.

Let's go on to multi-digit hex numbers. The first digit that you convert has the highest value and thus represents the highest nibble. To allow for this and to allow for an arbitrarily long number (actually not arbitrarily long, the number should fit in a long word—so it can only be eight digits long), you'll use a trick.

Take a look at the whole program. It handles the calculations and puts the result in D1. It assumes that A0 is a pointer to a string and that this string is ended by a null byte.

```
hexin:                              ;Converting a hex number
        clr.l   d1                  ;First erase D1
        move.l  #string, a0         ;Address of the string in A0
        jsr     hexinloop           ; test subroutine
        nop                         ; set break point here

hexinloop:
```

```
        tst.b   (a0)            ;Test digit
        beq     hexinok         ;Zero, then done
        bsr     nibblein        ;Convert digit
        lsl.l   #4,d1           ;Shift result
        or.b    d0,d1           ;Insert nibble
        bra     hexinloop       ;And continue
hexinok:
        rts
nibblein:                       ;Convert the nibble from (A0)
        clr.l   d0              ;Erase D0
        move.b  (a0)+,d0        ;Get digit, increment A0
        sub     #'A',d0         ;Subtract $41
        bcc     ischar          ;No problem: In the range A-F
        add     #7,d0           ;Else correct value
ischar:
        add     #10,d0          ;Correct value
        rts

string: DC.B "56789ABC',00      ;8 digit string, null byte
                                ; to be converted

        end
```

To test this subroutine, use AssemPro to assemble the routine, save the
program and load it into the debugger. Next set a breakpoint at the NOP,
to set the breakpoint in AssemPro select the correct address with the
mouse and press the right-Amiga-B keys. Start the program and watch the
contents of D1, the hex value is placed in this register.

The trick is to shift left four times, to shift one nibble. In this way, the
place of the last digit is incremented by one and there is room for the
nibble that comes back from the "nibblein" routine. The program uses the
TST.B instruction to check for the null byte at the end of the string,
when it encounters the null byte the program ends. The result is in the
D1 long word already!

To do some error checking, you need to make some changes in the program. You'll do this right after you come back from the "nibblein"
routine with the value of the current character.

If the value in D0 is bigger than $F, there is an error. You can detect this
in several ways. You chose the simplest one—you'll use CMP #$10,D0
to compare D0 with $10. If it is smaller, then the C flag is set (since
CMP uses subtraction) and everything is fine. If C is zero, there is an
error.

You can use this trick to skip the test for a null byte, since it's an invalid
character as well. The program looks like this:

```
;(4_3_3C) hex-conv2                Optional disk name
hexin:                            ;Converting a hex number
        clr.l    d1               ;First erase D1
        move.l   #string, a0      ;Address of the string in A0
        jsr      hexinloop        ;test subroutine
        nop                       ; set break point here


hexinloop:
        bsr      nibblein         ;Convert digit
        cmp      $10,d0           ;Test if good
        bcc      hexinok          ;No,then done
        lsl.l    #4,d1            ;Shift result
        or.b     d0,d1            ;Insert nibble
        bra      hexinloop        ;And continue
hexinok:
        rts
nibblein:                         ;Convert the nibble from (A0)
        clr.l    d0               ;Erase D0
        move.b   (a0)+,d0         ;Get digit, increment A0
        sub      #'A',d0          ;Subtract $41
        bcc      ischar           ;No problem: In the range  A-F
        add      #7,d0            ;Else correct value
ischar:
        add      #10,d0           ;Correct value
        rts

string: DC.B "56789ABC',00        ;8 digit string ending with a
                                  ; null byte to be converted
        end
```

To test this subroutine, use AssemPro to assemble the routine, save the program and load it into the debugger. Next set a breakpoint at the NOP, to set the breakpoint in AssemPro select the correct address with the mouse and press the right-Amiga-B keys. Start the program and watch the contents of D1, the hex value is placed in this register.

This is the method for converting hex to binary. If you convert decimal to binary, the conversion is not much harder.

4.3.4 Converting ASCII to decimal

You can use a very similar method to the one used above. Since you're not sure how many digits there are, you'll use a similar method for putting digits of a number in the next place up. You can't do this with shifting, but you can multiply by 10 and add the value of the digit.

Here's the program for converting decimal numbers.

```
decin:                              ;Converting a decimal number
        clr.l    d1                 ;First erase D1
        move.l   #string,a0         ;The string to convert
        jsr      decinloop          ;Test subroutine
        nop                         ;Breakpoint here
decinloop:
        bsr      digitin            ;Convert digit
        cmp      #10,d0             ;Test, if valid
        bcc      decinok            ;No, then done
        mulu     #10,d1             ;Shift result
        add      d0,d1              ;Insert nibble
        bra      decinloop          ;And continue

decinok:
        rts                         ;End of conversion

digitin:                            ;Converting the nibble from (A0)

        clr.l    d0                 ;Erase D0
        move.b   (a0)+,d0           ;Get digit, increment A0
        sub      #'0',d0            ;Subtract $30
        rts

string: dc.b '123456'               ;ASCII decimal string to convert


        end
```

To test this subroutine, use AssemPro to assemble the routine, save the program and load it into the debugger. Next set a breakpoint at the NOP, to set the breakpoint in AssemPro select the correct address with the mouse and press the right-Amiga-B keys. Select "Parameter-Output numbers-Decimal" so the registers are displayed as decimal numbers. Then start the program and watch the contents of D1, the decimal value is placed in this register.

This program can only convert numbers up to 655350, although the hex conversion routine can go higher. That's because the MULU command can only multiply 16-bit words. The last multiplication that can be done correctly is $FFFF*10--65535*10, which gives us the value 655350. Normally this is a large enough range, so you won't complicate the program further.

Chapter 5

Hardware Registers

5 Hardware Registers

You can get information about hardware functions without using library functions. You can use the hardware registers instead. These are memory locations at particular addresses that are neither in RAM nor in ROM. They are direct interfaces between the processor and its peripheral devices.

Each device has a number of hardware registers that the processor accesses to control graphics, sound and input/output. There are lots of possibilities for assembly language programmers. We'll only be able to go into a few examples.

The registers are generally used in byte-wise fashion. You'll find an example in the next chapter.

5.1 Checking for special keys

Load AssemPro and enter the debugger, select "Parameter-Display-From Address" and enter $BFEC00. Next select "Parameter-Display-HEX-Dump" to display the memory. (To use the SEKA assembler or a similar monitor program, enter "q $bfec00".)

You'll see a byte-wise listing of the addresses starting at $BFEC00 in which two bytes always repeat. These two bytes represent the status of two hardware registers.

The mirroring occurs because not all the address bits are used in decoding the address. In addressing this register, only the upper two bytes of the address and the low bit, bit 0, are used. The address of the two registers goes like this: $BFECxx, where the lower address byte xx doesn't contain any information in bits 1-7. Only bit 0 contains information about the desired register. You'll find this odd form of addressing with most hardware registers.

Let's look at the information in these registers. Let's look at the second register, $BFEC01. Hold down the <Alt> key and select "Parameter-Display-HEX-Dump" to re-display the screen. (SEKA owners must enter "q $bfec00" and press the <Alt> key right after pressing the <Return>

key.) You'll see that contents of every two bytes ($BFEC01, $BFEC03, etc...) have been changed to $37. This is the status of the special keys. This is also true for the other special keys. The following keys produce the bytes:

Shift left	$3F
Shift right	$3D
Control	$39
Alternate	$37
Amiga left	$33
Amiga right	$31

You can use this register to have a machine language program check if one of these keys was pressed and then respond by calling or ending a function. A program section might look like this:

```
skeys = $bfec01
        ...
        cmp.b   #$37,skeys      ;Alternate pressed?
        beq     function1       ;Yes!
        cmp.b   #$31,skeys      ;or right Amiga?
        beq     function2       ;Yes!
        ...                     ;and so on...
```

5.2 Timing

If you want to find out how much time elapsed between two events, you can use a hardware register to keep track of time quickly and precisely. The Amiga contains just such a time keeper: the I/O port componant. This chip has a 24 bit wide counter that has a 60 Hertz clock.

These 24 bits can't be read at once, for instance with a MOVE.L command, because the register is divided into three bytes. The low byte is at address $BFE801, the middle at $BFE901, and the high byte with bits 16-23 at $BFEA01.

Here's an example of a way to use this register: finding out how long a subroutine takes to run.

```
test:
        bsr     gettime         ;Put current time in D7
        move.l  d7,d6           ;Save it in D6
        bsr     routine         ;Routine to be timed
        bsr     gettime         ;Get the time again
        sub.l   d6,d7           ;Elapsed time in
        ...                     ;1/50 seconds is in D7!
        nop                     ; set breakpoint here to stop

routine:                        ; test routine
        move    #500,d0         ; delay counter
loop:
        dbra    d0,loop         ;count down
        rts

gettime:
        move.b  $bfea01,d7      ;HI-Byte in D0
        lsl.l   #4,d7           ;Shift twice by 4 bits,
        lsl.l   #4,d7           ;(8 bits shifted)
        move.b  $bfe901,d7      ;Get MID-Byte
        lsl.l   #4,d7
        lsl.l   #4,d7           ;Shift again
        move.b  $bfe801,d7      ;Get the LO-Byte
        rts                     ;Done
```

5.3 Reading the mouse - joystick

There are two hardware registers for the mouse and the joystick. They contain the state (or the position) of these input devices. It's interesting that the same port is used with both the mouse and the joystick even though they work completely different.

The joystick has four switches that are closed during movement and give off a potential (-) that is related to the movement of the joystick/mouse. The mouse's movements give off lots of quick signals—two for horizontal and two for vertical movement.

The computer must keep an eye on the ports so that it can evaluate the signals and calculate the new mouse position. This isn't the work of the processor though; it already has too much to do.

You find the status of the mouse/joystick port at address $DFF00A for port 1 and $DFF00C for port 2. The information in these words is for vertical mouse movement in the lower byte and for horizontal movement in the upper byte.

AssemPro owners be careful! Don't read these addresses, because for some reason that causes the computer to crash. This looks interesting (the screen begins to dance), but you can only recover by pressing <Reset> and loosing all of your data.

To read this register, let's write a short program.

```
;(5.3A) mouse

test:
        jsr     run             ;Test subroutine
        jmp     test            ;continue until broken
        nop                     ;Breakpoint here

joy = $dff00a
run:
        move    joy,d6          ;Data Item 1 in D6
        move    joy+2,d7        ;Data Item 2 in D7
        jmp     run             ;rts for Seka and other

        end
```

If you assemble the program and start Breakable in the debugger (SEKA - "j run"), D6 and D7 contain the contents of the two registers. Move the mouse a bit and watch the register contents.

As you see, the value in D6 is different. If you just move the mouse horizontally, only the lower byte's value is different, if just moved vertically only the upper byte is different.

You are not getting the absolute position of the mouse pointer on the screen. You can see that easily by moving the mouse into the upper left corner, then reading the value by restarting the program, and then move the mouse left again. As you can see, the register's contents are always relative.

Change the program as follows:

```
;(5.3B)                      mouse difference

test:
        jsr     run     ;Test subroutine
        jmp     test    ;continue until broken
        nop             ;Breakpoint here

joy = $dff00a
run:
        move    d7,d6   ;Old position in D6
        move    joy,d7  ;New position in D7
        sub     d7,d6   ;Difference in D6
        jmp     run     ;rts for Seka and other

        end
```

Start Breakable (right-Amiga-A) in the AssemPro debugger and watch D6, the result is zero or D7. (SEKA owners have to start the program two times. The result in D6 is zero.) If you move the mouse, D6 contains the difference between the old and new positions since the start. You'll find the vertical and horizontal position of the mouse relative to the last time you looked. In this way, you can use this register to find the relative mouse movement between two checks.

Now to check the joysticks. Put a joystick in port 2 and change the address $DFF00A to $DFF00C in the program. Start Breakable in the AssemPro debugger and watch D6, the result is zero or D7. (SEKA owners have to start the program two times. The result in D6 is zero.)

Move the joystick up. You'll get the value $FF00. One was subtracted from the upper byte. Let the joystick loose. This time you get the value $100—one is added. You'll get the same effect when you move the joystick left—after you let go, one is subtracted.

The individual movements and their effects on the joystick program are:

up	$FF00	HI-Byte -1
down	$FFFF	LO-Byte -1
left	$0100	HI-Byte +1
right	$0001	LO-Byte +1

These values aren't terribly reliable. If you move the joystick a lot and then look at the value, you'll find a crazy value in D6. This is because the input driver thinks that a mouse is attached. Nevertheless, this is the quickest way to read a joystick. In this way, an external device that gives off evaluatable TTL signals can be connected to the port and watched by a machine language program.

Now you just need to find out whether the fire button has been pressed, and you'll know how to get all the information you need from the joystick. The button's state is in bit 7 of the byte that is in memory location $BFE001. If the bit is set, the button wasn't pressed. That's true for the joystick connected to port 2. Bit 6 of this byte contains the button's state when the joystick is in port 1 or the state of the left mouse button.

Let's stay on port 2. You can test bit 7 to execute a function when the joystick button is pressed without any problems. Bit 7 is the sign bit. You can use this program segment:

```
        tst.b   $bfe001         ;Was fire button 2 hit?
        bpl     fire            ;Yes! Branch
```

The TST.B instruction tests the addressed byte and sets the Z and the N flag. If the N flag is set, you know that bit 7 of the tested byte is set. Since the fire button turns on LO potential, the bit is erased when the button is pressed. The N flag works that way with the TST command as well. The BPL command in the program above branches if the button was pressed. The PL stands for plus and it is set when the sign bit is cleared.

Here is the complete program to check the fire button and joystick difference:

```
;(5.3C)  fire button & joy difference

test:
        jsr     run             ;Test subroutine
        tst.b   $bfe001         ;Was fire button 2 hit?
        bpl     fire            ;Yes! Branch
        jmp     test            ;continue until broken

joy = $dff00a
run:
```

```
        move    d7,d6       ;Old position in D6
        move    joy,d7      ;New position in D7
        sub     d7,d6       ;Difference in D6
        jmp     run         ;rts for Seka and other

fire:
        nop                 ;Breakpoint here


        end
```

5.4 Tone production

It's fun to make noises and sounds. The Amiga let's you use Audio Devices and various I\O structures to play tones, noises and/or music pieces in the background. You'll leave this method to C or BASIC programmers, since you can use short machine language programs to directly program the audio hardware.

The Paula chip has all the capabilities needed for tone production. This chip can be accessed using the hardware registers of the processor. No library of any high level language can do more than you can—program the chip.

How does it work? Since the disk uses Direct Memory Access (DMA) to get information, you just need to tell it where to look for the tone or tone sequences that you would like played. You also need to tell it how to interpret the data.

Let's start with the easiest case—producing a constant tone. A tone like this consists of a single oscillation that is repeated over and over. If you make a diagram of the oscillation, you see the wave form of the oscillation. There are several standard waves: sine, square, triangle and saw tooth. The simplest is the square wave.

To produce a square wave, you just need to turn the loud speaker on and off. The frequency that occurs here is the frequency of the tone.

You want to produce such a tone using the Amiga. First you need to make a table that contains the amplitude of the tone you wish to produce. For a square wave, you only need two entries in the table, a large and a small value. Since the sound chip in the Amiga has amplitude values between -128 and +127, our table looks like this:

```
soundtab:
       dc.b -100,100
```

You need to give the address of the table to the sound chip. You have four choices, since the Amiga has four sound channels. The address of the hardware register in which the table address for channel 0 must be written is $DFF0A0; for channel 1 it is $DFF0B0; for channel 2 it's $DFF0C0; for channel 3 it's $DFF0D0. For stereo output, channels 0 and 3 control the left loud speaker. Channels 1 and 2 control the right loud speaker. For example, choose channel 0 and write the following:

```
move.l #soundtab,$DFF0A0      ;Address of the table
```

Next, you need to tell the sound chip how many items there are in the table. The data is read from beginning to end and sent to the loud speaker. Once it reaches the end, it starts over at the beginning. Since the sound chip gets this one word at a time, even though the data is in bytes, the table must always have an even number of bytes. The length that you give it is the number of words, the number of bytes/2.

You put the length for channel 0 in the register at address $DFF0A4 (for channel x just add x*$10!):

```
move #1,$dff0a4       ;Length of table in words
```

Now you have to tell it how quickly to read the data and output it to the loud speaker. This word determines the frequency. However, it does this "backwards". The larger the value, the lower the frequency. Choose the value 600 for this example:

```
move #600,$dff0a6     ;Read in rate
```

Now you need to decide the loudness level for the tone or noise. You have 65 different levels to choose from. Let's choose the middle level value 40 for our example.

```
move #40,$dff0a8      ;Loudness level
```

That's the data that the sound chip needs to produce the tone. However, nothing happens yet. What next? The chip can't tell if the data that's in the registers is valid, so it doesn't know if it should use the data.

You need to work with the DMA control register at address $DFF096 to let it know. You only need six bits of this word for your purposes:

Bit 15 ($8000)	If this bit is set, every bit that is written to this internal register is set. Otherwise the bits are erased. Zero bits aren't affected. This is very useful because this word also contains DMA information for disk operations that shouldn't be changed.
Bit 9 ($200)	This bit makes it possible for the chip to access DMA memory. If you want to start playing the tone, you need to set this bit.
Bits 0-3	Turn channel 0-3 on when the bits are set.

You'll start your tone by setting bits 15, 9 and 0:

```
        move #$8000+$200+1,$dff096      ;Start DMA
```

Here's an example of tone production—this time with a tone using a sine
wave:

```
;** Sound generation using hardware registers ** (5.5A)
ctlw = $dff096                      ;DMA Control
c0thi = $dff0a0                     ;Table address HI
c0tlo = c0thi+2                     ;Table address LO
c0tl = c0thi+4                      ;Table length
c0per = c0thi+6                     ;Read in Rate
c0vol = c0thi+8                     ;Loudness level
run:                                ;* Produce a simple tone
        move.l  #table,c0thi        ;Table beginning
        move    #8,c0tl             ;Table length--8 words
        move    #400,c0per          ;Read in rate
        move    #40,c0vol           ;Loudness level (Volume)
        move    #$8201,ctlw         ;DMA/Start Sound
        rts

 data                               ;>500K place in CHIP memory
 table:                             ;Sound table: sine
 dc.b -40,-70,-40,0,40,70,40,0

        end
```

To test this subroutine, use AssemPro to assemble the routine, save the
program and load it into the debugger. Next set a breakpoint at the RTS,
to set the breakpoint in AssemPro select the correct address with the
mouse and press the right-Amiga-B keys. Start the program and listen to
the tone. You need another routine to turn the tone off, turn your sound
down for now.

To turn the tone off, you just need to erase bit 0 of the DMA control
register. To do this, you just need to write a 0 in bit 15 and all the set
bits in this register are erased. To erase bit 0, just write a one to the
memory location: bit 15=0 => bit 0 is erased. Here's a small routine to
stop the tone coming from channel 0:

```
still:                              ;* Turn off tone
        move    #1,ctlw             ;Turn off channel 1
        rts
```

Now let's use the routine in a program to produce a short peep tone, that
you could, for instance, use as a key click:

```
;** Producing a peep tone **
ctlw  = $dff096                     ;DMA Control
c0thi = $dff0a0                     ;HI table address
c0tlo = c0thi+2                     ;LO table address
c0tl  = c0thi+4                     ;Table length
c0per = c0thi+6                     ;Read in rate
```

```
c0vol = c0thi+8                ;Volume
beep:                          ;* Produce a short peep tone
      move.l #table,c0thi      ;Table beginning
      move   #8,c0tl           ;Table length
      move   #400,c0per        ;Read in rate
      move   #65,c0vol         ;Volume
      move   #$8201,ctlw       ;Start DMA (Sound)
      move.l #20000,d0         ;Delay counter
loop:
      dbra d0,loop             ;Count down
still:
      move #1,ctlw             ;Turn off tone
      rts
table:                         ;Sound table
      dc.b 40,70,90,100,90,70,40,0,-4,0
      end
```

You can play up to four tones at the same time in such a way that they
are independent of each other. The Amiga also offers another method of
making the sound more interesting: you can modulate the tone.

Let's produce a siren tone. You could do this by figuring out the entire
sequence and programming it. However, as you can well imagine, that's a
lot of work.

It's much easier to use two tone channels. Let's use channel 1 for the
base tone and channel 0 for its modulation. Channel 0 needs to hold the
envelope of the siren tone. It needs to give the expanding and contracting
of the tone at the right speed.

You then have two ways that you can have channel zero work with
channel one. You can control the volume via channel 0, the read in rate
(frequency), or both. For our example, you'll use the frequency modulation.

Change the program as follows:

```
;** Modulated sound generation via hardware registers **
ctlw  = $dff096                ;DMA Control
adcon = $dff09e                ;Audio/Disk Control
c0thi = $dff0a0                ;HI table address
c0tlo = c0thi+2                ;LO table address
c0tl  = c0thi+4                ;Table length
c0per = c0thi+6                ;Read in rate
c0vol = c0thi+8                ;Volume
run:
      move.l #table,c0thi+16;Table start for channel 1
      move   #8,c0tl+16        ;Table length -- 8 words
      move   #300,c0per+16     ;Read in rate
      move   #40,c0vol+16      ;Volume

      move.l #table2,c0thi     ;Table start for channel 0
```

```
        move    #8,c0tl             ;Table length
        move    #60000,c0per        ;Read in rate
        move    #30,c0vol           ;Volume

        move    #$8010,adcon        ;Modulation mode: FM
        move    #$8203,ctlw         ;Start DMA
        rts
still:                              ;* Turn off tone
        move    #$10,adcon          ;No more modulations
        move    #3,ctlw             ;Turn off channels
        rts
table:                              ;Data for basic tone
dc.b -40,-70,-90,-100,-90,-70,-40,0
dc.b 40,70,90,100,90,70,40,0
table2:                            ;Data for Modulation
dc.w 400,430,470,500,530,500,470,430

        end
```

When you start the program, you'll hear a siren. You can change this tone to your heart's content.

Did you notice the added "adcon" register. This register controls the modulation of the audio channel as well as handling disk functions. The same technique is used here as for the DMA control register, bits can only be set if bit 15 is. As a result, you don't have to worry about the disk bits. I'd recommend against experimentation.

Control bit 15 isn't the only one of interest to you. You can also use bits 0-7, because they determine which audio channel modulates another channel. There is a restriction, though. A channel can only modulate the next higher numbered channel. For this reason, you use channel 1 for the basic tone and channel 0 for the modulation in the example. You can't, for example, modulate channel three with channel zero. Channel 3 can't be used to modulate any other channel.

Here is an overview of bits 0-7 of the "adcon" register.

Bit	Function
0	Channel 0 modulates the volume of channel 1
1	Channel 1 modulates the volume of channel 2
2	Channel 2 modulates the volume of channel 3
3	Turn of channel 3
4	Channel 0 modulates the frequency of channel 1
5	Channel 1 modulates the frequency of channel 2
6	Channel 2 modulates the frequency of channel 3
7	Turn off channel 3

In the example, you set bit 4, which put channel 0 in charge of channel one's frequency modulations.

When you've chosen a channel for use in modulating another channel, some of the parameters of the channel change. You don't need to give volume for this channel, so you can omit it. Now the table's data is looked at as words instead of as bytes. These words are read into the register of the modulated register at a predetermined rate. The Read in Rate Register determines the rate.

If you want to modulate the frequency and the volume of another channel (In the example, set bits 0 and 4 of "adcon"), the data is interpreted a little differently. The first word in the table is the volume, the second is the read in rate, and so on. It alternates back and forth. In this way, you can, for instance, produce the siren tone.

5.5 Hardware registers overview

The following tables should give you an overview of the most important hardware registers. There's not enough room to describe each register, so I'd recommend getting a hold of the appropriate technical literature. If you experiment with these registers, you should keep in mind that this can cause the computer to crash. Save your data to disk and then take the disk out of the drive, because you might cause the disk drive to execute some wierd functions.

Let's start with the PIAs. This covers the PIA type 8520. You should keep in mind that some functons and connection of the 8520 are integrated into the Amiga and so there are limitations on what you can do with the PIAs.

PIA A	PIA B	Register's Meaning
BFE001	BFE000	Data register A
BFE101	BFE100	Data register B
BFE201	BFE200	Data direction register A
BFE301	BFE300	Data direction register B
BFE401	BFE400	Timer A LO
BFE501	BFE500	Timer A HI
BFE601	BFE600	Timer B LO
BFE701	BFE700	Timer B HI
BFE801	BFE800	Event register Bits 0-7
BFE901	BFE900	Event register Bits 8-15
BFEA01	BFEA00	Event register Bits 16-23
BFEB01	BFEB00	Unused
BFEC01	BFEC00	Serial data register
BFED01	BFED00	Interrupt control register
BFEE01	BFEE00	Control register A
BFEF01	BFEF00	Control register B

Some internal meanings:

$BFE101	Data register for the parallel interface
$BFE301	Data direction register for the parallel interface
$BFEC01	State of the keyboard, contains the last special key pressed (Shift, Alternate, Control, Amiga)

Now come the registers that are used for tone production. The first two registers should be treated especially carefully—if they are used wrong, very nasty effects can occur.

These registers can be either read or written only. This information is included under R/W in the table.

Address	R/W	Meaning
DFF096	W	Write DMA Control
DFF002	R	Read DMA Control and Blitter Status
-- Audio channel 0 --		
DFF0AA	W	Data register
DFF0A0	W	Pointer to table beginning Bits 16-18
DFF0A2	W	Pointer to table beginning Bits 0-15
DFF0A4	W	Table length
DFF0A6	W	Read in Rate / Period
DFF0A8	W	Volume
-- Audio channel 1 --		
DFF0BA	W	Data register
DFF0B0	W	Pointer to table beginning Bits 16-18
DFF0B2	W	Pointer to table beginning Bits 0-15
DFF0B4	W	Table length
DFF0B6	W	Read in Rate / Period
DFF0B8	W	Volume
-- Audio channel 2 --		
DFF0CA	W	Data register
DFF0C0	W	Pointer to table beginning Bits 16-18
DFF0C2	W	Pointer to table beginning Bits 0-15
DFF0C4	W	Table length
DFF0C6	W	Read in Rate / Period
DFF0C8	W	Volume
-- Audio channel 3 --		
DFF0DA	W	Data register
DFF0D0	W	Pointer to table beginning Bits 16-18
DFF0D2	W	Pointer to table beginning Bits 0-15
DFF0D4	W	Table length
DFF0D6	W	Read in Rate / Period
DFF0D8	W	Volume

Now for the registers that contain information about the joystick, mouse or potentiometer. These addresses have been gone over in part previously.

Address	R/W	Meaning
DFF00A	R	Joystick/Mouse Port 1
DFF00C	R	Joystick/MousePort 2
DFF012	R	Potentiometer pair 1 Counter
DFF014	R	Potentiometer pair 2 Counter
DFF018	R	Potentiometer connection
DFF034	W	Potentiometer port direction

Chapter 6

The Operating System

6 The Operating System

Now let's take a step forward in your ability to write assembly language programs. It's not enough to put a piece of text in memory someplace. You want to be able to put it on the screen. Do you know how to write a character on the screen? Do you know how to draw a window on the screen that can be modified by the mouse? Actually, you don't have to have terribly precise knowledge about such topics.

Fortunately, the Amiga's operating system supplies routines that take care of common tasks like this. It can seem quite complicated due to the number of routines necessary. These routines are in libraries. We'll look at the libraries in some depth now.

6.1 Load libraries

Before you can use a library, it must be available. It has to be loaded into memory. Unfortunately, the whole library must be loaded, even if you only need one of the functions.

First you need to decide what the program must be able to do, so you can see which libraries you'll need. For simple I/O text, you don't need a library that contains routines for moving graphics!

There are a number of libraries on a normal Workbench disk. Here's an overview of the names and the sort of functions they contain:

exec.library This library is needed to load the other libraries. It is already in memory and doesn't need to be loaded. It's in charge of basic functions like reserving memory and working with I/O channels.

dos.library Contains all the functions for normal I/O operations, for instance screen or disk access.

intuition.library Used for working with screens, windows, menus, etc...

clist.library This contains routines for working with the Copper lists that are used for controlling the screen.

console.library   Contains graphics routines for text output in console windows.

diskfont.library   Used for working with the character fonts that are stored on the disk.

graphics.library   This library contains functions to control the Blitter (or graphics) chip. It's used for basic graphics functions.

icon.library   Used in the development and use of Workbench symbols (icons).

layers.library   Used for working with screen memory (layers).

mathffp.library   Contains basic math floating point operations.

mathieeedoubbas.library
Contains basic math functions for integers.

mathtrans.library
Contains higher level mathematical functions.

potgo.library   Used for evaluating analog input to the Amiga.

timer.library   Contains routines for time critical programs. They can be used to program exact time intervals.

translator.library   Contains the single function "Translate", that translates normal text written phonetically for the narrator, the speech synthesizer.

You can open (load) all these libraries of course. You should remember that this takes time and memory. For this reason, you should always think about which functions you need and which libraries they are in.

For example, let's say you want to write a program that does text input /output. You need the "dos.library", so it can be loaded.

The "exec.library" is in charge of loading. This library contains the Open-Lib function that can be called once you've passed the needed parameters. AssemPro Amiga includes all of the libraries necessary for the Amiga, it also includes files that contain the offsets for the operating system calls. The macros contained in AssemPro ease assembly language programming considerably. To make the programs in this book useful to the largest audience the following examples are written for generic assemblers and do not include AssemPro's macros. We have used the AssemPro ILABEL and the macros INIT_AMIGA and EXIT_AMIGA so AssemPro owners can start the programs from the desktop. If you are using a different assembler check your documentation for instructions on linking programs.)

6.2 Calling functions

Since this chapter is rather complex we'll first describe the fundamental routines necessary to use the Amiga's operating system, after a decsription a complete program is listed. Every library begins in memory with a number of JMP commands. These JMPs branch to the routines that are in the library. To call a function, you need to find the beginning of this JMP table and call function x by going to the xth JMP command. Usually you use an offset to get to the right JMP command. Normally, you don't start at the beginning but at the end of the JMP table, so use negative offsets.

It works out very easily. Now let's open the "dos.library" by using "exec.library's" base address. This address is $000004. To call a function from another library, you need to use another base address.

Now you need the offset for the function that you want. You want the OpenLib function that has -408 as an offset. You'll find a list of function offsets in the appendix.

You need a pointer to the name of the library you are loading for the OpenLib function (in this case "dos.library") and a long word in memory that you can use to store the base address of the DOS library. You get this back from the OpenLib function. You need to be sure to write the library name in lowercase letters (dos.library), otherwise you can't open it. I entered a name in capital letters once and spent a lot of time finding this error.

The routine looks like this:

```
;** Load the DOS library 'dos.library' (6.2A) **
ExecBase  = 4              ;Base address of the EXEC
                           ;library
OpenLib   = -408           ;Offset from the OpenLib
                           ;function

IoErr     = -132           ;Offset for IoErr information

init:
        move.l  ExecBase,a6    ;Base address in A6
        lea     dosname,a1     ;Address of library name
        moveq   #0,d0          ;Version number
        jsr     OpenLib(a6)    ;Open DOS library
        move.l  d0,dosbase     ;Save DOS base address
```

```
          beq      error           ;If zero, then error!
          ...                      ;Your program goes here
          ...                      ;More program...


error:                             ;Error
          move.l   dosbase,a6      ;Address of library name
          jsr      IoErr(a6)       ;Call IoErr for error info
          move.l   d0,d5
          ...                      ;Your error routine goes here
          rts



dosname:                           ;Name of the library to opened
          dc.b     'dos.library',0,0
          align                    ;Seka uses - even
dosbase:                           ;Storage for DOS base address
          blk.l    1


          end
```

This is the way to load the DOS library so that you can use it. All library
functions are called in this way. Parameters are put in registers and passed
to the function. When there is an error, when the function doesn't run
correctly, a zero is usually put in data register D0

Once your program is done with its work, you need to close the libraries
that are still open before you return to the CLI or Workbench. The
CloseLib function (offset -414) takes care of this job. This function is in
the EXEC library just like OpenLib. The only parameter it needs is the
base address of the library that is closed. To close "dos.library", do the
following:

```
CloseLib = -414,          ; (6.2 B)
          ...
          move.l   ExecBase,a6     ;EXEC base address
          move.l   dosbase,a1      ;DOS base address
          jsr      CloseLib(a6)    ;Close library
```

6.3 Program initialization

Before you can start a program, you need to initialize many things so that
the program can run.

Let's take an example program that does some text editing. A program
like this must be able to store text, so it needs to be able to access memory. It also needs to be able to accept keyboard input and to do screen
output, so it needs an output window.

To do this, you need to open one or more of the libraries that we talked
about earlier. Let's assume that you've loaded the DOS library, so that
you can do the next steps.

6.3.1   Reserve memory

There are several ways to get the operating system to assign you a chunk
of memory. You need to use one of them, so that during multitasking,
you don't have one program overwritting another programs memory area.

Let's look at the function that is normally used. This function is in the
resident EXEC library and has the name AllocMem (offset -$c6). It
reserves a memory area, using the value in D0 as the length. The address
that the memory area begins at is returned in the D0 data register. If it
returns zero, the program couldn't give you that much memory.

You can also use a mode word in D1 to determine whether the memory
area that is reserved should be erased or not.

The routine looks like this:

```
ExecBase = 4                    ;(6.3.1A)
AllocMem = -$c6
    ...
        move.l  #number,d0      ;Number of bytes to reserve
        move    #mode,a6        ;Mode word
        move.l  ExecBase,a6     ;DOS base address in A6
        jsr     AllocMem(a6)    ;Call function
        move.l  d0,address      ;Save memory's start address
        beq     error           ;Memory not reserved
```

...

The second way to reserve memory is to use the AllocAbs function (off-set -$CC). This function in contrast to the AllocMem function reserves a particular memory area. The D0 register contains the number of bytes that should be reserved. Address register A1 contains the desired start address. This function returns a zero in D0 if the memory area can't be reserved.

```
ExecBase = 4                            ;(6.3.1b)
AllocAbs = -$cc
    ...
    move.l  #number,d0      ;Number of bytes to reserve
    lea     address,a1      ;Desired start address
    move.l  execbase,a6     ;EXEC base address
    jsr     AllocAbs(a6)    ;Reserve memory
    tst.l   d0              ;Everything OK?
    beq     error           ;No!
    ...
```

When the program has done its work and must return to the CLI or the Workbench, it needs to return the memory it has reserved to the system. The FreeMem function (offset -$D2) handles this.

This function works like AllocAbs in that the number of bytes is put in D0 and the start address of the memory area is put in A1. If you try to free up a memory area that wasn't reserved, you usually crash the computer.

The routine to free up a memory area looks like this:

```
ExecBase = 4                            ;(6.3.1C)
FreeMem  = -$d2
    ...
    move.l  #number,d0      ;Number of bytes released
    lea     address,a1      ;Start address from AllocAbs
    move.l  ExecBase,a6     ;EXEC base address
    jsr     FreeMem(a6)     ;Free up memory
    tst.l   d0              ;Everything OK ?
    beq     error           ;No !
    ...
```

6.3.2   Opening a simple window

The title of this chapter may sound a bit strange. However, the differences between the two different methods of opening a window are so great that they should be handled in separate chapters.

The method of opening a window presented here is very simple, but it doesn't allow you to work with all of the gadgets. These gadgets include the close symbol in the upper left corner of a window and the size symbol in the lower left corner.

If you open the window in the simple manner, almost all the gadgets are present. However, the close symbol is not. As a result, this method isn't appropriate for every application. Now let's look at the method.

To open a window, use a function from the DOS library, so you need to open the library first (see the section "Load library"). This open function is an all purpose function that can be used for many things. For this reason, it makes good sense to put a "open" subroutine in your program. You can use it a lot. Let's do the basic steps:

```
;** Load the DOS library 'dos.library'   (6.3.2A) **
ExecBase = 4                    ;Base address of the EXEC
                                library
OpenLib  = -408                 ;Offset of OpenLib function
Open     = -30                  ;Offset of the DOS function OPEN
init:
        move.l  ExecBase,a6     ;Base address in A6
        lea     dosname(pc),a1  ;Address of library name
        moveq   #0,d0           ;Version number: unimportant
        jsr     OpenLib(a6)     ;Call the function
        move.l  d0,dosbase      ;Save DOS base address
        beq     error           ;If zero, then error !
        ...                     ;More of your program
        ...                     ;Now open window, etc...
        ...


error:
        ...                     ;Error occured
        ...                     ;Your error routine



Openfile:                       ;General OPEN function
        move.l  dosbase,a6      ;DOS base address in A6
        jsr     Open(a6)        ;Call OPEN function
        tst.l   d0              ;Test if OK
        rts                     ;Done, evaluate test later


dosname:                        ;Name of library to be opened
        dc.b    'dos.library',0,0
        align                   ;even
dosbase:                        ;Spot for DOS base address
        blk.l   1
```

You called the Openfile routine, because the label "Open" is already being used for the offset. This routine calls the Open function that is in the DOS library.

That isn't everything. The function must be given some parameters so that it knows what to open. The parameters are sent in registers D1 and D2. D1 points to a definition block that specifies what should be opened. You need to have a filename ended with a null byte there. D1 must be passed as a long word like all addresses. D2 contains the mode that the function should run in. There is an old (1005) and a new (1006) mode. This number must be passed in D2's long word.

Here's an overview of how windows are opened. Fortunately, AmigaDOS allows you to use input and and output channels in the same way. The standard channels are disk files, the console (keyboard and screen), the printer interface and the serial RS232 interface.

The console input/output is what you'll work with now. When you specify the console as the filename of the channel to be opened, a window is opened automatically.

The name must begin with CON: to do this. It's similar to DF0: for disk operations. A little more information about the window is still needed.

You need to specify the X and Y coordinates of the upper left and lower right corners of the window as well as the name that should appear in the title line of the window. A complete definition block for a window like this would appear like the following line:

```
consolname: dc.b 'CON:0/100/640/100/** Window **',0
```

To open this window, the line above needs to be inserted in the following program:

```
mode_old = 1005

lea     consolname(pc),a1    ;Console Definition
move.l  #mode_old,d0         ;mode
bsr     openfile             ;Console open
beq     error                ;didn't work
move.l  d0,conhandle

rts
        ...
conhandle:      dc.l 1       ;Space for handle
```

There are two points to clear up yet.

You should use mode_old as the mode when you open a window. Logically the window doesn't exist before opening so this seems weird but it doesn't hurt anything.

The parameter that returns from "openfile" in D0 is zero in the case of an error, in the case that opening didn't work. Otherwise the value is the identification number (handle number) of the opened channel. You need to store it away, because every function that wants to use this channel must give the handle number. In the example, you stored this number in the "conhandle" long word.

As mentioned, the window you've opened doesn't have a close symbol, but it can be made bigger and smaller and moved forward and back. The manipulations that are carried out using the mouse are completely taken care of by the Amiga (in contrast to the ATARI ST where the programmer has to take care of these things).

An important function that uses the handle number is the one that closes the channel (in your case the window). This function is also in the DOS library and is called "Close". Its offset is -36 and it only needs one parameter; the handle number of the channel that is closed must be in the D1 register.

After your work is done, you need to put the following lines in your program to close the window:

```
Close = -36                    ;(6.3.2C)
    ...
    move.l  conhandle,d1    ;Handle number in D1
    move.l  dosbase,a6      ;DOS base address in A6
    jsr     Close(a6)       ;Close channel!
```

The window disappears!

Now for a few remarks about opening and closing the window in this way. If you open several windows in the same way, you'll get several windows and thus several handle numbers. In this way, you can put as many windows on the screen as you'd like. You can do your work with them and then close them indivudally.

Here is the complete program to open and close a simple window in AssemPro format (We have used the AssemPro ILABEL and the macros INIT_AMIGA and EXIT_AMIGA so AssemPro owners can start the programs from the desktop. If you are using a different assembler check your documentation for instructions on starting and exiting programs.):

```
;***** 6.3.2 S.D. *****

OpenLib          =-30-378
closelib         =-414
;ExecBase        =4                              ; Defined in AssemPro
                                                 Macros

* calls to Amiga Dos:

Open             =-30
Close            =-30-6
IoErr            =-132
mode_old         = 1005
alloc_abs        =-$cc


ILABEL Assempro:includes/Amiga.l        ;AssemPro only

 INIT_AMIGA                             ;AssemPro only

run:
        bsr     init                    ;Initialization
        bra     test                    ;System-Test

init:                                   ;System initialization
                                        and open
        move.l  ExecBase,a6             ;Number of Execute-
                                        library
        lea     dosname(pc),a1
        moveq   #0,d0
        jsr     openlib(a6)             ;Open DOS-Library
        move.l  d0,dosbase
        beq     error

        lea     consolname(pc),a1       ;Console Definition
        move.l  #mode_old,d0
        bsr     openfile                ;Console open
        beq     error
        move.l  d0,conhandle

        rts

test:

        bra qu                          ;quit and exit


error:
        move.l  dosbase,a6
        jsr     IoErr(a6)
        move.l  d0,d5

        move.l  #-1,d7                  ;Flag
qu:
        move.l  conhandle,d1            ;Window close
        move.l  dosbase,a6
        jsr     close(a6)
```

```
        move.l   dosbase,a1              ;DOS.Lib close
        move.l   ExecBase,a6
        jsr      closelib(a6)

        EXIT_AMIGA                       ;AssemPro only

openfile:                               ;Open File
        move.l   a1,d1                   ;Pointer to I/O-
                                         Definition-Text

        move.l   d0,d2
        move.l   dosbase,a6
        jsr      open(a6)
        tst.l    d0
        rts


dosname: dc.b 'dos.library',0,0
        Align.w
dosbase: dc.l 0
consolname: dc.b 'CON:0/100/640/100/** CLI-Test **',0
        Align.w
conhandle: dc.l 0


        end
```

There is another way to open a window easily. Just use RAW: instead of CON: as the channel designator. All the other parameters and operations remain the same.

If you try them both out, you won't see any differences between the two windows. They both look the same and can be worked with in the same way with the mouse. The difference comes when you input to the window. In the **RAW:** window, the cursor keys are ignored. In the **CON:** window and in CLI, they do work.

6.4 Input/Output

Besides managing and making calculations with data, the most important work of a program is to input and output the data. There are many methods of data transfer in and out of the computer, for instance screen or printer output, keyboard input, using the serial or the parallel interface, tone or speech output and finally disk operations.

You want to learn about all these methods of data input and output for programming and applications. We've written some programs as subroutines that should be useful for later programs. It makes good sense to make a library of these subroutines that can either be directly integrated in a new program or linked to a program. At the end of the sections there is a list of a complete program so you can see how the subroutines are used.

To prepare for input/output, you need to have data to output and space to input data. To get this ready, you need a correct program beginning in which the EXEC and DOS libraries are opened and memory is reserved. After this, you begin most programs by outputing some text. The text can be a program title or the instruction to input data over the keyboard. Let's start looking at screen output.

6.4.1   Screen output

For a computer like the Amiga the first question is where should the screen output be sent? The answer is simple for many computers; they only have one screen, and output goes there. You need to specify which window to write to when you use the Amiga, however.

There are two possibilities:

1. Output to the CLI window

2. Output to another window

The first possibility only exists if the program that makes the output was started from CLI. If not, you need to open your own custom window for your program. If so, you can use the window that was opened by the CLI for output.

If you use the second method, you need to open a window. As you've already seen, there are three methods. For simple text and character output, the difference between the three sorts of windows isn't very great. Here you have a free hand in determining which sort of window to use. Let's open a CON: window and put its handle number in "conhandle".

You've opened your window and want to output a title. You choose text to output and then put it in memory using a code segment like this:

```
title: dc.b "** Welcome to this program ! **"
titleend:
align           ;even
```

The "align" (even) is a pseudo-op that should follow text when it is followed by either word data or program lines. It causes the assembler to insert a null byte if necessary to make the next address even.

To output this text you need another DOS function: Write. This has an offset of -48 and needs three parameters:

In D1   the handle of an opened output channel that should be written to (in your case, this is the handle number that you got back from the Open command when you opened your window.).

In D2   the address of the text to be output (in the example, the address "title").

In D3   the number of characters to be output in bytes.

To find the number of bytes to output, you need to count the number of characters in your text. Use "titleend" to calculate this. Using this label, the assembler can calculate the length of your text for itself (after all, why should you count when you have a computer?) if you write:

```
move.l #titleend-title,d3
```

The advantage of specifying the length is that you can put control characters between the beginning and end of the text. In this way, you can execute certain functions using text output. You'll learn about the control characters in a bit.

Here's the routine:

```
Write = -48                         ;(6.4.1A)
      ...                           ;Open window
      ...
      move.l  dosbase,a6            ;DOS base address
      move.l  conhandle,d1          ;Pass handle
      move.l  #title,d2             ;Text address
      move.l  #titleend-title,d3    ;And length
      jsr     Write(a6)             ;Call function
```

```
      ...

      title: dc.b "** Welcome to this program ! **"
      titleend:
      align                                    ;event
            end
```

You'll certainly use this function a lot. You'll often want to output just
one character though. To allow you to do this and similar text related
tasks, there are four subroutines, each of which do a different sort of output:

pmsg   Outputs the text from (D2) to the first null byte.

pline   Is the same as the routine above except that the text is automatically fol-
              lowed by a CR, the cursor is positioned at the beginning of the next line.

pchar   Outputs the character in D0.

pcrlf   Puts the cursor at the beginning of the next line.

Here's the subroutine package:

```
      Write = -48                      (6.4.1B
            ...

      pline:                           ;* Output line and then a CR
            bsr     pmsg               ;Output line
      pcrlf:                           ;* Move cursor to the next line
            move    #10,d0             ;Line feed
            bsr     pchar              ;Output
            move    #13,d0             ;and CR
      pchar:                           ;* Output character in D0
            move.b  d0,outline         ;Character in output buffer
            move.l  #outline,d2        ;Address of the character
      pmsg:                            ;*Output line (D2) up to null
            move.l  d2,a0              ;Address in A0
            clr     d3                 ;Length = 0
      ploop:
            tst.b   (a0)+              ;Null byte ?
            beq     pmsg2              ;Yes: length found
            addq.l  #1,d3              ;Else Length+1
            bra     ploop              ;And continue looking
      pmsg2:
            move.l  dosbase,a6         ;DOS base address in A6
            move.l  conhandle,d1       ;Our window handle
            jsr     Write(a6)          ;Call Write function
            rts                        ;Done !
      outline:    dc.w 0               ;Output buffer for 'pchar'
      conhandle:  dc.l 0               ;Window's handle
```

Here is an example program to open and close a simple window and output a text message in AssemPro format (We have used the AssemPro macros INIT_AMIGA and EXIT_AMIGA so AssemPro owners can start the program from the desktop. If you are using a different assembler check your documentation for instructions on starting and exiting programs.):

Here is the complete program in AssemPro format:

```
;***** 6.4.1C.asm S.D. *****

OpenLib     =-30-378
closelib    =-414
;ExecBase    =4                          ; Defined in AssemPro
                                         ; Macros

* calls to Amiga Dos:

Open        =-30
Close       =-30-6
Write       =-48
IoErr       =-132
mode_old    = 1005
alloc_abs   =-$cc

            ILABEL AssemPro:includes/Amiga.l ;AssemPro only

            INIT_AMIGA                  ;AssemPro only

run:
      bsr    init                       ;Initialization
      bsr    test                       ;System-Test
      nop
      bra qu                            ;quit and exit

test:
      move.l #title,d0
      bsr    pmsg
      bsr    pcrlf
      bsr    pcrlf


      rts


init:                                   ;System initialization
                                        and open
      move.l ExecBase,a6                ;Number of Execute-
                                        library
      lea    dosname(pc),a1
      moveq  #0,d0
      jsr    openlib(a6)                ;Open DOS-Library
      move.l d0,dosbase
      beq    error
```

```
              lea      consolname(pc),a1      ;Console Definition
              move.l   #mode_old,d0
              bsr      openfile               ;Console open
              beq      error
              move.l   d0,conhandle

              rts


pmsg:                                          ;Print message (d0)
              movem.l  d0-d7/a0-a6,-(sp)
              move.l   d0,a0
              move.l   a0,d2
              clr.l    d3
ploop:
              tst.b    (a0)+
              beq      pmsg2
              addq.l   #1,d3
              bra      ploop                  ;length calculate
pmsg2:
              move.l   conhandle,d1
              move.l   dosbase,a6
              jsr      write(a6)
              movem.l  (sp)+,d0-d7/a0-a6
              rts


pcrlf:
              move     #10,d0
              bsr      pchar
              move     #13,d0
pchar:                                         ;output char in D)
              movem.l  d0-d7/a0-a6,-(sp)      ;save all
              move.l   conhandle,d1
pch1:
              lea      outline,a1
              move.b   d0,(a1)
              move.l   a1,d2
              move.l   #1,d3 ;1 letter
              move.l   dosbase,a6
              jsr      write(a6)
              movem.l  (sp)+,d0-d7/a0-a6      ;restore all
              rts


error:
              move.l   dosbase,a6
              jsr      IoErr(a6)
              move.l   d0,d5

              move.l   #-1,d7                 ;Flag
qu:
              move.l   conhandle,d1           ;Window close
              move.l   dosbase,a6
              jsr      close(a6)

              move.l   dosbase,a1             ;DOS.Lib close
```

```
        move.l  ExecBase,a6
        jsr     closelib(a6)

        EXIT_AMIGA                      ;AssemPro only

openfile:                               ;Open File
        move.l  a1,d1                   ;Pointer to I/O-
                                        Definition-Text
        move.l  d0,d2
        move.l  dosbase,a6
        jsr     open(a6)
        tst.l   d0
        rts


dosname: dc.b 'dos.library',0,0
        Align.w
dosbase: dc.l 0
consolname: dc.b 'CON:0/100/640/100/** CLI-Test **',0
        Align.w

conhandle: dc.l 0
title: dc.b '** Weclome to this program! **'
titleend:
        align
outline: dc.w 0                         ;Output buffer for pchar
        end
```

Using this program, you can very easily put whatever you want in the
CON: window. These functions also work in a **RAW**: window. You
should rename "conhandle" as "rawhandle", so that you don't get things
mixed up later.

Let's stay with the **CON**: window. As mentioned earlier, you can output
special characters that execute functions or change parameters for output.
These characters are called control characters.

You've already learned about one of these control characters, Line Feed
($A). This character isn't just output; instead, it calls a function that
moves the cursor into the next line and moves the screen up. This is very
useful, but there are much more interesting control characters.

Here's a list of control characters that execute functions. These characters
are given in hex.

Control Sequence	Sequence	Function
	08	Backspace
	0A	Line Feed, Cursor down
	0B	Move cursor up a line
	0C	Clear screen
	0D	Carriage Return, cursor in the first column
	0E	Turn on normal characters (Cancels OF effects)
	0F	Turn on special characters
	1B	Escape

The following sequences begin with $9B, the CSI (Control Sequence Introducer). The characters that follow execute a function. The values in square brackets can be left off. The n's you see represent one or more digit decimal numbers given using ASCII characters. The value that is used when n is left off, is given in the parenthesis that follow n in the description of the function in the table.

Control Sequence Introducer	Sequence	Function
	9B [n] 40	Insert n blanks
	9B [n] 41	Move cursor n (1) lines up
	9B [n] 42	Move cursor n (1) lines down
	9B [n] 43	Move cursor n (1) characters to the right
	9B [n] 44	Move cursor n (1) characters to the left
	9B [n] 45	Move cursor down n (1) lines into column 1
	9B [n] 46	Move cursor up n (1) lines and into column 1
	9B [n] [3B n] 48	Cursor in line; Set column
	9B 4A	Erase screen from the cursor
	9B 4B	Erase line from the cursor
	9B 4C	Insert line
	9B 4D	Delete line
	9B [n] 50	Delete n characters starting at cursor
	9B [n] 53	Move up n lines
	9B [n] 54	Move down n lines
	9B 32 30 68	Line Feed => Line Feed + Return
	9B 32 30 6C	Line Feed => just Line Feed
	9B 6E	Sends the cursor position! A string of the following form is returned: 9B (Line) 3B (Column) 52

	Sequence	Function
Control	9B (Style);(Foreground color);(Background color) 6D	
Sequence		The three parameters are decimal numbers in
Introducer		ASCII format. They mean:
		Style: 0 = normal
		1 = bold
		3 = italic
		4 = underlined
		7 = inverse
		Foreground color: 30-37
		Color 0-7 for Text
		Background color: 40-47
		Color 0-7 for background
	9B (Length) 74	sets the maximum number of lines to be displayed
	9b (Width) 75	sets the maximum line length.
	9B (Distance) 78	defines the distance in pixels from the left border of the window to the place where output should begin
	9B (Distance) 79	defines the distance in pixels from the upper border of the window to the place where output should begin
		The last four functions yield the normal values if you leave off the parameters.
	9B 30 20 70	Make cursor invisible
	9B 20 70	Make cursor visible
	9B 71	Sends window construction A string of the following form is returned: 9B 31 3B 31 3B (Lines) 3B (Columns) 73

To see how the control characters work, have "pmsg" output this text to your window:

```
mytext: dc.b $9b,"4;31;40m"           ; (6.3.2D)
        dc.b "Underline"
        dc.b $9b,"3;33;40m",$9b,"5;20H"
        dc.b "** Hello, World ! **",0
```

The parameters for the control sequence are put in quotation marks so they are treated as an ASCII string. Now you see, just how easy it is to do text output!

Here is the complete program to open and output the text and control codes to your window in AssemPro format (We have used the AssemPro macros INIT_AMIGA and EXIT_AMIGA so AssemPro owners can start the programs from the desktop. If you are using a different assembler check your documentation for instructions on starting and exiting programs):

```
;***** 6.4.1D.ASM S.D. *****

OpenLib    =-30-378
closelib   =-414
;ExecBase  =4                        ; Defined in AssemPro
                                     Macros

* calls to Amiga Dos:

Open       =-30
Close      =-30-6
Write      =-48
IoErr      =-132
mode_old   = 1005
alloc_abs  =-$cc

          ILABEL AssemPro:includes/Amiga.l ;AssemPro only

          INIT_AMIGA                 ;AssemPro only

run:
          bsr    init                ;Initialization
          bsr    test                ;System-Test
          nop
          bra qu                     ;quit and exit

test:
          move.l #mytext,d0
          bsr    pmsg
          bsr    pcrlf
          bsr    pcrlf


          rts


init:                                ;System initialization
                                     and oprn
          move.l ExecBase,a6         ;Number of Execute-
                                     library
          lea    dosname(pc),a1
          moveq  #0,d0
          jsr    openlib(a6)         ;Open DOS-Library
          move.l d0,dosbase
          beq    error

          lea    consolname(pc),a1   ;Console Definition
          move.l #mode_old,d0
          bsr    openfile            ;Console open
          beq    error
          move.l d0,conhandle
```

```
            rts


pmsg:                                               ;Print message (d0)
            movem.l d0-d7/a0-a6,-(sp)
            move.l  d0,a0
            move.l  a0,d2
            clr.l   d3
ploop:
            tst.b   (a0)+
            beq pmsg2
            addq.l  #1,d3
            bra ploop
pmsg2:
            move.l  conhandle,d1
            move.l  dosbase,a6
            jsr write(a6)
            movem.l (sp)+,d0-d7/a0-a6
            rts


pcrlf:
            move    #10,d0
            bsr     pchar
            move    #13,d0
pchar:                                              ;output char in D0
            movem.l d0-d7/a0-a6,-(sp)    ;save all
            move.l  conhandle,d1
pch1:
            lea     outline,a1
            move.b  d0,(a1)
            move.l  a1,d2
            move.l  #1,d3 ;1 letter
            move.l  dosbase,a6
            jsr     write(a6)
            movem.l (sp)+,d0-d7/a0-a6    ;restore all
            rts


error:
            move.l  dosbase,a6
            jsr     IoErr(a6)
            move.l  d0,d5

            move.l  #-1,d7          ;Flag
qu:
            move.l  conhandle,d1        ;Window close
            move.l  dosbase,a6
            jsr     close(a6)

            move.l  dosbase,a1         ;DOS.Lib close
            move.l  ExecBase,a6 jsr    closelib(a6)

            EXIT_AMIGA                 ;AssemPro only
```

```
openfile:                                   ;Open File
        move.l  a1,d1                       ;Pointer to I/O-
                                            Definition-Text

        move.l  d0,d2
        move.l  dosbase,a6
        jsr     open(a6)
        tst.l   d0
        rts


dosname: dc.b 'dos.library',0,0
        Align.w
dosbase: dc.l 0
consolname: dc.b 'CON:0/100/640/100/** CLI-Test **',0
        Align.w

conhandle: dc.l 0
mytext :dc.b $9b,'4;31;40m'                  ;
        dc.b 'Underline
        dc.b $9b,'3;33;40m',$9b,'5;20H'
        dc.b '** Hello World !! **',0


        align
outline: dc.w 0                              ;Output buffer for pchar
        end
```

Now that you've done text and character output, its time to move on to text input.

6.4.2   Keyboard input

You can read keyboard input very easily. You just need to open the I/O channel of the CON: window and read from it. You need the READ function from the DOS library to do this. Its offset is -42.

This function has three parameters just like the WRITE function.

In D1   the handle number that you get from the OPEN function
In D2   the address that the data read in is to start at
In D3   the number of bytes to read

Here is a subroutine that reads the number of characters from the keyboard that it finds in D3. It puts them in a buffer.

```
Read     = -42                              ;(6.4.2A)
        ...
getchr:                                     ;* Get (D3) characters from the
                                            keyboard
```

```
          move.l  #inbuff,d2      ;Address of buffer in D2
          move.l  dosbase,a6      ;DOS base address in A6
          move.l  conhandle,d1    ;Our window handle
          jsr     Read(a6)        ;Call Read function
          rts                     ;Done!
inbuff:           blk.b 80,0      ;Buffer for keyboard input
```

This routine returns to the main program when <Return> is entered. If more then D3 characters are entered, "inbuff" only gets the first characters. The routine gets the remaining characters when called a second time.

This sort of input is fairly easy. You can backspace, because only the characters that should be there are put in the memory block starting at "inbuff". The number of characters moved into "inbuff" is put in D0.

Try the program out as follows:

After opening the CON: window, put the following lines in the main program:

```
     move   #80,d3       ;Read 80 characters (6.4.2B)
     bsr    readchr      ;Get line from keyboard
     lea    inline,a0    ;Address of the line in A0
     clr.b  0(a0,d0)     ;Null byte on the end
     bsr    pmsg         ;Output line again
bp:
```

After this comes the code segment that closes the window again. After loading the program into the AssemPro debugger, make "bp" a breakpoint and start the program. (SEKA users start the program with "g run" and enter "bp" as the breakpoint) The program quits at the breakpoint and you can take a look at the results on the screen. Then you can continue the program (SEKA with "j bp") and let the window close.

After starting the program and opening the window, the cursor appears in the upper left corner of the window. Enter some text and press <Return>. The string that you just entered is output again on the screen.

You use the "pmsg" routine from the previous chapter to do the output. This routine needs a null byte at the end of the text to be output. You put a null byte there by putting the address of the input buffer in A0 and then erasing the byte at A0+D0 using the CLR.B command. Since D0 contains the number of characters that were entered, this byte is the first unused byte.

Since you're in the debugger you can redisplay the disassembled output when the program ends to see what "getchar" put in "inbuff" (SEKA owners can use "q inbuff" when the program ends to see what "getchr" put there.) You'll find the characters that you typed plus a closing $A. The

123

$A stands for the <Return> key and it's counted too, so if you enter a 12 and then hit <Return>, for example, D0 will contain a three.

Try this again with a **RAW**: window. Change the window definition from CON: to RAW: and reassemble the program. You'll notice the difference right away. After you've entered one character, a return is executed. D0 always has a one in it.

The advantage of this form of input is that cursor and function keys can be recognized. Using your own routine, you can repeatedly accept input of characters using "getchr" and then work with the special characters.

There's another form of keyboard input: checking for a single key. This is important when a program is about to execute an important function and the user must say he wants it executed by entering a "Y" for yes. This can be treated as normal input, but in some cases, there is a better method.

There is a function in the DOS library that waits a certain specified length of time for a key to be pressed, and returns a zero (FALSE) if no key was hit in this time period. It returns a -1 ($FFFFFFFF = TRUE) if one was. To find out which key it takes another function. The WaitForChar function, is only good for tasks like waiting for the user to let the program know that it can continue scrolling text.

The function needs two parameters:

In D1   the handle number of the window or file from which the character should be read. It can also wait for a character from an interface.

In D2   you pass the length of time in microseconds that you should wait for a key stroke.

To wait one second for one key to be hit, you can use the following routine:

```
WaitForCh=-30-174                ; (6.4.2C)
        ...
scankey:                         ;* Wait for a key stroke
        move.l  conhandle,d1     ;In our window
        move.l  #1000000,d2      ;Waiting time: one second
        move.l  dosbase,a6       ;DOS base address
        jsr     waitforch(a6)    ;Wait ...
        tst.l   d0               ;Test result
        rts
```

The TST command at the end of the program allows the calling routine to use a BEQ or BNE command to evaluate the results of the routine—BEQ branches if no key was hit. BNE doesn't.

Here is an example program in AssemPro format covering what you have
learned so far. Opening and closing a window, displaying text in the window and inputting text:

```
;***** 6.4.2A.ASM S.D. *****

OpenLib    =-30-378
closelib   =-414
;ExecBase  =4                      ; Defined in AssemPro
                                   ; Macros

* calls to Amiga Dos:

Open       =-30
Close      =-30-6
Read       =-42
Write      =-48
IoErr      =-132
mode_old   = 1005
alloc_abs  =-$cc

        ILABEL AssemPro:includes/Amiga.l ;AssemPro only

        INIT_AMIGA                 ;AssemPro only

run:
        bsr    init                ;Initialization
        bsr    test                ;System-Test
        nop
        bra qu                     ;quit and exit

test:
        move.l #mytext,d0
        bsr    pmsg
        bsr    pcrlf
        bsr    pcrlf
        move.l #80,d3              ;80 characters to read
                                   (D3)
        bsr    getchr              ;get character
        bsr    pmsg                ;output line

        rts


init:                             ;System initialization
                                  and open
        move.l ExecBase,a6        ;Number of Execute-
                                  library
        lea    dosname(pc),a1
        moveq  #0,d0
        jsr    openlib(a6)         ;Open DOS-Library
        move.l d0,dosbase
        beq    error

        lea    consolname(pc),a1   ;Console Definition
```

```
              move.l  #mode_old,d0
              bsr     openfile              ;Console open
              beq     error
              move.l  d0,conhandle

              rts


pmsg:                                        ;Print message (d0)
              movem.l d0-d7/a0-a6,-(sp)
              move.l  d0,a0
              move.l  a0,d2
              clr.l   d3
ploop:
              tst.b (a0)+
              beq pmsg2
              addq.l #1,d3
              bra ploop                      ;Check length
pmsg2:
              move.l  conhandle,d1
              move.l  dosbase,a6
              jsr write(a6)
              movem.l (sp)+,d0-d7/a0-a6
              rts


pcrlf:
              move #10,d0
              bsr pchar
              move #13,d0
pchar:                                       ;Character in D0 output
              movem.l d0-d7/a0-a6,-(sp)      ;Save all
              move.l  conhandle,d1
pch1:
              lea outline,a1
              move.b  d0,(a1)
              move.l  a1,d2
              move.l  #1,d3                   ;1 letter
              move.l  dosbase,a6
              jsr     write(a6)
              movem.l (sp)+,d0-d7/a0-a6       ;Restore all
              rts


getchr:                                       ;Get character for
                                              keyboard
              move.l  #1,d3                   ;1 Character
              move.l  conhandle,d1
              lea     inbuff,a1               ;Buffer-Address
              move.l  a1,d2
              move.l  dosbase,a6
              jsr     read(a6)
              clr.l   d0
              move.b  inbuff,d0
              rts
```

```
error:
        move.l  dosbase,a6
        jsr     IoErr(a6)
        move.l  d0,d5

        move.l  #-1,d7                  ;Flag
qu:
        move.l  conhandle,d1            ;Window close
        move.l  dosbase,a6
        jsr     close(a6)

        move.l  dosbase,a1             ;DOS.Lib close
        move.l  ExecBase,a6 jsr        ;closelib(a6)

        EXIT_AMIGA                      ;AssemPro only


openfile:                              ;Open File
        move.l  a1,d1                  ;Pointer to I/O-
                                        Definition-Text

        move.l  d0,d2
        move.l  dosbase,a6
        jsr     open(a6)
        tst.l   d0
        rts


dosname: dc.b 'dos.library',0,0
        Align.w
dosbase: dc.l 0
consolname: dc.b 'CON:0/100/640/100/** CLI-Test **',0
        Align.w

conhandle: dc.l 0
mytext:dc.b '** Hello World !! **',0


        align
outline:    dc.w 0                     ;Output buffer for pchar
inbuff:     blk.b 8                    ;Input buffer
        end
```

6.4.3   Printer control

Now that you've looked at console I/O, let's look at outputting data from
the computer. The first device that we'll discuss is the printer.

It's very easy to use the printer. You just need to open another channel. It
goes just the way you learned it with **CON:** and **RAW:** windows; the
only difference is you enter **PRT:** instead.

You open this channel using the same lines that you used above for the window except that the pointer is to the channel name PRT: in D1. You pass the mode "new" (1006) in D2 in the "do_open" routine as well. Save the handle number that comes back at a label called "prthandle".

Now you can use the same output routines that you used with windows to send text to the printer. You need to put "prthandle" instead of "conhandle" in the line with the "move.l conhandle,d1" command.

Actually it would be better to eliminate this line from the routine totally. Then you can use the same routine for window and printer output. The calling procedure would then need to put "conhandle" in D1 for window output. It would put "prthandle" in D1 for printer output. This is a very flexible output routine that can be used for window and printer output now. You can't accept input from the printer, because the printer doesn't send data. It just accepts it and prints it.

6.4.4   Serial I/O

It's just as easy to use the serial interface as the printer. Just enter SER: as the filename. Now you can use the DOS functions READ and WRITE just as before to do I/O with the channel you've just opened. You can set the parameters for the interface (like Hand shake and Transfer rate) with the Preferences program.

6.4.5   Speech output

The Amiga has a speech synthesizer built in. This isn't quite as easy to program as the I/O devices discussed earlier, however. You use the "narrator.device" to do this.

This device requires several program steps to install it and then causes it to speak. You need to open the device, start the I/O, etc... Let's look at how to translate the text into the proper form and then output the text.

First we need to do some initialization. Let's define the constants now. Some of them are new.

```
;***** Narrator Basic Functions 3/87 S.D. *****  (6.4.5A)

OpenLib    =-408
closelib   =-414
```

```
ExecBase    =4

Open        =-30              ;Open File
Close       =-36              ;Close File
mode_old    =1005            ;Old Mode

OpenDevice  =-444            ;Open Device
CloseDev    =-450            ;Close Device

SendIo      =-462            ;Start I/O
AbortIO     =-480            ;Abort I/O

Translate   =-30             ;Translate text
```

The initialization routine follows:

```
init:                       ;Initialize and open system

;* Open DOS library *

        move.l  execbase,a6     ;Pointer to EXEC library
        lea     dosname,a1      ;Pointer to DOS name
        moveq   #0,d0           ;Version: unimportant
        jsr     openlib(a6)     ;Open DOS library
        move.l  d0,dosbase      ;Save handle
        beq     error           ;Error handle

;* Open translator.library

        lea     transname,a1    ;Pointer to translator name
        clr.l   d0
        jsr     openlib(a6)     ;Open translator
        move.l  d0,tranbase     ;Save handle
        beq     error           ;Error handling

;* Set up I/O area for Narrator *

        lea     talkio,a1       ;Pointer to I/O area in A1
        move.l  #nwrrep,14(a1)  ;Enter port address
        move.l  #amaps,48+8(a1) ;Pointer to audio mask
        move    #4,48+12(a1)    ;Number of the mask
        move.l  #512,36(a1)     ;Length of the output area
        move    #3,28(a1)       ;Command: write
        move.l  #outtext,40(a1) ;Address of output area

;* Open Narrator device *

        clr.l   d0              ;Number 0
        clr.l   d1              ;No flags
        lea     nardevice,a0    ;Pointer to device name
        jsr     opendevice(a6)  ;Open narrator.device
        tst.l   d0              ;Error ?
        bne     error           ;Yes !

;* Open window *
```

```
move.l  #consolname,d1 ;Console definition
move.l  #mode_old,d2   ;Old mode
move.l  dosbase,a6     ;DOS base address
jsr     Open(a6)       ;Open window
tst.l   d0             ;Error ?
beq     error          ;Yes !
move.l  d0,conhandle   ;Else save handle
```

After you've done this initialization, you can have the computer save the text you have prepared for it. To see what the Amiga is saying, use the "pmsg" function to have the text written in the window:

```
       move.l  #intext,d2            ;Text for Amiga to say
       bsr     pmsg                  ;Output in window also

sayit:                               ;Have the text said

;*Translate the text into a form that the computer can use*

       lea     intext,a0            ;Address of the text
       move.l  #outtext-intext,d0   ;Length of the text
       lea     outtext,a1           ;Address of output area
       move.l  #512,d1              ;Length of output area
       move.l  tranbase,a6          ;Translator base address
       jsr     Translate(a6)        ;Translate text

;* Speech output *

       lea     talkio,a1            ;Address of I/O structure
       move.l  #512,36(a1)          ;Length of output area
       move.l  execbase,a6          ;EXEC base address
       jsr     SendIO(a6)           ;Start I/O (speech output)
```

Once the program ends, the I/O stops as well, so you need to put in something that keeps the program going longer. You'll use the "getchr" function that you programmed earlier to take care of this:

```
       bsr     getchr               ;Wait for keyboard input
```

The computer waits until the <Return> key is pressed. Now you can listen to what the Amiga has to say. Once the <Return> key is pressed, the program stops.

```
qu:                                 ; (6.4.5C)
       move.l  execbase,a6          ;EXEC base address
       lea     talkio,a1            ;Pointer to I/O area
       jsr     abortio(a6)          ;Stop the I/O

       move.l  conhandle,d1
       move.l  dosbase,a6
       jsr     close(a6)            ;Close window
```

```
          move.l   dosbase,d1
          move.l   execbase,a6
          jsr      closelib(a6)    ;Close DOS library

          lea      talkio,a1
          jsr      closedev(a6)    ;Close narrator.device

          move.l   tranbase,a1
          jsr      closelib(a6)    ;Close translator library

          rts                      ;* End of program
```

Now comes the data that you need for the program above:

```
mytext:       dc.b     'This is a test text ! ',10,13,10,13,0,0
dosname:      dc.b     'dos.library',0,0
transname:    dc.b     "translator.library",0
consolname:   dc.b     'RAW:0/100/640/100/** Test window',0
nardevice:    dc.b     'narrator.device',0
     align
dosbase:      dc.l     0
tranbase:     dc.l     0
amaps:        dc.b     3,5,10,12
     align
conhandle:    dc.l     0
talkio:       blk.l    20,0
nwrrep:       blk.l    8,0
intext:       dc.b     'hello, i am the amiga talking to you',0
     align
outtext:      blk.b    512,0
```

This is quite a bit of work, but it's worth it because it opens so many
possibilities for you. There are a lot of variations possible if you modify
parameters. These parameters are entries in the I/O area starting at the
"talkio" label. The area is built as follows:

Offset	Length	Meaning
** Port Data **		
0	L	Pointer to next block
4	L	Pointer to last block
8	B	I/O type
9	B	Priority
10	L	Pointer to I/O name
14	L	Pointer to port
18	W	Length
** I/O Data **		
20	L	Pointer to Device
24	L	Pointer to Device Unit
28	W	Command word
30	B	I/O flags
31	B	I/O status
32	L	I/O pointer
36	L	I/O length
40	L	Pointer to data
44	L	I/O offset
** Narrator data items **		
48	W	Speech speed
50	W	Highness of voice
52	W	Speech mode
54	W	Sex (male/female voice)
56	L	Pointer to audio mask
60	W	Number of mask
62	W	Volume
64	W	Read in rate
66	B	Flag for producing graphics (0=off)
67	B	Actual mask (internal use)
68	B	Channel used (internal use)

We wouldn't recommend experimenting with the data in the first two blocks. If you do, you can easily cause a system crash. You can use the last entries of the structure to produce some interesting effects though.

Here's an overview of the parameters you can use to vary the speech output. The value in parenthesis is the standard value, the value set when narrator.device is opened.

Speech speed (150)

You can use this to set the speed of speech. The pitch of the voice is not affected by this value.

Pitch of voice (110)

You can choose a value between 65 and 320 for the pitch (from Goofy to Micky Mouse).

Speech mode (0)

The zero gives half-way natural speech. A one lets the Amiga speak in monotone like a robot.

Sex (0)   A zero means masculine and a one means feminine (more or less ...).

Volume (64)   The volume can range from 0 to 64. The standard value is the loudest possible.

Read in rate (22200)

By lowering this value, the voice is lowered. If you change this very much, you'll get some weird voices!

You can experiment a bit until you find an interesting voice. Have fun!

Here is a complete talking program in AssemPro format:

```
;***** Speech output S.D. *****

OpenLib      =-30-378
closelib     =-414
;ExecBase     =4                        ;defined by AssemPro

* calls to Amiga Dos:

Open         =-30
Close        =-30-6
opendevice   =-444
CloseDev     =-450
addport      =-354
RemPort      =-360
;DoIo         =-456
SendIO       = -462
AbortIO      = -480
Read         =-30-12
Write        =-30-18
;MyInput      =-30-24
;Output       =-30-30
;CurrDir      =-30-96
;Exit         =-30-114
WaitForCh    =-30-174
FindTask     =-294
Translate    =-30
mode_old     =1005
;mode_new     =1006
;alloc_abs    =-$cc
;free_mem     =-$d2
```

133

```
;!!! when > 500KB !!!  or place in chip memory
; org $40000
; load $40000
;!!!!!!!!!!!!!!!!!!!!!

        ILABEL AssemPro:includes/Amiga.l ;AssemPro only

        INIT_AMIGA                      ;AssemPro only

run:
        bsr    init                     ;Initialization
        bra    test                     ;System-Test

init:                                   ;System initialization
                                        ;and open
        move.l ExecBase,a6              ;Pointer to EXEC library
        lea    dosname(pc),a1           ;Pointer to DOS name
        moveq  #0,d0                    ;Version: not important
        jsr    openlib(a6)              ;Open DOS-Library
        move.l d0,dosbase               ;Save handle
        beq    error                    ;Error routine
;*                                      ;Open translator
                                        library
        move.l ExecBase,a6              ;Pointer to EXEC library
        lea    transname,a1             ;Pointer to translator
                                        ;name
        clr.l  d0
        jsr    openlib(a6)              ;Open Translator
        move.l d0,tranbase              ;Save handle
        beq    error                    ;Error routine
;*                                      ;Set up
        sub.l  a1,a1
        move.l ExecBase,a6
        jsr    FindTask(a6)             ;Find Task
        move.l d0,nwrrep+2

        lea    nwrrep,a1
        jsr    addport(a6)              ;Add Port
;*                                      ;Open narrator device
        lea    talkio,a1                ;Pointer to I/O area in
                                        ;A1
        move.l #nwrrep,14(a1)           ;Enter Port address
        clr.l  d0                       ;Number 0
        clr.l  d1                       ;No flags
        lea    nardevice,a0             ;Pointer to device name
        jsr    opendevice(a6)           ;Open Narrator.device
        tst.l  d0                       ;Error?
        bne    error                    ;Yes!
;*                                      ;Setup I/O for narrator
                                        ;device
bp:
        lea    talkio,a1                ;Pointer to I/O in A1
        move.l #nwrrep,14(a1)           ;Enter port address
        move.l #amaps,48+8(a1)          ;Pointer to audio mask
        move   #4,48+12(a1)             ;Size of Mask
```

```
        lea     consolname(pc),a1     ;Console-Definition
        move.l  #mode_old,d0
        bsr     openfile              ;Console open
        beq     error
        move.l  d0,conhandle

        rts

test:
        move.l  #MyText,d0
        bsr     pmsg                  ;Test-Text output

        bsr     sayit                 ;Say text

        bsr     readln                ;Input
        move    #10,d0
        bsr     pchar                 ;LF output
        move.l  #inline+2,d0
        bsr     pmsg                  ;and again
        bsr     pcrlf
        bra     qu

error:
        move.l  #-1,d7               ;Flag
qu:
        move.l  ExecBase,a6 lea    talkio,a1
        jsr     abortio(a6)

        move.l  conhandle,d1         ;Window close
        move.l  dosbase,a6
        jsr     close(a6)

        move.l  dosbase,a1           ;DOS.Lib close
        move.l  ExecBase,a6
        jsr     closelib(a6)

        lea     nwrrep,a1
        jsr     RemPort(a6)          ;Remove port
        lea     talkio,a1
        jsr     closedev(a6)         ;close narraror device
        move.l  tranbase,a1
        jsr     closelib(a6)         ;Close translator
                                     ;library

        EXIT_AMIGA                   ;AssemPro only

openfile:                           ;Open File
        move.l  a1,d1               ;pointer to I/O-
                                     Definition-Text

        move.l  d0,d2
        move.l  dosbase,a6
        jsr     open(a6)
        tst.l   d0
        rts

pmsg:                               ;Print message (d0)
```

```
          movem.l  d0-d7/a0-a6,-(sp)
          move.l   d0,a0
          move.l   a0,d2
          clr.l    d3
mess1:
          tst.b    (a0)+
          beq      mess2
          addq.l   #1,d3
          bra      mess1                    ;Length calculate
mess2:
          move.l   conhandle,d1
          move.l   dosbase,a6
          jsr      write(a6)
          movem.l  (sp)+,d0-d7/a0-a6
          rts


pcrlf:
          move     #10,d0
          bsr      pchar
          move     #13,d0
pchar:                                      ;Output character in D0
          movem.l  d0-d7/a0-a6,-(sp)        ;save all
          move.l   conhandle,d1
pch1:
          lea      chbuff,a1
          move.b   d0,(a1)
          move.l   a1,d2
          move.l   #1,d3                    ;1 letter
          move.l   dosbase,a6
          jsr      write(a6)
          movem.l  (sp)+,d0-d7/a0-a6        ;restore all
          rts


scankey:                                    ;Test key
          move.l   conhandle,d1
          move.l   #500,d2                  ;Wait value
          move.l   dosbase,a6
          jsr      waitforch(a6)
          tst.l    d0
          rts


readln:                                     ;Input from keyboard
          movem.l  d0-d7/a0-a6,-(sp)        ;save registers
          lea      inline+2,a2              ;Pointer to input buffer
          clr.l    (a2)
inplop:
          bsr      getchr
          cmp.b    #8,d0
          beq      backspace
          cmp.b    #127,d0                  ;Delete ?
          beq      backspace
          bsr      pchar                    ;Character output
          cmp.b    #13,d0
          beq      inputx
          move.b   d0,(a2)+
          bra      inplop
```

```
inputx:
        clr.b   (a2)+
        sub.l   #inline,a2
        move    a2,inline               ;Lenght in inline+1
        movem.l (sp)+,d0-d7/a0-a6       ;Registers
        rts

backspace:
        cmp.l   #inline,a2              ;At the beginning?
        beq     inplop                  ;yes
        move.b  #8,d0
        bsr     pchar                   ;Backspace
        move    #32,d0
        bsr     pchar                   ;Blank
        move    #8,d0
        bsr     pchar                   ;Backspace
        clr.b   (a2)
        subq.l  #1,a2
        bra     inplop

getchr:                                 ;Get one character from
                                        ;keyboard
        move.l  #1,d3                   ;One character
        move.l  conhandle,d1
        lea     inbuff,a1               ;Buffer-Address
        move.l  a1,d2
        move.l  dosbase,a6
        jsr     read(a6)
        clr.l   d0
        move.b  inbuff,d0
        rts

sayit:
        lea     intext,a0
        move.l  #outtext-intext,d0
        lea     outtext,a1
        move.l  #512,d1
        move.l  tranbase,a6
        jsr     Translate(a6)

p:
        lea     talkio,a1
        move    #3,28(a1) ;??
        move.l  #512,36(a1)
        move.l  #outtext,40(a1)
        move.l  ExecBase,a6
        jsr     sendio(a6)

        rts

MyText:     dc.b 'This is our Test-Text !',10,13,10,13,0,0
dosname:    dc.b 'dos.library',0,0
transname:  dc.b "translator.library",0
    align.w
dosbase:    dc.l 0
tranbase:   dc.l 0
```

```
consolname:        dc.b 'CON:0/100/640/100/* Speech-Test S.D.* ',0
nardevice:         dc.b 'narrator.device',0
amaps:             dc.b 3,5,10,12,0,0
    align.w
conhandle:         dc.l 0
inbuff:            blk.b 8
inline:            blk.b 180,0
chbuff:            blk.b 82,0
narread:           blk.l 20,0
talkio:            blk.l 20,0
nwrrep:            blk.l 8,0
intext:            dc.b 'hello, i am the amiga computer',0
    align.w
outtext:           blk.l 128,0

    end
```

6.5 Disk operations

The most important peripheral device for a computer like the Amiga is the disk drive. You use it to save data, so that you don't lose it when you turn off the computer. We'll look at saving and retrieving data in this chapter.

Let's first look at the simple disk operations that are used for data management. To gain access to a file, you must open it first. This is done using the OPEN function from the DOS library, a function that you're already familiar with. I'll assume in the following examples, that you've already opened the DOS library.

6.5.1   Open files

The OPEN function needs a parameter for the mode. The mode has a particular meaning. If the file is opened for reading, it must already exist. The mode for the OPEN function must be "old" (1005) in this case.

If you want to produce a file, you must open it first. Since it doesn't exist, you use the "new" (1006) mode. If a file is opened for writing using this mode even though a file with this name already exists, the old file with this name is erased and replaced. To avoid loss of data, you should check if a file by that name already exists and then output an error message if it does.

You're going to start with a subroutine that opens a file. Let's assume that the filename starts at the label "filename", and that it is closed with a null byte. You just need to pass the mode in register D2.

The routine puts the file handle number in "filehd" and returns to the main program. Since the operation with the handle is the last one performed by the subroutine, the status of the operation can be evaluated once the return has been executed. If the operation went smoothly and the file is opened, the handle number has a non-zero value. If it is zero and "bsr openfile" is followed by "beq error", you can branch to an error handling routine when problems occur.

Here is the subroutine for opening and closing a file.

```
Open        = -30;                      (6.5.1A)
Close       = -36
Mode_old    = 1005
Mode_new    = 1006
    ...
openfile:                       ;* Open file, mode in D0
    move.l  dosbase,a6          ;DOS base address in A6
    move.l  #filename,d1        ;Pointer to file name
    jsr     Open(a6)            ;Open file
    move.l  d0,filehd           ;Save handle
    rts
closefile:                      ;* Close file
    move.l  dosbase,a6          ;DOS base address in A6
    move.l  filehd,d1           ;File handle in D1
    jsr     Close(a6)           ;Close file
    rts
filehd:     dc.l   0            ;Storage for File handle
filename:   dc.b   "Filename",0 ;File to be opened
    align                       ;even
```

To use these routines, you must look at how you can load and save data.

6.5.2   Reading and writing data

Let's write a new file. To start, write the following lines:

```
move.l  #Mode_new,d2    ;Open new file (6.5.2A)
bsr     openfile        ;Open file
beq     error           ;Didn't work!
```

For the filename, write a name like "Testfile" in the line labled "filename". After calling the "openfile" routine, a file with this name is created on the disk. If one existed already, it is erased.

Let's assume you want to write a short text to the file. For the example let's use:

```
text:   dc.b    "This is a test text for the Testfile",0
textend:
```

The "textend" label is used so that you can calculate the number of data bytes by subtracting "text".

You want to write this text in the file. Use the WRITE function which needs three parameters:

In D1   the file handle that you got back from the OPEN function

In D2   a pointer to the data that should be written

In D3   the number of bytes to be written

For the example, you'll need another segment of code to put the pointer to the data in D2 and the number of bytes in D3:

```
Write   = -48                   ; (6.5.2B)
        ...
writedata:                      ;* Write data in the file
        move.l  dosbase,a6      ;DOS base address in A6
        move.l  filehd,d1       ;File handle in D1
        jsr     Write(a6)       ;Write data
        rts
```

After opening the file, you can call the subroutine from the main program with the following lines:

```
        move.l  #text,d2            ;Pointer to data
        move.l  #textend-text,d3    ;Number of bytes
        bsr     writedata           ;Write data in the file
```

Then close the file with:

```
        bsr     closefile       ;Close file
        bra     end             ;End program
```

After running the program, look at the directory of the diskette, you should find the file "testfile". It is just as long as your text. You want to read this file in, to make sure that it contains the right data.

You need the DOS function READ, which needs the same parameters as the WRITE function. You can use parameters for the number of bytes to read just part of the file. If you give a larger number than the file contains, the whole file is loaded. You'll find the number of bytes read in D0.

Let's set up a field that has enough space for the data you want to read. You can do this with the following line:

```
field: blk.b  100     ;Reserve 100 bytes
```

For the example data, this is plenty. If you want to load another file, you may need to reserve more space.

Now let's write a subroutine to read the data. You always want to load whole files. You just need to pass the address of the buffer so the data is loaded into the subroutine. In the example, it's the address "field".

Here's the subroutine that reads the entire opened file into the memory area pointed to by D2:

```
Read    = -42                    ; (6.5.2C)
        ...
readdata:                        ;* Read file
        move.l  dosbase,a6       ;DOS base address in A6
        move.l  filehd,d1        ;File handle in D1
        move.l  #$ffffff,d3      ;Read an arbitrary number of
                                 bytes
        jsr     Read(a6)         ;Read data
        rts
```

To use this routine to load the file into the buffer "field", use the following main program:

```
        move.l  #Mode_old,d2     ;Old file
        bsr     openfile         ;Open file
        beq     error            ;Didn't work !
        move.l  #field,d2        ;Pointer to data buffer
        bsr     readdata         ;Read file
        move.l  d0,d6            ;Save number of bytes in D6
        bsr     closefile        ;Close file
        bra     end              ;Program end
```

After assembling and starting this program, you can use the debugger to look at the data buffer that you filled with data from the file. In D6, you'll find the number of bytes that were read from the file.

6.5.3   Erase files

Once you've experimented enough with the program above, you'll certainly want to erase the "Testfile" file. The DELETEFILE function in the DOS library has an offset of -72. It only needs one parameter. The parameter is passed in D1. The parameter is a pointer to the filename. The name must be closed with a null byte.

To erase "Testfile", use the following lines:

```
DeleteFile    = -72              ; (6.5.3)
        ...
        move.l  dosbase,a6       ;DOS base address in A6
        move.l  #filename,d1     ;Pointer to file name in
                                 D1
        jsr     DeleteFile(a6)   ;Erase file
```

The file is deleted. You can't save the file with normal methods if you accidently erase it! You can use a trick that saves the data. We'll take a look at this trick later. It's used in lots of programs.

6.5.4   Rename files

When a text editing program writes a text that has been altered back to disk, the old file usually isn't erased. Often the old file is renamed. For example, it might get the name "Backup". Then the new file is written to disk with the old name.

The function in the DOS library that allows you to change the names of programs is called RENAME and has -78 as an offset. You need to pass two parameters—D1 as a pointer to the old name and D2 as a pointer to the new name of the file.

To rename "Testfile" as "Backup" (before you erase it), use the following lines:

```
Rename = -78
        ...
        move.l   dosbase,a6       ;DOS base address in A6
        move.l   #oldname,d1      ;Pointer to old name in D1
        move.l   #newname,d2      ;Pointer to new name in D2
        jsr      Rename(a6)       ;Rename file
        ...
oldname: dc.b    "Testfile",0
newname: dc.b    "Backup",0
```

6.5.5   CLI directory

Let's pretend that you've programmed a text editor and started it. Now you want to load a text from disk and edit it—but what's the name of that file?

You need a function to read and display the directory of a disk. There are several ways to do this. First let's use the easiest method. It doesn't require much programming and can be quite useful.

The trick is to call the Dir or List programs that are in the C directory. You'll use the CLI commands. The DOS library contains a command called "Execute" with offset -222 that allows you to execute CLI commands.

The function needs three parameters:

In D1   a pointer to a string closed with a zero that contains the name of the command to be executed. This string must contain the same command that you would give in the CLI. It can be a null pointer as well.

In D2   the input file is determined. Normally there's a zero here. If, however, you give the file handle of a text file, though, this file is read and interpreted as a command sequence. If you define a window as the input medium, you've programmed a new CLI window!

In D3   the output file is determined. If there's a zero here, the output of the commands (for example, DIR output) is sent to the standard CLI window.

To try this out, insert this subroutine in a program that has already opened the DOS library and a window.

```
Execute   = -222                  ; (6.5.5)
          ...
dir:
          move.l  dosbase,a6      ;DOS base address in A6
          move.l  #command,d1     ;Pointer to command line
          clr.l   d2              ;No input (CLI window)
          move.l  conhandle,d3    ;Output in our window
          jsr     Execute(a6)     ;Execute command
          rts
command:
          dc.b    "dir",0
```

This program works with the List command as well. The disadvantage of this method is that the disk that the Workbench is loaded from must be in the drive or the system requests you to put it in. The Dir command is just a program, and the Amiga must load it before it can run.

This disadvantage isn't too great. The program is short, and it allows you to use any CLI command in a program.

Here is the complete program in AssemPro format that calls the Dir program:

```
;***** 6.5.5 ADIR.ASM S.D. *****

OpenLib         =-408
closelib        =-414
;ExecBase        =4                        ; Defined in AssemPro
                                           Macros

* calls to Amiga Dos:
```

```
Open            =-30
Close           =-36
Execute         = -222
IoErr           =-132
mode_old        = 1005
alloc_abs       =-$cc


        ILABEL AssemPro:includes/Amiga.l ;AssemPro only

        INIT_AMIGA                        ;AssemPro only

run:
        bsr     init                      ;Initialization
        bra     test                      ;System-Test

init:                                     ;System initialization
                                          ;and open
        move.l  ExecBase,a6               ;Number of Execute-
                                          ;library
        lea     dosname(pc),al
        moveq   #0,d0
        jsr     openlib(a6)               ;Open DOS-Library
        move.l  d0,dosbase
        beq     error

        lea     consolname(pc),al         ;Console Definition
        move.l  #mode_old,d0
        bsr     openfile                  ;Console open
        beq     error
        move.l  d0,conhandle

        rts

test:
        bsr dir                           ;do directory
        bra qu                            ;quit and exit

dir:
        move.l  dosbase,a6                ;DOS base address in A6
        move.l  #command,d1               ;Pointer to command line
        clr.l   d2                        ;No input (CLI window)
        move.l  conhandle,d3              ;output in our window
        jsr     Execute(a6)               ;execute command
        rts


error:
        move.l  dosbase,a6
        jsr     IoErr(a6)
        move.l  d0,d5

        move.l  #-1,d7                    ;Flag
qu:
        move.l  conhandle,d1              ;Window close
        move.l  dosbase,a6
        jsr     close(a6)
```

```
                move.l   dosbase,a1           ;DOS.Lib close
                move.l   ExecBase,a6
                jsr      closelib(a6)

                EXIT_AMIGA                    ;AssemPro only

openfile:                                     ;Open File
                move.l   a1,d1                 ;Pointer to I/O-
                                              ;Definition-Text

                move.l   d0,d2
                move.l   dosbase,a6
                jsr      open(a6)
                tst.l    d0
                rts


dosname: dc.b 'dos.library',0,0
        Align.w
dosbase: dc.l 0
consolname: dc.b 'CON:0/100/640/100/** CLI-Test **',0
        Align.w
conhandle: dc.l 0
command:
        dc.b     "dir",0

        end
```

6.5.6   Read directory

Now, let's look at another method that doesn't need the CLI. In this way, you can read the directory of any disk without having to play Disk Jockey.

You need to write a program that does what CLI's Dir program does. There are several steps.

First you must give the system a key to the desired directory. That means you must call DOS' Lock function. It needs two parameters:

In D1   pass a pointer to a text that contains the name of the directory you wish to read. If, for example, you want to read the contents of the RAM disk, the text would be 'RAM:',0.

In D2   put the mode that determines whether to read or write. Let's use the "Read" (-2) mode.

You call the Lock function (Offset -84) and get either a pointer to the key or a zero returned to you in the D0 register. If you get a zero, the call didn't work, the file wasn't found. This function can be used to find if a file is on the disk. You use this function with the name and see if D0 comes back zero. If not, the file exists.

Let's assume the file or path exists. You need to save the value that came back in D0. You'll need it for both functions that you'll call.

The next function you need is called Examine. You use it to search the disk for an acceptable entry. It returns parameters like name, length and date that correspond to the entry. You need to reserve a memory block for this information and put the beginning of the block in D2 before calling the Examine function. Put the key that you got from the Lock function in the D1 register.

The memory area that is filled with information is called a FileInfoBlock. It's 260 bytes long and contains information about the file. The name starts in the 9th byte and ends with a null byte, so you can easily print it with our "pmsg" routine. The information that Examine gives isn't about a particular file, but about the disk. The name in FileInfoBlock is the disk name.

The Examine function sends the status back in the D0 register. Since the Lock function already tested if the file existed, evaluating the status really isn't necessary.

Now to the function that you can use to read individual files from the directory. The function is called ExNext (Examine Next). This function searches for the next entry that fits the key every time it is called. ExNext gets the same parameters as Examine gets. However, the return parameter in D0 is more important here.

The ExNext function is always called in the same way. It always gets the next entry of the directory. If no more entries exist in the directory, Ex-Next puts a zero in the D0 register.

You need to continue performing this operation until there aren't any more entries. You can find this using the IoErr function from the DOS library.

This function doesn't need any parameters. It returns the status of the last I/O operation that was performed in the D0 register. After the last Ex-Next, this value is 232, which means no_more_Entries.

Here's a complete routine for reading the directory of the disk in drive
DF0: and displaying the contents in the window.

```
;6.5.5B.ASM
;***** DOS-Sample function 3/87 S.D. *****

OpenLib     =-30-378
closelib    =-414
ExBase      =4

* calls to Amiga Dos:

Open        = -30
Close       = -30-6
Read        = -30-12
Write       = -30-18
MyInput     = -30-24
Output      = -30-30
CurrDir     = -30-96
Lock        = -30-54
Examine     = -30-72
ExNext      = -30-78
Exit        = -30-114
IoErr       = -30-102
WaitForCh   = -30-174
Mode        = 0
mode_old    = 1005
mode_new    = 1006
alloc_abs   = -$cc
free_mem    = -$d2

            ILABEL AssemPro:includes/Amiga.l ;AssemPro only

            INIT_AMIGA                       ;AssemPro only

run:
            bsr     init                ;Initialization
            bra     test                ;System-Test

init:                                   ;System initialization
                                        ;and open
            move.l  ExBase,a6           ;Pointer to EXEC library
            lea     dosname(pc),a1
            moveq   #0,d0
            jsr     openlib(a6)         ;Open DOS-Library
            move.l  d0,dosbase
            beq     error

            lea     consolname(pc),a1   ;Console-Definition
            move.l  #mode_old,d0
            bsr     openfile            ;Console open
            beq     error
            move.l  d0,conhandle

            rts
```

```
test:
        move.l  #MyText,d0
        bsr     pmsg                    ;Test-Text output

        move.l  dosbase,a6
        move.l  #name,d1
        move.l  #-2,d2
        jsr     Lock(a6)
        move.l  d0,d5
        tst.l   d0
        beq     error
        move.l  d0,locksav

        move.l  dosbase,a6
        move.l  locksav,d1
        move.l  #fileinfo,d2
        jsr     Examine(a6)
        move.l  d0,d6
        tst.l   d0
        beq     error
loop:
        move.l  dosbase,a6
        move.l  locksav,d1
        move.l  #fileinfo,d2
        jsr     ExNext(a6)
        tst.l   d0
        beq     error

        move.l  #fileinfo+8,d0
        bsr     pmsg
        bsr     pcrlf
        bra     loop

error:
        move.l  dosbase,a6
        jsr     IoErr(a6)
        move.l  d0,d6

        move.l  #presskey,d0
        bsr     pmsg
        bsr     getchr
        move.l  #-1,d7                  ;Flag
qu:
        move.l  conhandle,d1           ;Window close
        move.l  dosbase,a6
        jsr     close(a6)

        move.l  dosbase,a1             ;DOS.Lib close
        move.l  ExBase,a6
        jsr     closelib(a6)

        EXIT_AMIGA                     ;AssemPro only

openfile:                             ;Open File
```

149

```
              move.l  a1,d1                    ;pointer to I/O-
                                               ;Definition-Text
              move.l  d0,d2
              move.l  dosbase,a6
              jsr     open(a6)
              tst.l   d0
              rts

      pmsg:                                    ;Print message (d0)
              movem.l d0-d7/a0-a6,-(sp)
              move.l  d0,a0
              move.l  a0,d2
              clr.l   d3
      mess1:
              tst.b   (a0)+
              beq     mess2
              addq.l  #1,d3
              bra     mess1
      mess2:
              move.l  conhandle,d1
              move.l  dosbase,a6
              jsr     write(a6)
              movem.l (sp)+,d0-d7/a0-a6
              rts

      pcrlf:
              move    #10,d0
              bsr     pchar
              move    #13,d0
      pchar:                                   ;Character in D0 output
              movem.l d0-d7/a0-a6,-(sp)         ;save all
              move.l  conhandle,d1
      pch1:
              lea     chbuff,a1
              move.b  d0,(a1)
              move.l  a1,d2
              move.l  #1,d3
              move.l  dosbase,a6
              jsr     write(a6)
              movem.l (sp)+,d0-d7/a0-a6          ;restore all
              rts

      scankey:                                 ;Test key
              move.l  conhandle,d1
              move.l  #500,d2                   ;Wait value
              move.l  dosbase,a6
              jsr     waitforch(a6)
              tst.l   d0
              rts

      readln:                                  ;Input from keyboard
              movem.l d0-d7/a0-a6,-(sp)          ;Registers
              lea     inline+2,a2               ;Pointer to input buffer
              clr.l   (a2)
      inplop:
              bsr     getchr
```

```
          cmp.b    #8,d0
          beq      backspace
          cmp.b    #127,d0                  ;Delete ?
          beq      backspace
          bsr      pchar                    ;Character output
          cmp.b    #13,d0
          beq      Inputx
          move.b   d0,(a2)+
          bra      inplop
Input:
          clr.b    (a2)+
          sub.l    #inline,a2
          move     a2,inline                ;Length in inline+1
          movem.l  (sp)+,d0-d7/a0-a6        ;Registers
          rts

backspace:
          cmp.l    #inline,a2               ;at beginning?
          beq      inplop                   ;yes
          move.b   #8,d0
          bsr      pchar                    ;Backspace
          move     #32,d0
          bsr      pchar                    ;Blank
          move     #8,d0
          bsr      pchar                    ;Backspace
          clr.b    (a2)
          subq.l   #1,a2
          bra      inplop

getchr:                                     ;Get one character from
                                            ;keyboard
          move.l   #1,d3                    ;1 character
          move.l   conhandle,d1
          lea      inbuff,a1                ;Buffer-Address
          move.l   a1,d2
          move.l   dosbase,a6
          jsr      read(a6)
          clr.l    d0
          move.b   inbuff,d0
          rts


MyText:    dc.b 'Directory of diskette: DF0:',10,13,10,13,0,0
dosname:   dc.b 'dos.library',0,0
presskey:  dc.b 'Press the RETURN key!!',0
          align.w
dosbase:    dc.l 0
consolname: dc.b 'CON:0/100/640/100/** Directory-Test **',0
name:       dc.b 'DF0:',0
          align.w
locksav:    dc.l 0
fileinfo:   ds.l 20
conhandle:  dc.l 0
inbuff:     DS.B 8
inline:     DS.B 180
chbuff:     DS.B 82
```

```
end
```

The FileInfoBlock contains the following entries:

Offset	Name	Meaning
0	DiskKey.L	Disk number
4	DirEntryType.L	Entry type (+ = Directory, - = File)
8	FileName	108 bytes with the filename
116	Protection.L	File protected?
120	EntryType.L	Entry type
124	Size.L	Length of file in bytes
128	NumBlocks.L	Number of blocks
132	Days.L	Creation day
136	Minute.L	Creation time
140	Tick.L	Creation time
144	Comment	116 bytes with comments

If you want to have the program output the file length as well, you can read the length with "move.l fileinfo+124,d0" and then use a conversion routine to produce a decimal number. You can output this result with the name.

6.5.7   Direct access to disk

There isn't a simple function in the library for accessing single disk sectors. Here, you must work with a device just like you did with speech output. This time you'll be working with the trackdisk.device.

You want to work with this device to directly program the disk drives. Once you've built up the necessary program machinery, you can experiment with various commands for disk access. Remember that an error can cause the disk to be modified and thus unusable. Make sure you're using a non-essential disk. Don't use one which contains your only copy of something.

The initialization here is similar to that for speech output. Here's the initialization routine for the program:

```
;** Direct disk access via trackdisk.device **  (6.5.6)
OpenLib    =-408
closelib   =-414
ExecBase   =4
Open       =-30
Close      =-36
```

```
opendevice  =-444
CloseDev    =-450
SendIo      =-462
Read        =-30-12
Write       =-30-18
WaitForCh   =-30-174
mode_old    =1005
run:
        bsr     init                    ;Initialization
        bra     test                    ;System test
init:                                   ;Initialize and open
                                        ;system
        move.l  execbase,a6             ;Pointer to EXEC library
        lea     dosname,a1
        moveq   #0,d0
        jsr     openlib(a6)             ;Open DOS library
        move.l  d0,dosbase
        beq     error
        lea     diskio,a1               ;Pointer to disk I/O area
        move.l  #diskrep,14(a1)         ;Pointer to port
        clr.l   d0                      ;Drive 0 (built in)
        clr.l   d1                      ;No flags
        lea     trddevice,a0            ;Pointer to device name
        jsr     opendevice(a6)          ;Open trackdisk.device
        tst.l   d0                      ;Error?
        bne     error                   ;Yes!
        move.l  #consolname(pc),d1      ;Console definition
        move.l  #mode_old,d2            ;Old mode
        move.l  dosbase,a6              ;DOS base address
        jsr     open(a6)                ;Open window
        tst.l   d0                      ;Error?
        beq     error                   ;Yes!
        move.l  d0,conhandle            ;Else save handle
        rts                             ;Done
test:                                   ;Place for test routine
```

And now for the functions that take care of the various messages at the end of the program.

```
error:
        move.l  #-1,d7                  ;Flag for error (for SEKA)
qu:
        move.l  execbase,a6             ;EXEC base address
        lea     diskio,a1               ;Pointer to disk I/O
        move.l  32(a1),d7               ;IO_ACTUAL in D7 (for testing)
        move    #9,28(a1)               ;Command: motor on/off
        move.l  #0,36(a1)               ;0=off, 1=on, so turn motor
        jsr     sendio(a6)              ;off
        move.l  conhandle,d1            ;Close window
        move.l  dosbase,a6
        jsr     close(a6)
        move.l  dosbase,d1              ;Close DOS.Lib
        move.l  execbase,a6
        jsr     closelib(a6)
        lea     diskio,a1
```

```
        jsr     closedev(a6)    ;Close trackdisk.device
        rts
```

Let's not forget the routine that waits for the user to press <Return>, so that you can watch the effects of the test function in peace:

```
getchr:                         ;Get a character from keyboard
        move.l  #1,d3           ;1 character
        move.l  conhandle,d1    ;Window handle
        move.l  #inbuff,d2      ;Buffer address
        move.l  dosbase,a6      ;DOS base address
        jsr     read(a6)        ;Read character
        rts                     ;That's it
```

The last thing you need is the section of code that declares the text and data fields that your program needs:

```
dosname:        dc.b            'dos.library',0
        align
consolname:     dc.b            'RAW:0/100/640/50/** Wait
                                Window',0
        align
trddevice:      dc.b            'trackdisk.device',0
        align
dosbase:        dc.l  0         ;DOS base address
conhandle:      dc.l  0         ;Window handle
inbuff:         blk.b 80,0      ;Keyboard buffer
diskio:         blk.l 20,0      ;I/O structure
diskrep:        blk.l 8,0       ;I/O port
diskbuff:       blk.b 512*2,0   ;Place for 2 sectors
```

There, now you're done with the set-up work. Let's look at how you can give commands to the disk drives. The first and easiest command, is the one for turning the drive motor on and off. You've already seen this command in the program. This is command number nine. This number goes in the command word of the I/O structure (bytes 28 and 29 of the structure).

You need to pass a parameter that lets the computer know whether to turn the motor off or on. This information goes in the I/O long word that starts at byte 36; it's zero for off, and one for on.

You already chose the motor that should be turned on or off when you opened the device. You put the number of the chosen disk drive in D0—in your case you put a zero there because you are using the DF0: disk drive.

Here's an overview of the commands you can use to access information on the disk:

No.	Name	Function
2	READ	Read one or more sectors
3	WRITE	Write sectors
4	UPDATE	Update the track buffer
5	CLEAR	Erase track buffer
9	MOTOR	Turn motor on/off
10	SEEK	Search for a track
11	FORMAT	Format tracks
12	REMOVE	Initialize routine that is called when you remove the disk
13	CHANGENUM	Find out number of disk changes
14	CHANGESTATE	Test if disk is in drive
15	PROTSTATUS	Test if disk is write protected

You've already learned about command number nine. Let's look at the three commands you can use to make tests. These are the last three commands. They put a return value in the long word that begins in the 32nd byte in the I/O structure. This value was written to D7 in the program above for testing purposes. You can read its contents directly if you ran the program with AssemPro.

Here is a simple routine that you can use to run one of these commands with:

```
test:                       ;(6.5.6B)
        lea     diskio,a1    ;Pointer to I/O structure
        move    #13,28(a1)   ;Pass command (for example,13)
        move.l  execbase,a6  ;EXEC base address in A6
        jsr     SendIO(a6)   ;Call function
```

If CHANGENUM (command 13) is executed, in D7 you'll get the number of times a disk was taken out and put in the drive. If you call the program, you'll get a value back. If you take the disk out and put it back in, the number is two higher the next time you call the program.

The CHANGESTATE command (command 14) tells whether a disk is in the drive or not. If one is, a zero comes back. Otherwise, a $FF is returned.

You get the same values back from the PROTSTATUS function (command 15). Here a zero means that the disk isn't write protected, while $FF means that it is.

Now let's look at the READ and WRITE functions. These operations need a few more parameters than the status functions. You need to pass the following parameters:

The address of the I/O buffer in the data pointer, the number of bytes to be transferred in I/O length, and the data address on the disk in I/O offset.

The number of data bytes must be a multiple of 512, since every sector is 512 bytes, and only whole sectors can be read.

The data address is the number of the first byte in the sector. If you want to use the first sector, the offset is zero. For the second sector, it's 512, etc... The formula is:

$$Offset = (Sector\_number - 1) * 512$$

Here is a routine that loads the first two sectors of the disk into the buffer:

```
test:   (6.5.6C)
        lea    diskio,a1
        move   #2,28(a1)              ;Command: READ
        move.l #diskbuff,40(a1)       ;Buffer
        move.l #2*512,36(a1)          ;Length: 2 sectors
        move.l #0*512,44(a1)          ;Offset: 0 sectors
        move.l execbase,a6            ;EXEC base address
        jsr    SendIO(a6)             ;Start function
```

Start the program from the debugger and then look at the buffer's contents after the program ends. You can find out the format of the disk here. If you want to read a sector that's being used, change the 0 in the offset definition to 700 and start again. It's highly probable that there's some data there.

To modify and write back the data that you've read from the disk, you need command three, the WRITE command. The parameters are the same.

If you've execute the WRITE command, you're probably wondering why the disk light didn't go on. That's because the Amiga writes a track that has been read into a buffer of its own. It WRITEs data there as well. It won't write the data to disk until another track is accessed.

You can have the data updated directly as well using command four, the UPDATE command.

Command 11, the FORMAT command, is also quite interesting. This command needs a data field that is 11*512=5632 bytes long—the length of a track. The offset must be a multiple of this number so that you start at the beginning of a track.

The length must be a multiple of 5632 as a result. If several tracks are formatted, each track is filled with the same data.

You can use this function to easily write a disk copy program. You READ the source disk and then FORMAT the corresponding track on the destination disk. That's how the DiskCopy program works—it reformats the destination disk.

Command ten, the SEEK command, just needs the offset. It moves the Read/Write head of the drive to the position specified without making a disk access or testing if it's at the right position.

Command 12, the REMOVE command, is used to install an interrupt routine that is called when the disk is removed from the disk drive. The address of the interrupt structure is passed in the data pointer of the I/O structure. If there's a zero here, the interupt routine is turned off.

Here is a complete example program in AssemPro format:

```
;***** Track disk-Basic function 10/86 S.D. *****

        ILABEL ASSEMPRO:Includes/amiga.l ;AssemPro only

OpenLib        =-30-378
closelib       =-414
;ExecBase       =4                        ;defined in INIT_AMIGA


* calls to Amiga Dos:

Open           =-30
Close          =-30-6
opendevice     =-444
CloseDev       =-450
SendIo         =-462
Read           =-30-12
Write          =-30-18
WaitForCh      =-30-174
mode_old       =1005


        INIT_AMIGA                        ;AssemPro only

run:
        bsr    init                       ;Initialization
        bra    test                       ;System-Test

init:                                     ;System initialization
                                          and open
        move.l ExecBase,a6                ;Pointer to EXEC-library
        lea    dosname,a1
        moveq  #0,d0
        jsr    openlib(a6)                ;Open DOS-Library
        move.l d0,dosbase
        beq    error

        lea    diskio,a1
        move.l #diskrep,14(a1)
```

```
                clr.l    d0
                clr.l    d1
                lea      trddevice,a0
                jsr      opendevice(a6)        ;Open trackdisk.device
                tst.l    d0
                bne      error

        bp:
                lea      consolname(pc),a1     ;Console-Definition
                move.l   #mode_old,d0
                bsr      openfile              ;Console open
                beq      error
                move.l   d0,conhandle

                rts

        test:
                bsr      accdisk

                bsr      getchr                ;wait for character
                bra      qu

        error:
                move.l   #-1,d7                ;Flag
        qu:
                move.l   ExecBase,a6 lea       diskio,a1
                move     #9,28(a1)
                move.l   #0,36(a1)
                jsr      sendio(a6)

                move.l   conhandle,d1          ;Window close
                move.l   dosbase,a6
                jsr      close(a6)

                move.l   dosbase,a1            ;DOS.Lib close
                move.l   ExecBase,a6
                jsr      closelib(a6)

                lea      diskio,a1
                move.l   32(a1),d7
                jsr      closedev(a6)

                EXIT_AMIGA                     ;AssemPro only

        openfile:                             ;Open File
                move.l   a1,d1                 ;Pointer to the I/O-
                                               Definition-Text
                move.l   d0,d2
                move.l   dosbase,a6
                jsr      open(a6)
                tst.l    d0
                rts

        scankey:                              ;Test for key
                move.l   conhandle,d1
                move.l   #500,d2               ;Wait value
```

```
          move.l  dosbase,a6
          jsr     waitforch(a6)
          tst.l   d0
          rts

getchr:                                        ;Get one character from
                                               keyboard
          move.l  #1,d3                        ;1 character
          move.l  conhandle,d1
          lea     inbuff,a1                    ;Buffer-Address
          move.l  a1,d2
          move.l  dosbase,a6
          jsr     read(a6)
          clr.l   d0
          move.b  inbuff,d0
          rts

accdisk:
          lea     diskio,a1
          move    #2,28(a1)                    ;Command: READ
          move.l  #diskbuff,40(a1)             ;Buffer
          move.l  #2*512,36(a1)                ;Length: 2 Sectors
          move.l  #20*512,44(a1)               ;Offset: n Sectors
          move.l  ExecBase,a6 jsr              sendio(a6)
          rts

dosname:        dc.b 'dos.library',0,0
        align.w
dosbase:        dc.l 0
consolname:     dc.b 'RAW:0/100/640/100/** Test-Window S.D.
                V0.1',0
trddevice:      dc.b 'trackdisk.device',0
        align.w
conhandle:      dc.l 0
inbuff:         ds.b 8
diskio:         ds.l 20,0
diskrep:        ds.l 8,0
diskbuff:       ds.b 512*2,0

        end
```

Chapter 7

Working with Intuition

7 Working with Intuition

Now that you've learned so much about machine language, let's look at the special features of the Amiga. Let's look at the operating system Intuition that is in charge of windows, screens, the mouse and lots of other things. Before taking a look at these beautiful features, there's some bad news.

First, though, let's hear the good news. Since Intuition has so many functions, it allows you to be very creative in programming your ideas. The disadvantage is that the flexibility means that you have to use a lot of parameters, and that makes for a lot of tedious work.

However, this is no grounds for a panic. Once you've built up the necessary routines, the programming and experimentation become increasingly interesting. Before you try out new program variations, you should save your source code to disk, because Intuition get's fairly upset about bad parameters and often responds by crashing the system.

Now let's get to work. To start working with Intuition, you need the Intuition library. You can load it with the OpenLibrary function from the EXEC library. Here's the subroutine that takes care of initialization.

```
OpenLib  = -408
ExecBase = 4
run:
        bsr     openint             ;Load Intuition library
        ...
openint:                            ;* Initialize and open system
        move.l  ExecBase,a6         ;EXEC base address
        lea     IntName,a1          ;Name of Intuition
                                    ;library
        jsr     OpenLib(a6)         ;Open Intuition
        move.l  d0,intbase          ;Save Intuition base address
        rts
IntName: dc.b "intuition.library",0
        align
intbase: dc.l 0                     ;Base address of
                                    ;Intuition
```

When your program is finished, you need to close the screens, the window and the library. To do this, use the CloseLibrary function from the EXEC library. It has an offset of -414. Here's the subroutine:

```
CloseLibrary  = -414
       ...
closeint:                          ;* Close Intuition
      move.l  execbase,a6          ;EXEC base address in A6
      move.l  intbase,a1           ;Intuition base address
                                in A1
      jsr     CloseLibrary(a6)  ;Close Intuition
      rts                          ;Done
```

Now that you've got that taken care of, you can finally start working
with Intuition.

7.1 Open screen

Intuition is a graphics operating system. For this reason, you'll be working with the screen. It's even more interesting to work with several screens at the same time. However, you only have one monitor on the Amiga.

You can open as many screens as you like (at least, as long as there's some memory available). You can open a window, display menus and do I/O's there. The individual screens are fully independent. You can work with all of them simultaneously on the monitor.

You can move individual screens forward and back to your heart's content. You can also press the left <Amiga> key and then an "m" to return to the Workbench screen after getting into the different screens.

You want to begin programming Intuition by setting up a screen. You've already loaded the Intuition library, so you can use the OpenScreen function.

Wait a minute! What should the screen look like, where should it go, and what form should it have? You need to look at the options for the form of the screen you have available.

The input to the screen is in the form of a table that has 13 entries. Let's take a look at the parameters that you need for our screen.

You'll start the table with the label "screen_defs" which must be at an even address:

```
        align
screen_defs:              ;* The screen table begins here
```

The first bit of information that the screen needs is the position and size. Let's have it start in the upper left corner and fill the entire screen. You'll use the positions X=0 and Y=0, the width 320 and the height 200. This means that your screen is the maximum size.

```
x_pos:          dc.w    0       ;X-Position
y_pos:          dc.w    0       ;Y-Position
width:          dc.w    320     ;Width
height:         dc.w    200     ;Height
```

Next you need to decide which colors should be displayed. That depends on the number of bit planes, on the depth. Let's choose two. That means you have 2^2 (4) colors available. If the depth was one, you'd only have two colors available. Let's choose two, since four colors is usually plently.

```
depth:          dc.w    2       ;Number of bit planes
```

Next you need to choose the color of the title line and the function symbols. Give the number of the color register:

```
detail_pen:     dc.b    0       ;Color of the text, etc...
```

Now for the color of the text background:

```
block_pen:      dc.b    1       ;Background color
```

Make sure that these two inputs fit in a byte. The colors are normally the following (if the standard values haven't been changed). You'll notice that the number of colors depends on the number of bit maps.

Pen	Color
0	Background (blue)
1	White
for two bit planes	
2	Black
3	Red
for three bit planes	
4	Blue
5	Violet
6	Turquoise
7	White
for four bit planes	
8	Black
9	Red
10	Green
11	Brown
12	Blue
13	Blue
14	Green
15	Green

The next word contains the bits that decribe the appearance of the screen. The bits are:

Bit	Value	Name	Meaning
1	2	GENLOCK_VIDEO	
2	4	INTERLACE	Puts the screen in Interlace mode. The resolution and thus the maximum screen size are doubled.
6	$40	PFBA	
7	$80	EXTRA_HALFBRITE	
8	$100	GENLOCK_AUDIO	
10 and	$400	DBLPF	Divides the screen into a border character area.
11	$800	HOLDNMODIFY	Turns on Hold-and-Modify mode
13	$2000	VP_HIDE	
14	$4000	SPRITES	Allows sprites to be used
15	$8000	MODE_640	Turns on the highest resolution graphics for the screen (640x400)

Choose the value two (normal) for your example screen:

```
view_modes:    dc.w    2        ;Representation mode
```

The following word is constructed in such a way that each bit has its own meaning. Use this to set what sort of screen it is. Choose 15 so the screen is a "Custom screen", which allows you all of the options.

```
screen_type:   dc.w    15       ;Screen type: custom screen
```

Next there's a pointer to the character set to be used for all output to the screen. If you don't want to install your own character set, just put a zero here, and the standard character set is used.

```
font:          dc.l    0        ;Character set: Standard
```

Next there's a pointer to the text that's used as the name of the screen. The text ends with a zero, just like window names must.

```
title:         dc.l    name     ;Pointer to title text
```

Next comes a long word that defines the gadgets. These gadgets represent the functions, like "Bring forward", that can be accessed via a mouse click in the screen. The long word in this table is a pointer to a list which specifies the gadgets. These aren't the system gadgets. However, you're only using system gadgets here, so put a zero here.

```
gadgets:       dc.l    0        ;No gadgets
```

Finally there's a long word that you only need if you want to use a special bit map just for your screen. Since this isn't the case, just put a zero here.

```
bitmap:         dc.l    0        ;No bit map
```

That's it for the list entries that you need to define the screen. You still need the text for the name of the screen. Enter the following:

```
sname:          dc.b    'Our Screen',0 ;Screen title
```

Here's a quick overview of the list:

```
        align
screen_defs:                      ;* The screen ta
x_pos:          dc.w    0         ;X-Position
y_pos:          dc.w    0         ;Y-Position
width:          dc.w    320       ;Width
height:         dc.w    200       ;Height
depth:          dc.w    2         ;Number of bit planes
detail_pen:     dc.b    0         ;Color of the text, etc...
block_pen:      dc.b    1         ;Background color
view_modes:     dc.w    2         ;Representation mode
screen_type:    dc.w    15        ;Screen type: custom
                                  ;screen
font:           dc.l    0         ;Character set: Standard
title:          dc.l    sname     ;Pointer to title text
gadgets:        dc.l    0         ;No gadgets
bitmap:         dc.l    0         ;No bit map
sname:          dc.b    'Our Screen',0 ;Screen title
```

Once you've decided on the parameters, it's very easy to open the screen. You need Intuition's OpenScreen function. It's offset is -198, and it only needs one parameter, the address of the parameter table. The program fragment looks like this:

```
OpenScreen = -198
        bsr     openint           ;Open Intuition
        bsr     scropen           ;Open screen
        ...
scropen:                          ;* Open screen
        move.l  intbase,a6        ;Intuition base address
                                  ;in A6
        lea     screen_defs,a0    ;Pointer to table
        jsr     openscreen(a6)    ;And open
        move.l  d0,screenhd       ;Save screen handle
        rts                       ;Return to main program
        ...
screen_defs:                      ;Table info follows
```

Now the Amiga's Workbench screen is covered by your screen. Now you can do what you want with it until the program is done. Afterwards, the screen must be closed again, so that you can see the Workbench screen again.

Use the CloseScreen function (offset -66) to do this. The only parameter it needs is the pointer to the screen structure you got back from the Open-Screen function.

```
CloseScreen = -66
        ...
scrclose:                          ;*Close screen
        move.l  intbase,a6         ;Intuition base address
                                   ;in A6
        move.l  screenhd,a0        ;Screen handle in A0
        jsr     CloseScreen(a6)    ;Close screen
        rts                        ;Done
```

The long word that OpenScreen returned to you is a pointer to a screen structure that contains all the needed data about the screen. Besides the data which was given, there is a pointer in the screen area for individual bit planes, etc...

The form of this structure is fairly complicated and contains some data that you can't use. Several of the parameters are interesting, however. Here's a selection of the usable parameters:

No.	Name	Function
0	(NextScreen.L)	Pointer to next screen
4	(FirstWindow)	Pointer to first window structure
8	(LeftEdge.W)	
$A	(TopEdge.W)	Position of the screen
$C	(Width.W)	Width
$E	(Height.W)	Height
$10	(MouseY.W)	
$12	(MouseX.W)	Mouse position in the screen
$14	(Flags.W)	Screen flags
$16	(Title.L)	Pointer to title text
$1A	(DefaultTitle)	Pointer to normal title
$28	(Font.L)	Pointer to character set
$C0	(Plane0.L)	Pointer to the bit plane 0
$C4	(Plane1.L)	Pointer to the bit plane 1
$C8	(Plane2.L)	Pointer to the bit plane 2
$CC	(Plane3.L)	Pointer to the bit plane 3

An example of an application for the plane pointer is writing and using your own character routine. Next you want to move the address of a plane into an address register as follows:

```
        move.l  screenhd,a5     ;Screen pointer in A5
        move.l  $c0(a5),a5      ;Bit plane 0-pointer in A5
```

If you want to try this, do the following:

```
        move.l  screenhd,a5      ;Screen pointer in A5
        move.l  $c0(a5),a5       ;Bit plane 0-pointer in A5
        move    #$20,d0          ;Counter D0=$20
lop1:
        move    d0,(a5)          ;Write counter bits in picture
        add.l   #80,a5           ;Address +80, next line
        dbra    d0,lop1          ;Continue until D0<0
```

This program draws a white, square pattern that corresponds to the bit pattern for the numbers $20 to 0. This isn't a particularly useful program, but it shows how easy it is to write from a machine language program directly to the screen. If you change the offset in the second line to $C4, the pattern is read.

You can move the entire screen with the normal technique of moving the mouse pointer into the upper border and moving it up and down with the left mouse key depressed. You can do the same thing with a program.

Let's move the screen without the mouse. Use the joystick for demonstration purposes. Put the joystick in port two. As you saw in the chapter on the hardware register, you can read memory location $DFF00C to find information about the joystick. You can find the direction the screen should be moved here.

Moving the screen requires another Intuition function. You use the MoveScreen function which has an offset of -162 and needs three parameters to do this. The parameters are:

In A0   the pointer to the screen structure that you got back in D0 when you opened the screen. (You saved it in "screenhd".)
In D1   the desired movement in the Y-direction, the vertical direction
In D0   the horizontal movement in the X-direction. The variant doesn't work so you can only move the screen vertically.

Insert the following lines in your program:

```
MoveScreen      =-162
        ...
scrmove:                         ;* Move screen D0 to the right
                                 ;  and D1 down
        move.l  intbase,a6       ;Intuition base address in A6
        move.l  screenhd,a0      ;Screen handle in A0
        clr.l   d0               ;No horizontal movement
        jsr     MoveScreen(a6)   ;Move screen
        rts                      ;Done
```

Now your looking at a complete program that goes through the following
steps:

1.   Opens the Intuition library
2.   Opens a screen.
3.   Moves the screen in the direction specified by the joystick in
        port two.
4.   Closes the screen when the fire button is hit.
5.   Closes the Intuition library.
6.   Ends.

Here is the complete program including the subroutines, so you'll have it
all in one spot:

```
;** Demo programm to open and move a screens **
MoveScreen      = -162
OpenScreen      = -198
CloseScreen     = -66
CloseLibrary    = -414
OpenLib         = -408                  ;Open library
ExecBase        = 4                     ;EXEC base address
joy2            = $dff00c               ;Joystick 2 Data
fire            = $bfe001               ;Fire button 2: Bit 7
run:
        bsr     openint                 ;Open Intuition
        bsr     scropen                 ;Open screen
        move    joy2,d6                 ;Save joystick info
loop:
        tst.b   fire                    ;Test fire button
        bpl     ende                    ;Pressed down: done
        move    joy2,d0                 ;Basic info in D0
        sub     d6,d0                   ;Subtract new data
        cmp     #$0100,d0               ;Up ?
        bne     noup                    ;No
        move.l  #-1,d1                  ;dy=-1 direction y
        bsr     scrmove                 ;Move up
        bra     loop
noup:
        cmp     #$0001,d0               ;Down ?
        bne     loop                    ;No
        move.l  #1,d1                   ;dy=1
        bsr     scrmove                 ;Move down
        bra     loop
ende:
        bsr     scrclose                ;Close screen
        bsr     closeint                ;Close Intuition
        rts                             ;Done !
openint:                                ;* Initialize and open system
        move.l  ExecBase,a6             ;EXEC base address
        lea     IntName,a1              ;Name of Intuition library
        jsr     OpenLib(a6)             ;Open Intuition
        move.l  d0,intbase              ;Save Intuition base address
        rts
```

```
closeint:                              ;* Close Intuition
        move.l  execbase,a6            ;EXEC base address in A6
        move.l  intbase,a1            ;Intuition base address in A1
        jsr     CloseLibrary(a6)      ;Close Intuition
        rts                           ;Done
scropen:                               ;* Open screen
        move.l  intbase,a6            ;Intuition base address in A6
        lea     screen_defs,a0        ;Pointer to table
        jsr     openscreen(a6)        ;Open
        move.l  d0,screenhd           ;Save screen handle
        rts                           ;Return to main program
scrclose:                              ;* Close Screen
        move.l  intbase,a6            ;Intuition base address in A6
        move.l  screenhd,a0           ;Screen handle in A0
        jsr     CloseScreen(a6)       ;Close screen
        rts                           ;Done
scrmove:                               ;Move screen D0 right/D1 down
        move.l  intbase,a6            ;Intuition base address in A6
        move.l  screenhd,a0           ;Screen handle in A0
        clr.l   d0                    ;No horizontal movement
        jsr     MoveScreen(a6)        ;And move
        rts                           ;Done
        Align
screen_defs:                           ;* Screen table begins here
x_pos:          dc.w    0              ;X-position
y_pos:          dc.w    0              ;Y-position
width:          dc.w    320            ;Width
height:         dc.w    200            ;Height
depth:          dc.w    2              ;Number of bit planes
detail_pen:     dc.b    1              ;Text color = white
block_pen:      dc.b    3              ;Background color = red
view_modes:     dc.w    2              ;Representation mode
screen_type:    dc.w    15             ;Screen type: Custom  screen
font:           dc.l    0              ;Standard character set
title:          dc.l    sname          ;Pointer to title text
gadgets:        dc.l    0              ;No gadgets
bitmap:         dc.l    0              ;No bit map
intbase:        dc.l    0              ;Base address of
                                            Intuition
screenhd:       dc.l    0              ;Screen handle
IntName:        dc.b    'intuition.library',0
        align
sname:          dc.b    'Our Screen',0 ;Screen title
        align
        end
```

From this example, you can see how easy scrolling actually is. Another easy thing to do is to use the DisplayBeep function. It has offset -96; the only parameter it needs is the screen pointer that you stored in the "screenhd" memory block. This function covers the screen with an orange color for a short while. The screen isn't changed. The beep function can be used as follows:

```
DisplayBeep = -96
      ...
      move.l  intbase,a6          ;Intuition base address in A6
      move.l  screenhd,a0         ;Screen pointer in A0
      jsr     DisplayBeep(a6)     ;Light up screen
```

If you put a zero instead of a screen pointer in A0, the whole screen
blinks.

Good, now you have your own screen that you can move up and down.
What good is it if you can't put anything on it? Let's open a window on
the screen!

7.2 Open window

As you saw in the chapter on program initialization, it's easy to open a window with the DOS library. You can't use this method on your own screen however. You need to use another method that can open any window on any screen.

Intuition has a function called OpenWindow which handles this sort of work. It has an offset of -204 and needs only one parameter, a pointer to a window definition table. This pointer goes in register A0.

This table is very similar to the one used to define the screen. The first four values specify the X- and Y-positions, the width, and the height of the window to be opened. Here's an example:

```
    align
window_defs:
        dc.w    10      ;X-position
        dc.w    20      ;Y-position
        dc.w    300     ;Width
        dc.w    150     ;Height
```

Next come two bytes that define the color of the letters and the background:

```
        dc.b    1       ;White letter color
        dc.b    3       ;On a red background
```

The next long words contain the IDCMP flag in its bits. The bits determine the circumstances under which Intuition sends a message to the program. The bits have the following meaning:

Bit	Value	Name	Meaning (Report if)
0	$000001	SIZEVERIFY	
1	$000002	NEWSIZE	Window size changed
2	$000004	REFRESHWINDOW	
3	$000008	MOUSEBUTTONS	Mouse key hit
4	$000010	MOUSEMOVE	Mouse moved
5	$000020	GADGETDOWN	A special gadget chosen
6	$000040	GADGETUP	Same as above
7	$000080	REQSET	
8	$000100	MENUPICK	A menu item chosen
9	$000200	CLOSEWINDOW	A window closed
10	$000400	RAWKEY	A key pressed
11	$000800	REQVERIFY	
12	$001000	REQCLEAR	
13	$002000	MENUVERIFY	
14	$004000	NEWPREFS	Preferences modified
15	$008000	DISKINSERTED	A disk put in
16	$010000	DISKREMOVED	A disk taken out
17	$020000	WBENCHMESSAGE	
18	$040000	ACTIVEWINDOW	A window activated
19	$080000	INACTIVEWINDOW	A window deactivated
20	$100000	DELTAMOVE	Report relative mouse movement

If you want your first window to respond only by clicking on the close symbol, write the following:

```
dc.l    $200    ;IDCMP flags: CLOSEWINDOW
```

Next comes a long word whose bits determine the window's type. You can use this to construct a window to your exact specifications. This is quite different from windows opened with the DOS function. The bits mean:

Bit	Value	Name	Meaning (Report if)
0	$0000001	WINDOWSIZING	Window size is changeable
1	$0000002	WINDOWDRAG	Window is moveable
2	$0000004	WINDOWDEPTH	Window covering is possible
3	$0000008	WINDOWCLOSE	Window close symbol
4	$0000010	SIZEBRIGHT	
5	$0000020	SIZEBBOTTOM	
6	$0000040	SIMPLE_REFRESH	New drawing manual
7	$0000080	SUPER_BITMAP	Save the window's contents
8	$0000100	BACKDROP	Move window back
9	$0000200	REPORTMOUSE	Report mouse coordinates
10	$0000400	GIMMEZEROZERO	
11	$0000800	BORDERLESS	Window without border
12	$0001000	ACTIVATE	Window active
13	$0002000	WINDOWACTIVE	
14	$0004000	INREQUEST	
15	$0008000	MENUSTATE	
16	$0010000	RMBTRAP	Right mouse key: no menu
17	$0020000	NOCAREREFRESH	No refresh message
24	$1000000	WINDOWREFRESH	
25	$2000000	WBENCHWINDOW	

To refresh is to rebuild the window contents when necessary, for instance when the window's size is changed. If none of the refresh bits are set, you're in Smart-Refresh-Mode. In this case, Intuition takes care of refreshing the window. This is the easiest method.

If you choose the value $100F as the type for your example window, the window is active once it's opened, and it has all the system gadgets:

```
dc.l    $100f   ;ACTIVATE and all gadgets
```

The next long word in the list allows you to use your own gadgets in the window. This long word is a pointer to the structure of a your gadget. Since you don't want this, just put a zero here.

```
dc.l    0       ;First gadget:no gadgets of our own
```

The next long word is a pointer to a graphics structure so you can design your own symbol for checking menu points. Put a zero here. You'll use the standard sign:

```
dc.l    0       ;CheckMark: Standard
```

The next list entry is a pointer to the text for the window name. This text must be closed by a null byte.

```
dc.l    windowname   ;Pointer to window name
```

The next long word is a pointer to the screen structure that you got back after calling the OpenScreen function. The easiest way to do this is to save the pointer to this location in the buffer:

```
screenhd:    dc.l    0        ;Screen pointer
```

The next long word is a pointer to a bit map if you want one of your own for the window. Since you don't want one, put a zero here:

```
        dc.l    0               ;No bitmap of our own
```

Next come four values that set the maximum and minimum width and height of the window:

```
        dc.w    150     ;Smallest width
        dc.w    50      ;Smallest height
        dc.w    320     ;Maximum width
        dc.w    200     ;Maximum height
```

The last value in the list is the screen type of the screen the window is located in. Put a 15 here. You're using our screen as a Custom screen:

```
        dc.w    15      ;Screen type: custom screen
```

Here's a quick overview of the whole list:

```
    align
window_defs:
            dc.w    10          ;X-position
            dc.w    20          ;Y-position
            dc.w    300         ;Width
            dc.w    150         ;Height
            dc.b    1           ;White print color
            dc.b    3           ;On a red background
            dc.l    $200        ;IDCMP flags: CLOSEWINDOW
            dc.l    $100f       ;ACTIVATE and all gadgets
            dc.l    0           ;First gadget: no gadgets
                                ;of our own
            dc.l    0           ;CheckMark: Standard
            dc.l    windowname  ;Pointer to window name
screenhd:   dc.l    0           ;Screen pointer
            dc.l    0           ;No bitmap of our own
            dc.w    150         ;Smallest width
            dc.w    50          ;Smallest height
            dc.w    320         ;Maximum width
            dc.w    200         ;Maximum height
            dc.w    15          ;Screen type: custom
                                ;screen
;And here comes the window name:
windowname: dc.b 'Our Window',0
    align
```

Insert these lines in the program you listed above. Here are the two subroutines for opening and closing the window:

```
OpenWindow      = -204
CloseWindow     = -72
        ...
windopen:
        move.l  intbase,a6          ;Intuition base address in A6
        lea     windowdef,a0       ;Pointer to window definition
        jsr     openwindow(a6)     ;Open window
        move.l  d0,windowhd        ;Save window handle
        rts
windclose:
        move.l  intbase,a6          ;Intuition base address in A6
        move.l  windowhd,a0        ;Window handle
        jsr     closewindow(a6)    ;Close window
        rts
        ...
windowhd:       dc.l    0           ;Window handle
```

Now you can insert a "bsr windowopen" after the "bsr scropen" and a "bsr
windclose" before the "bsr scrclose" command. Once you've started the
program, move the window around in the screen. You'll find that you
can't move the window out of the screen with the mouse.

The window in the example has the close gadget in the upper left corner.
Normally if you click it, the window is closed. Try clicking it. You'll
find that nothing happens.

The display of this and all other gadgets, as well as other events must be
programmed in, since Intuition doesn't know which action causes which
event. We'll take a look at how to handle this in the next chapter.

7.3 Requesters

If you only have one disk drive, you've certainly seen the Amiga message, "Please insert xxx in unit 0", a lot. This window is another window that has two fields for clicking. This sort of message with a choice of options is called a requester.

You want to take a look at how to program a requester. First, you need a window for the requester to appear in. You opened a window of this sort in the example program.

To display a requester, use the Intuition function AutoRequest (offset -348). It takes care of drawing and managing the requester. This function needs the following parameters:

In A0   The pointer to the window structure that you put in "windowhd"
In A1   A pointer to the text structure that should stand over the choice buttons
In A2   Same as above for the text of the left button.
In A3   Same as above for the right button.
In D0   The IDCMP flag which lets you know what event should go with the clicking of the left button
In D1   Same as above for the right button.
In D2   The width of the whole requester.
In D3   The height of the requester.

Insert the following lines in your program:

```
AutoRequest = -348
        ...
request:
        move.l  windowhd,a0         ;Pointer to window structure
        lea     btext,a1
        lea     ltext,a2           ;Pointer to text structure
        lea     rtext,a3
        move.l  #0,d0              ;Left activates by clicking
        move.l  #0,d1              ;Right activates by
                                   clicking
        move.l  #180,d2            ;Width and
        move.l  #80,d3             ;Height of the Requester
        move.l  intbase,a6         ;Intuition base address
        jsr     autorequest(a6)    ;Display Requester
        rts
```

The flags passed in D0 and D1 offer some interesting possibilities. The system messages that tells you to enter a particular disk are overlooked when the DISKINSERTED flag is similar. Putting a disk in brings about the same responce as clicking the "Retry" button.

What's new is the use of a text structure. Use three of them. Text structures are lists that contain entries for the text that you need.

These lists begin with two bytes that are used to define the color. The first byte is the color of the text. The second is for the background color. Here this doesn't have any meaning.

```
btext:
        dc.b    2       ;Black text color
        dc.b    0       ;Background color
```

The next byte specifies the character mode. A zero means that the text is output normally. A four means the text is output inverted.

```
        dc.b    0       ;Normal text representation
```

The next entries are words. For this reason the addresses must be even, so you need to either insert another byte or use the "align" pseudo-op. The following words are the X- and Y-position of the text relative to the upper left corner of requester.

```
        dc.w    10      ;X-position
        dc.w    5       ;Y-position relative to upper corner
```

Next, there's a pointer to the character set that is used. Put a zero here to use the standard set.

```
        dc.l    0       ;Standard character set
```

Next you need to give the address of the text that should be output. This text must be closed with a null byte.

```
        dc.l    text    ;Pointer to text
```

You need a long word at the end of the list that is either a pointer to another text or a zero if no more text is needed.

```
        dc.l    0       ;No more text
```

Here are the three text structures that you need for the example:

```
btext:                                  ;Text structure for the title
                dc.b 0,1                ;Color
                dc.b 0                  ;Mode
                align
                dc.w 10,10              ;Text position
                dc.l 0                  ;Standard font
                dc.l bodytxt            ;Pointer to text
                dc.l 0                  ;No more text
bodytxt:        dc.b  "Requester Text",0
                align
ltext                       ;Text structure of the left button
                dc.b 0,1                ;Color
                dc.b 0                  ;Mode
                align
                dc.w 5,3                ;Text position
                dc.l  0                 ;Standard font
                dc.l lefttext           ;Pointer to text
                dc.l  0                 ;No more text
lefttext:       dc.b "left",0
                align
rtext:
                dc.b 0,1                ;Color
                dc.b 0                  ;Mode
                align
                dc.w 5,3                ;Text position
                dc.l  0                 ;Standard font
                dc.l  righttext         ;Pointer to text
                dc.l  0                 ;No more text
righttext:      dc.b "right",0
                align
```

After calling the requester, D0 contains the information about which of
the buttons were pressed, and in which button the event took place. If D0
is zero, it was the right button. If it is one, it was the left button.

7.4 Event handling

Pretend you've opened a window that has the close symbol, and you want the program to react to this symbol being clicked. You need a signal from Intuition that lets you know that an event has taken place. This signal is called a message.

The IDCMP flag of the window specifies which events should cause Intuition to send a message. By setting the bits for WINDOWCLOSE, you can allow a message to be sent when the close symbol is clicked.

To get the message, you can use the EXEC function GetMsg (offset - 372). It needs the source address of the event as a parameter. Here the source is the User port (which doesn't have anything to do with the User port on old Commodore computers).

The user port contains a table which has entries which specify the events that have taken place and related things like mouse position and time.

How do you find the User port? Use the pointer to the window structure that you got back from the OpenWindow function and stored in the "windowhd" memory block.

This pointer points to the window structure of this window. This structure consists of a number of entries. Some are copies of the parameters from our window definition table. We won't cover all the entries, because most won't be interesting to you. You're more interested in the pointer to the user port. It's in the window structure.

You can find this in the long word that begins in the 86th byte of the structure. You can get this long word with the following lines of code:

```
move.l  windowhd,a0    ;Pointer to structure in A0
move.l  86(a0),a0      ;User port pointer in A0
```

You can call the GetMsg function with this pointer in A0 by using the following lines of code in your program:

```
GetMsg = -372
        ...
        move.l  windowhd,a0     ;Pointer to structure in A0
        move.l  86(a0),a0       ;User port pointer in A0
        move.l  ExecBase,a6     ;EXEC base address in A6
        jsr     GetMsg(a6)      ;Get message
```

This function returns a value in the D0 register. This value is a pointer to another structure, the Intuition Message Structure. If there's a zero in D0, no event has taken place.

The long word that starts at the 20th byte in this structure contains the information about which event took place. Evaluating the information is easy, since the bits of this long word have the same meaning as the IDCMP flag that you described when you looked at opening windows.

Put the lines above after "loop" and then insert the following:

```
        move.l  d0,a0           ;Message pointer in A0
        move.l  20(a0),d6       ;Save event in D6
        tst.l   d0              ;Did an event take place?
        bne     end             ;Yes!
```

Now you can end this program by clicking the close symbol. This way you can find out if an event has taken place. You can use D6 to determine what event took place. In the example, D6 contains the number $00000200, which means that the close symbol was clicked.

To see if this works with other events, change the $200 IDCMP flag to $10200 in the window definition table. When you've assembled and started this version, take the disk out of the drive—the program terminates.

The IDCMP flags that you've got now cause the clicking of the close symbol and the taking out of the disk (DISKREMOVED) to be reported. If you want to find out which of the events took place, you can look in D6. It has a $200 in it if the window was closed, a $10000 if the disk was removed.

7.5 Menu programming

Now let's look at one of Intuition's more interesting capabilities: menu programming. By using menus, you can make your programs extremely user-friendly.

There are a lot of ways for you to use menus. You can make menu points unusable, output submenus, choose the type of menu entries (allow text or pictures to be output), etc... To have lots of options, you need some parameters.

Let's produce a menu with the SetMenuStrip function (offset -264) of Intuition. The function only needs two parameters, a pointer to the menu structure of the window to be drawn and a pointer to the window structure of the window in which the menu is to function. Each window can have its own menu that is active when the window is activated.

Here's the subroutine to set up the menu:

```
SetMenuStrip = -264
      ...
setmenu:                            ;* Initialize a menu
      move.l  intbase,a6           ;Intuition base address in A6
      move.l  windowhd,a0          ;Pointer to window structure
      lea     menu,a1              ;Pointer to menu structure
      jsr     SetMenuStrip(a6)     ;Call function
      rts
```

Here's a routine to erase the menu:

```
ClearMenuStrip = -54
      ...
clearmenu:
      move.l  intbase,a6           ;Intuition base address in A6
      move.l  windowhd,a0          ;Pointer to window structure
      jsr     ClearMenuStrip(a6)
      rts
```

You've already got the pointer to the window structure. Let's look at the menu structure you need for the menu. You need to build a structure like this for each menu—for each menu title that appears when you press the right mouse key.

This structure is a table with the following form:

First there is a long word that points to the menu structure of the next menu. If the current menu is the last one, a zero goes here.

```
    align
menu:
        dc.l       menu1       ;Pointer to the next menu
```

Next come two words which contain the X- and Y-position of the menu title:

```
        dc.w          20       ;X-position
        dc.w           0       ;Y-position
```

Next, use two words to store the menu title's width and height in pixels:

```
        dc.w          50       ;Width
        dc.w          10       ;Height of menu title
```

The next word contains the flag bit that determines whether the menu is available or not. An unavailable menu either has gray entries or they are drawn weakly. If the flag bit, bit 0, is set the menu is available. Otherwise, it is not.

```
        dc.w           1       ;Menu available
```

Now comes a long word which functions as a pointer to the text which is used as the menu title. Make sure that the length isn't larger than the width entry allows! Otherwise unpleasant things will happen.

```
        dc.l    menutext       ;Pointer to title text
```

Next comes a long word which functions as a pointer to the structure of the first menu entry of this menu. Each menu entry needs its own structure.

```
        dc.l    menuitem01     ;Pointer to the first menu item
```

The last entries in the table are four words that are reserved for internal functions. They must be here.

```
        dc.w    0,0,0,0        ;Reserved words
```

That's the structure of the first menu. This structure's first long word points to the next structure which has the same form. The pointer is set to zero in the last menu.

You still need the structure of the menu entries. These structure tables have the following form:

They start with a pointer to the next menu item. This pointer is set to zero for the last entry.

```
    align
menuitem01:
        dc.l    menuitem02      ;Pointer to next menu item
```

Next come four words: the X- and Y-position, the width, and the height of the box the menu entry goes in. The size becomes obvious when the item is chosen by having the right mouse key clicked on it. Then the box becomes visible. As you can see, the next word is determined in the flags. First let's set the position and size of the menu point, though:

```
        dc.w    0       ;X-position of an entry
        dc.w    0       ;Y-position
        dc.w    90      ;Width in pixels
        dc.w    10      ;Height in pixels
```

The position entries are relative to the upper left corner of the menu that is pulled down.

The following word was described above: it contains flags for entries to this menu item. There are several interesting variations possible. The following flag bits are contained in this word:

Bit	Value	Name	Meaning when set
0	$0001	CHECKIT	Point is checked when chosen
1	$0002	ITEMTEXT	Text menu item
2	$0004	COMMSEQ	Choice can be made with keys as well
3	$0008	MENUTOGGLE	Check turned on and off
4	$0010	ITEMENABLED	Menu item available
6	$0040	HIGHCOMP	Item inverted when chosen
7	$0080	HIGHBOX	Item framed when chosen
8	$0100	CHECKED	Item is checked

Here's a description of the bits:

CHECKIT   If this bit is set, a check or a user-defined drawing is put in front of the text when the item is chosen. The text should begin with two blanks.

ITEMTEXT   The menu item is a normal text if this bit is set. Otherwise a drawing is output.

COMSEQ   By setting this bit and entering a character, this menu point can be chosen by pressing the right <Amiga> key and the key that was input. The input character is then displayed in the menu with the Amiga symbol. There needs to be space available for this.

MENUTOGGLE   If this bit is set and checking is allowed (bit 0), the second time this point is chosen the check is erased, the next time it is displayed again, etc...

ITEMENABLED   Erasing this bit makes the menu item unavailable.

HIGHCOMP   If this bit is set, the box you've defined is inverted when this menu item is chosen by the mouse pointer.

HIGHBOX   In this mode, the box is framed when it is chosen.

The two previous bits determine the mode of the chosen menu item. The following combinations are possible:

HIGHIMAGE   If both bits are cleared, choosing the bit causes a self-defined drawing to be output.

HIGHNONE   When both bits are set, there isn't any reaction to choosing this item.

CHECKED   This bit can be set by either the program or Intuition. It lets you know if the menu text has a check next to it or not. You can use this to find out if the item was checked by testing bit eight. If it's set, the item was checked. You can also use it to cause the item to be checked.

You're chosing the mode CHECKIT, ITEMTEXT, COMMSEQ, MENU-TOGGLE, ITEMENABLED and HIGHBOX for the example:

```
dc.w    %10011111    ;Mode flag
```

Let's get back to the structure of the menu items. After the flag word, there is a long word whose flag bits determine whether this menu point can turn off another one. Set this to zero:

```
dc.l    0            ;No connection
```

Now comes the pointer to the structure of the text that should be displayed. If the ITEMTEXT bit isn't set, this pointer must point to the structure of a drawing. If nothing should be shown, you can set this to zero. Use a text in the example and write the following:

```
dc.l    menu01text    ;Pointer to menu text structure
```

The following long word only has a meaning if the HIGHIMAGE flag is set. Then this long word points to the text or the drawing that should be displayed when the menu item's box is clicked. Otherwise the long word is ignored, so insert a zero:

```
dc.l            0        ;No drawing when clicked
```

The next entry is a byte that is used for input of keyboard characters, which together with the right <Amiga> key can be used to choose the menu item. This only works if the COMMSEQ bit is set. Place a character here:

```
dc.b            'A'      ;Choose item using <AMIGA>/'A'
```

Since the next item is a long word, you need an "align" pseudo-op here. Next comes the long word that points to the menu item structure of a submenu. The submenu is automatically shown when this menu item is clicked. You can't nest them any deeper, however, so this long word is ignored for submenus.

If you don't want a submenu to this item, put a zero here:

```
align
   dc.l    0      ;No submenu
```

The next and final long word is written to by Intuition if you choose several menu items. In this case, the menu number of the next menu item chosen goes here.

```
dc.l    0      ;Preparation
```

That's the structure for a menu item. You still need the text structure for the text of the item. This isn't complicated, but it makes you get into fine details about the form of the menu. You've already learned about this text structure when you looked at requesters, so we'll skip an explanation.

Here is the complete structure of an example menu. You can use two menus, each with two subpoints. The second menu point of the left menu has a submenu with two entries. You ought to type this program in, so that you can experiment with it. You can also use this example to evaluate the clicked menu item.

```
;** Complete menu structure for example menu**
menu:
        dc.l menu1              ;No next menu
        dc.w 10,30              ;X/Y
        dc.w 50,10              ;Width/Height
        dc.w 1                  ;Menu enabled
        dc.l menuname           ;Menu title
        dc.l menuitem01         ;Menu entry
        dc.w 0,0,0,0
menuname:
        dc.b "Menu 1",0         ;First menu name
    align
menu1:
        dc.l 0                  ;No further menu
        dc.w 80,0               ;See above
        dc.w 50,10
        dc.w 1
        dc.l menuname1
        dc.l menuitem11
        dc.w 0,0,0,0
menuname1:
        dc.b "Menu 2",0         ;Second menu name
    align
menuitem01:                     ;First menu item
        dc.l menuitem02         ;Pointer to next entry
        dc.w 0,0                ;X,Y
        dc.w 130,12             ;Width, Height
        dc.w $9f                ;Flags
        dc.l 0                  ;Exclude
        dc.l text01             ;Pointer to text structure
        dc.l 0                  ;Select fill
        dc.b "1"                ;Command
    align
        dc.l 0                  ;Subitem: none
        dc.w 0                  ;Next select: no
text01:
        dc.b 0,1                ;Colors
        dc.b 0                  ;Mode: overwrite
    align
        dc.w 5,3                ;X/Y position
        dc.l 0                  ;Standard character set
        dc.l text01txt          ;Pointer to text
        dc.l 0                  ;No more text
text01txt:
        dc.b " Point 0.1",0
    align
menuitem02:                     ;Second menu item
        dc.l 0
        dc.w 0,10
        dc.w 130,12
        dc.w $57
        dc.l 0
        dc.l text02
        dc.l 0
        dc.b "2"                ;Activate with <Amiga>/'2'
    align
```

```
        dc.l 0
        dc.w 0
text 02:
        dc.b 0,1
        dc.b 0
    align
        dc.w 5,3
        dc.l 0
        dc.l text02txt
        dc.l 0
text02txt:
        dc.b " Point 0.2",0
    align
menuitem11:                         ;First menu point of the 2nd menu
        dc.l menuitem12             ;Pointer to second menu point
        dc.w 0,0
        dc.w 90,12
        dc.w $52
        dc.l 0
        dc.l text11
        dc.l 0
        dc.b 0
    align
        dc.l 0
        dc.w 0
text11:
        dc.b 0,1
        dc.b 0
    align
        dc.w 5,3
        dc.l 0
        dc.l text11txt
        dc.l 0
text11txt:
        dc.b "Point 1.1",0
    align
menuitem12:                         ;Second menu item of second menu
        dc.l 0                      ;No more items
        dc.w 0,10
        dc.w 90,12
        dc.w $92
        dc.l 0
        dc.l text12
        dc.l 0
        dc.b 0
    align
        dc.l submenu0               ;Pointer to submenu
        dc.w 0
text12:
        dc.b 0,1
        dc.b 0
    align
        dc.w 5,3
        dc.l 0
        dc.l text12txt
        dc.l 0
```

```
text12txt:
        dc.b "Point 1.2",0
    align
submenu0:                           ;First point of submenu
        dc.l submenu1               ;Pointer to next point
        dc.w 80,5
        dc.w 90,12
        dc.w $52
        dc.l 0
        dc.l texts0
        dc.l 0
        dc.b 0
    align
        dc.l 0
        dc.w 0
texts0:
        dc.b 0,1
        dc.b 0
    align
        dc.w 5,3
        dc.l 0,texts0txt,0
texts0txt:
        dc.b "S Point 1",0
    align
submenu1:                           ;Submenu, second item
        dc.l 0
        dc.w 80,15
        dc.w 90,12
        dc.w $52
        dc.l 0
        dc.l texts1
        dc.l 0
        dc.b 0
    align
        dc.l 0
        dc.w 0
texts1:
        dc.b 0,1
        dc.b 0
    align
        dc.w 5,3
        dc.l 0
        dc.l texts1txt
        dc.l 0
texts1txt:
        dc.b "S Point 2",0
    align
```

The menu items in this example have the following properties as a result of their flags:

Menu 1   The first item, "Point 0.1", can be chosen using the right <Amiga> key and the "1" key. This point alternates between checked and not checked, which can easily be used to check out the key function. If the item is

191

checked and you hit both keys, the check disappears and vice versa. The box at this point is framed when the mouse pointer clicks on it.

The second item, "Point 0.2" can be chosen using the right <Amiga> key and the "2" key. This item is checked the first time it is chosen. However, in contrast to the item above, it can't be erased. The box of this item is inverted when clicked.

Menu 2

These two points can't be chosen using keys. The box of the upper item is inverted when clicked on; the lower one is framed. When you click the second item, "Point 1.2", a submenu with two entries is displayed.

Experiment with this structure a little bit. Change some values and see what happens. As you can see, menu programming isn't as bad as you thought, and it offers a lot of options (but you'll have to do lots of typing!).

When you're done experimenting, you'll want to produce your own program with menus. How does the program find whether a menu item in a menu has been clicked on?

You already looked at one way to find out the menu state. You can test the CHECKED bit in the flag word of a menu item. If this is set, the user clicked on this item with the mouse.

This only works if checking is allowed for the item being tested. You could allow all the menu items to be checked, but this still isn't a good solution—it requires testing all the flag bits of all the menus one after the other. That makes for very boring programming.

You've already learned about finding about events from Intuition. You've moved the message about which event took place into D6, and you can look at it to find out what happened.

If you set the the eighth bit, the MENUPICK bit, of the IDCMP flag long word in the window definition, the choice of a menu point is reported. Put the following lines in your loop in the main program.

```
loop:
        move.l  execbase,a6     ;EXEC base address in A6
        move.l  windowhd,a0     ;Window structure pointer
        move.l  86(a0),a0       ;User point pointer in A0
        jsr     GetMsg(a6)      ;Get message
        tst.l   d0              ;What happened?
        beq     loop            ;Nothing happened
        move.l  d0,a0           ;Message pointer in A0
        move.l  $14(a0),d6      ;Event in D6
```

If the program makes it out of the loop, an event has taken place. You have the event's flag in the D6 register. You can evaluate the event using CMP or BTST to find out which flag bits are set. You can then execute the function corresponding to the set bit. You can use lines like the following ones:

```
cmp    #$200,d6      ;WINDOWCLOSE?
beq    ende          ;Yes: program end
```

These lines terminate the program when the window is closed.

If the user chose a menu item, there is a $100 in the D6 register. You now need to determine which item it was.

You can find this information in a word that comes right after the long word with the event flags in the message structure. Write:

```
move   $18(a0),d7
```

You now have the code for the clicked menu item in the D7 register. If the user just pressed the right key and let it go without choosing a menu item, you'll find a $FFFF here. This word doesn't contain just one, but three pieces of information:

•   Which menu was the item chosen from?
•   Which menu item?
•   Which submenu?

The information is divided in three bit groups. The division is as follows:

Bits   0 - 4   Menu title number
Bits   5 - 10   Menu item number
Bits   11 - 15 Submenu item number

The numbering begins with zero—ie the first menu point of the first menu has the numbers 0 and 0.

To try this out insert the following lines:

```
move   d7,d6         ;Move code into D6
lsr    #8,d7         ;Shift right 11 times
lsr    #3,d7         ;Submenu item now in D7
clr.l  d5
roxr   #1,d6         ;Bit 0 in X-flag
roxl   #1,d5         ;Menu number now in D5
and.l  #$7f,d6       ;Issolate lower bits
cmp    #$7f,d6       ;No menu item?
beq    loop          ;No: continue
lsr    #4,d6         ;Else menu item in D6
```

ende:

By making a test run with AssemPro, you can easily see if this works
right—just look at the registers after the program is over.

If you, for example, want to write a program with four menus with 10
menu items each, this sort of method is to much work—there are 44
tables. For this reason, let's look at a short program that takes care of the
necessary structure table itself.

The menu structure is built very simply—it doesn't offer submenus or
the option of choosing items via the keyboard. If you want these extras,
you can still use this program, but you'll have to use MOVE commands
to insert the desired flags and pointers.

The input that this program needs is a list of the menu names and the
items in each menu. The addresses of the menu texts go in a table with
the following simple form:

```
dc.l     Menu title 1
dc.l     Point1, Point2, Point3, ...,0
dc.l     Menu title 2
dc.l     Point1, Point2, Point3, ...,0
dc.l     Menu title 3 oder 0
```

This program is set up in such a way that up to four menus can lie next
to each other (in normal screen resolution), which is often plenty. The
table above ends by putting a zero instead of a pointer to the next menu
title. As you can see, it's pretty simple.

This program is inserted into your big program right behind the
"setmenu" label. After the "bsr setmenu" command is executed, the menu
structure is built and initialized at the same time. You don't need to
change the rest of the program, it'll be shorter that way.

Here's the program fragment for the complete "setmenu" routine:

```
setmenu:                            ;* Initialize menu structure
        lea     mentab,a0           ;Pointer to text pointer in A0
        lea     menu,a1             ;Pointer to menu field in A1
        move    #10,d1              ;Horizontal menu position=10
menuloop:
        clr.l   d2                  ;Vertical menu position=0
        move.l  a1,a2               ;Save address for pointer
        tst.l   (a0)                ;Another menu there?
        beq     setmenu1            ;No: quit
        clr.l   (a1)+               ;"No more menus" preparations
        move    d1,(a1)+            ;Set X-position
        add.l   #70,d1              ;And increment
        move.l  #50,(a1)+           ;Y-position and width
```

```
        move.l   #$a0001,(a1)+    ;Height and flag
        move.l   (a0)+,(a1)+      ;Menu title
        lea      12(a1),a3
        move.l   a3,(a1)+         ;Pointer to menu item
        clr.l    (a1)+            ;Reserved words
        clr.l    (a1)+
itemloop:
        tst.l    (a0)             ;Last entry?
        beq      menuend          ;Yes: menu done
        lea      54(a1),a3
        move.l   a3,(a1)+         ;Pointer to next item
        move.l   d2,(a1)+         ;X- and Y-position
        add      #10,d2           ;Y-position +10
        move.l   #$5a000a,(a1)+   ;Width/Height
        move     #$52,(a1)+       ;Flag: normal
        clr.l    (a1)+            ;No connection
        lea      16(a1),a3
        move.l   a3,(a1)+         ;Text structure pointer
        clr.l    (a1)+            ;No fill structure
        clr.l    (a1)+            ;No command, no submenu
        clr.l    (a1)+            ;And no continuation
        move     #$1,(a1)+        ;Set text structure: color
        clr      (a1)+            ;Mode 0
        move.l   #$50003,(a1)+    ;X- and Y-positon
        clr.l    (a1)+            ;Standard character set
        move.l   (a0)+,(a1)+      ;Text pointer
        clr.l    (a1)+            ;No continuation
        bra      itemloop         ;Next item...
menuend:                          ;Eventual transfer to next menu
        clr.l    -54(a1)          ;Erase pointer to next item
        tst.l    (a0)+            ;Increment table pointer
        tst.l    (a0)             ;Another menu there?
        beq      setmenu1         ;No: done
        move.l   a1,(a2)          ;Pointer to next menu
        bra      menuloop         ;And continue
setmenu1:                         ;* Initialize menu (like before)
        move.l   intbase,a6       ;Intuition base address in A6
        move.l   windowhd,a0      ;Window structure in A0
        lea      menu,a1          ;Pointer to menu structure
        jsr      SetMenuStrip(a6)
        rts
```

You need three things yet for this program: the memory to be used for the structure, the table of text pointers and the text. Here's an example:

```
mentab:
        dc.l menu1               ;First menu title
        dc.l mp11,mp12,mp13      ;Menu items
        dc.l 0                   ;End of menu 1
        dc.l menu2               ;Second menu title
        dc.l mp21,mp22,mp23      ;Menu items
        dc.l 0                   ;End of menu 2
        dc.l 0                   ;You're out of menus!
;** Menu Text **
menu1:  dc.b "Menu 1",0
```

```
mp11:    dc.b "Point11",0
mp12:    dc.b "Point12",0
mp13:    dc.b "Point13",0
menu2:   dc.b "Menu 2",0
mp21:    dc.b "Point 21",0
mp22:    dc.b "Point 22",0
mp23:    dc.b "Point 23",0
    align
;** Storage space for menu structure **
menu:    blk.w 500
```

Make sure that the memory area reserved for the menu structure is big enough and change the entry "blk.w 500" to the calculated value.

If you use this program, and want to build some special features into the menu (for instance key commands), you can make entries in the menu structure table while the program is running. You can find the word (or byte or long word) that interests you in the table as follows:

For example, to find the keyboard command byte of the second entry in the first menu, calculate as follows:

```
Address = Start_address + Menu*30 + (Entry-1)*54 + 26
```

which in the example comes to:

```
Address  = menu + 30 + 54 + 26
         = menu + 110
```

The 26 is the distance from the beginning of the MenuItem structure to the desired byte, the command byte. In this way, you can calculate the addresses and use MOVE commands to modify the menu to fit your wishes. By the way, in the example above, the corresponding flag bit must be set as well, so that the keyboard command is recognized!

Now let's get back to the window. It's nice to have a window that you can change and close, but you really want to be able to output text in a window!

7.6 Text output

It's very easy to use Intuition's text output function. Use the PrintIText function (offset -216). It needs four parameters.

In A0   A pointer to the RastPort of the window. You can find this in the window structure.

In A1   A pointer to the text structure of the text that should be output

In D0   The X-position

In D1   The Y-position of the text in the window

It's very easy to enter the X- and Y-positions. You've already used the text structure twice (for requesters and menus).

What's new is accessing the windows's RastPort. The RastPort is a structure that describes the window. The address is needed by several Intuition functions.

The pointer to the RastPort starts at the 50th byte in the window structure. You can access it as follows:

```
move.l  windowhd,a0     ;Address of window structure
move.l  50(a0),a0       ;RastPort address in A0
```

Now you've got the address of the RastPort. Let's write a routine that prints a text. The X- and Y-positions are in D0 and D1 respectively and the address of the text structure in A1 before the routine is called:

```
PrintIText = -216
       ...
print:
       move.l  intbase,a6      ;Intuition base address in A6
       move.l  windowhd,a0     ;Address of window structure
       move.l  50(a0),a0       ;RastPort address in A0
       jsr     PrintIText(a6) ;Call function
       rts
```

You can try out this routine by using the requester's text that is still in a structure of the program. Write the following lines before the "loop" label:

```
lea      btext,a1        Pointer to text structure in A1
move.l   #10,d0          ;X-position
move.l   #30,d1          ;Y-position of text
bsr      print           ;Output text
```

Start the program and the text appears in the middle of the window. If this doesn't happen, check the color of the text in the text structure. It's probably zero. Just change it to three, and the text appears in red the next time you start the program.

7.7 Images

An Image is a drawing that goes in a rectangular field and is defined bitwise. The disk symbol of the Intuition screen and the system gadgets in the screen and window borders are examples of such Images.

The rectangle that the drawing goes in can be arbitrarily large, but each pixel in the rectangle needs its own bit, so programming screen-sized Images isn't advisable. You'll stick to an Image that requires about 32x16 bits—an Image that's about 3x1 cm.

You can make all sorts of images as you've seen looking at window gadgets. There is an Intuition function that draws an Image: It is the DrawImage function (offset -114) and it needs 4 parameters:

In A0   The address of the RastPort image is drawn in. You've already learned how to access this address in the section on the text function.

In A1   The structure address of the Image to be drawn

In D0   The relative X-position

In D1   The relative Y-position of the drawing

Let's draw this picture in your window. It just takes a simple routine. You just need to put the address of the Image structure in A1 and the position of the image in D0 and D1 before you call it.

```
DrawImage = -114
      ...
draw:                         ;* Draw Image
      move.l  intbase,a6      ;Intuition base address in A6
      move.l  windowhd,a0     ;Pointer to window structure
      move.l  50(a0),a0       ;Now, RastPort address in A0
      jsr     DrawImage(a6)   ;Draw image
      rts
```

Now you need the structure of Image. The structure contains nine entries which have the following meanings:

The first two entries are words which specify the distance in the X- and Y-direction from the coordinates that were given to tell where the Image should be drawn. You'll just put two zeros here:

```
image:
        dc.w    0,0      ;X- and Y-position
```

Next come two words which specify the width and height of the Image in pixels. Let's draw a 32x13 point Image. Enter:

```
        dc.w    32,13    ;Width and height of the Image
```

The next word in the list specifies the number of planes in the drawing. If it's a simple Image that only uses two colors, just enter a one. For more colors, you'll need a correspondingly bigger number. When more colors are worked with, the bit pattern of the Image must have more data. Let's just have one bit plane:

```
        dc.w    1        ;One bit plane: 2^1=2 colors
```

Next comes a long word that points to the data for the Image:

```
        dc.l    imgdata      ;Pointer to image data
```

The next two bytes are very interesting. The first byte, the PlanePick byte, tells which plane of the window or screen the Image data should be written in. Since you only have one plane, you need to enter the bit plane of the window. This information is found in the bits of this byte—bit 0 stands for plane 0, bit 1 for plane 1, etc... You also define the color of the Image with this input. If you enter a two, every set bit of your Image represents a red point.

```
        dc.b    2            ;Drawing red: plane 1
```

The second byte, the PlaneOnOff byte, is an interesting enhancement. Each bit of the window bit plane corresponds to a whole number here. The only bytes that are interesting though are the ones that are cleared in the PlanePick byte. If the bit is set in PlaneOnOff, every bit of the Image in the corresponding plane is set. Otherwise they are cleared. To make sure that each bit of the Image that isn't set appears white, enter a one. All the bits of the Image that aren't set, are set in Plane 1 and appear white.

```
        dc.b    1        ;Background: white
```

The last entry of the structure is a long word that points to another Image. You don't need this, so set the long word to zero:

```
        dc.l    0        ;No more Images
```

Here's a quick overview of the Image structure:

```
image:
        dc.w    0,0             ;X- and Y-position
        dc.w    32,13           ;Width and height of the Image
        dc.w    1               ;One bit plane: 2^1=2 colors
        dc.l    imgdata         ;Pointer to image data
        dc.b    2               ;Drawing red: plane 1
        dc.b    1               ;Background: white
        dc.l    0               ;No more'lImages
```

Now let's produce the Image data. Each Image row uses a word, long word, or several of these to represent the pattern. The set points of the Image correspond to the set bits. This is repeated as often as the height of the Image requires. The data on each line must begin on a word border, on an even address.

For the example, it's easy to decide on the data, since you're going 32 points across—that corresponds to exactly one long word. It's easiest to program the Image using the binary representation of the data.

Let's use, as an example, an image that repressents a switch in "OFF" mode. This form is chosen for a good reason, so you should type it in. In the chapter on gadgets that's coming up, we'll show you how to turn the switch on. Here is the example data for the switch Image:

```
imgdata:    ;Data for switch in "OFF" mode
    dc.l    %00000000000000000000000000000000
    dc.l    %00000000000000000000111000000000
    dc.l    %00011101110111000001111100000000
    dc.l    %00010101000100000001111100000000
    dc.l    %00010101100110000001111000000000
    dc.l    %00011101000100000011100000000000
    dc.l    %00000000000000000111000000000000
    dc.l    %00000000000000001110000000000000
    dc.l    %00000000000111111111100000000000
    dc.l    %00000000000111111111110000000000
    dc.l    %00000000000111111111110000000000
    dc.l    %00000000000110000001100000000000
    dc.l    %00000000000000000000000000000000
```

Once you've typed this data, you can experiment with displaying it on the screen. Enter the following lines before the "loop" label:

```
        move.l  image,a1        ;Pointer to Image structure
        move    #30,d0          ;X-position in window
        move    #50,d1          ;Y-position
        bsr     draw            ;Draw image
```

How do you like the Image on the screen? You'll run into this switch again when we talk about putting the switch in the "ON" state when discussing gadgets. You need to look at other methods of drawing in the window first, though.

7.8 Borders

A border is a collection of lines that are connected. They can be of any length or at any angle. Intuition lets you draw borders to do things like put frames around windows and screens. They are used to put borders around pictures or text, especially for use with string gadgets. We'll talk about that later, though.

It's easy to draw borders. Just use the Intuition function DrawBorder (off-set -108) which needs four parameters:

In A0   The RastPort address of the output medium the lines should be drawn in. Use your window.

In A1   The address of the border structure. We'll look at the form of this structure shortly.

In D0   The relative X-coordinate which is used with the X- and Y-coordinate list to calculate the actual line coordinates.

In D1   The relative Y-coordinates. Relative, here too, means that this is relative to the upper left corner of the screen.

Let's write a short routine that is called with three parameters. The structure address is in A1 and the X- and Y-coordinates are in D0 and D1 respectively when the routine is called. The border is drawn in the window whose structure address is in "windowhd".

```
DrawBorder = -108
     ...
borderdraw:                     ;* Draw several lines
     move.l  intbase,a6         ;Intuition base adcdress in A6
     move.l  windowhd,a0        ;Pointer to window structure
     move.l  50(a0),a0          ;Now RastPort address is in A0
     jsr     DrawBorder(a6)     ;Draw lines
     rts
```

Now let's look at the border structure. The list needs the eight following parameters:

First, you need two words for the vertical and horizontal distance from the coordinates given in the function call. To avoid losing sight of some of the many distance entries, put zeros here:

```
border:
        dc.w    0       ;Horizontal distance
        dc.w    0       ;Vertical distance
```

Next come two bytes that determine the color. Use a red frame:

```
        dc.b    3       ;Red frame
        dc.b    0       ;Background (unused)
```

As you can see, the background color isn't used. You have two modes to choose between for drawing the lines. The following mode determines the mode that is used. If it is zero, each line is drawn in the color chosen, no matter what was before. This is the JAM1 mode. The other mode is the XOR mode which ignores both color entries. In this mode, all the points that lie under the line have their color value inverted. As a result, a white point becomes black, and a blue one becomes red. That is mode two. Let's use the JAM1 mode for the example:

```
        dc.b    0       ;Mode: JAM1 (2=XOR)
```

The next entry specifies how many coordinate pairs there are in the list. Since this word must be on an even address, you need to use the "align" pseud-op first. Then enter the number of pairs. Remember that you need three points to draw two lines: beginning, corner and end point. To draw a rectangular frame, you need five pairs:

```
        dc.b    5       ;5 X,Y pairs used together
```

The next item is a pointer to the coordinate table that contains a list of points to be connected:

```
        dc.l    coord   ;Pointer to coordinates table
```

The border structure's final entry is a long word that can point to another border structure. If you don't have any more structures to be pointed to, just enter a zero here. The pointer is useful for connecting two independent border structures—for example, to produce a two colored frame that really stands out. You don't need this pointer in the example, though:

```
        dc.l    0       ;No more structures
```

That's the border structure. Now let's look at the coordinate list. For the example, it consists of five pairs of numbers which represent a rectangle. I recommend entering these values, because you'll use them in example programs further down the line.

```
coord:                          ;Coordinates for rectangular frame
        dc.w    -2,-2
        dc.w    80,-2
        dc.w    80, 9
        dc.w    -2, 9
        dc.w    -2,-2
```

Here's a quick overview of the border structure:

```
border:
        dc.w    0           ;Horizontal distance
        dc.w    0           ;Vertical distance
        dc.b    3           ;Red frame
        dc.b    0           ;Background (unused)
        dc.b    0           ;Mode: JAM1 (2=XOR)
        dc.b    5           ;5 X,Y pairs used together
        dc.l    coord       ;Pointer to coordinates table
        dc.l    0           ;No more structures
coord:                      ;Coordinates for rectangular frame
        dc.w    -2,-2
        dc.w    80,-2
        dc.w    80, 9
        dc.w    -2, 9
        dc.w    -2,-2
```

Once you've typed this in, you can try the whole thing out. Type the following lines before the "loop" label in the program:

```
lea     border,a1       ;Address of the border structure
move    #20,d0          ;X base position
move    #80,d1          ;Y base position
bsr     borderdraw      ;Draw frame
```

As you can see, using enough X- and Y-coordinates, you can draw the Eiffel tower. That's enough about simple drawings. You want to put some life into your drawings and text. Let's manipulate them with the mouse!

7.9 Gadgets

We already talked a bit about gadgets when you looked at screen construction. Looking at system gadgets like the window close symbol, you can activate by clicking and causes a program function to be executed.

You can make your own gadgets as well. Intuition allows you a lot of interesting possiblities.

There are four types of gadgets:

- Boolean gadgets are used in Yes/No situations. You can click and activate it (Yes) or deactivate it (No).
- String gadgets are used to accept input of text of a specified length.
- Integer gadgets are a special sort of string gadgets which accept the input of a decimal number. Intuition converts the value into a long word and sends it to the program.
- Proportional gadgets let you choose an analog value with the mouse. You can move these around with the mouse.

7.9.1   Boolean gadgets

Let's start with the simplest type, the boolean gadget. An example of this sort of gadget is the close symbol of the window. The only status it differentiates between are clicked and not clicked. Let's develop a gadget of this type step by step. The flags and other parameters are similar for the other gadgets.

Each gadget needs a structure containing fifteen entries. There is a pointer to this structure in window, screen or requester that the gadget is to appear in. There's always a long word available for this purpose. Up to this point, you've just put a zero there. If there is an address of a gadget structure there, the gadget or gadgets are displayed when the window is opened.

A gadget structure has the following entries:

The first long word is a pointer to the next gadget to be installed. The gadgets are displayed in a row, like pearls on a string. This pointer is the first gadget in this linked list of gadgets. If you just want one gadget in your window, put a zero here:

```
gadget1:
      dc.l     0          ;No more gadgets
```

The next two words determine the position of the gadget in the window. There are several ways to determine the position. Use flags to access the various possibilities. Let's start with a gadget that stays in one spot:

```
      dc.w     40         ;X- and
      dc.w     50         ;Y-position of the gadget
```

The next two words determine the size of the gadget's Hit box. This box isn't the visible size of the gadget (that depends on the Image data). It is the size of the rectangle that Intuition should watch. If the mouse pointer is moved into this box and the left button is pressed, the gadget is activated. Clicking on parts of the gadget that are outside this box have no effect!

```
      dc.w     32         ;Width and
      dc.w     13         ;Height of the Hit box
```

Next, comes the word whose bits determines the properties of the gadget. Bits 0 and 1 determine what should happen when this object's hit box is clicked on. The meanings of the various values of these bits go as follows:

Bit 0	1	Value	Name	Meaning
0	0	0	GADGHCOMP	The gadget inverted
0	1	1	GADGHBOX	The gadget framed
1	0	2	GADGHIMAGE	Another Image appears
1	1	3	GADGHNONE	No reaction

Bit 2 determines whether the gadget should consist of a drawing or a border. If it is set (Value +4), it is treated as an image; otherwise it's treated like a border.

The next bit determines if the gadget should appear in the upper or lower border of the frame. If it is set (Value +8), the position is relative to the lower border; otherwise it is relative to the upper border. The next bit has the same meaning for the horizontal position. If set (Value +$10), it is a relative positioning. Otherwise, it is an absolute positioning.

Notice that when you define a gadget to be relative, you must have a negative value in the position input in the first word of the structure. Since the desired positon isn't under, but is over this position!

In this way, you can choose either absolute or relative positioning of the gadget. An example of a gadget that is positioned absolutely is the system gadget, close window. An example of a relative gadget is the symbol for changing the size.

The width and height of the gadget's hit box can also be relative to the window size. Specify this by using bit 5 for width (Value +$20) and bit 6 for the height (Value +$40). A set bit means a relative size.

Bit 7 (Value +$80) makes the object active as soon as the window is opened.

Bit 8 (Value +$100) determines whether the gadget can be used or not. If this bit is set, the gadget can't be activated.

For the example, you'll use absolute positioning and size, the inverted appearance for the activated gadget, and the representation of the object as an image. That means you must use the value four:

```
dc.w    4        ;Flags: Image, invert
```

Next comes a word whose bits are used as flags. This flag is called the Activation Flag. It determines the functions of the gadget. The bits, their values and meanings follow:

Bit	Value	Name	Meaning
0	1	RELVERIFY	Causes the gadget to be activated only when the left mouse key is let loose over the gadget
1	2	GADGIMMEDIATE	Let's the gadget be active as soon as there is a click.
2	4	ENDGADGET	Let's you choose to end this choice and have it disappear if this is a Requester gadget.
3	8	FOLLOWMOUSE	Let's the gadget know the mouse position at regular intervals from the time it is selected until the time it is deselected. You can use this to move the gadget with the mouse when you want to change the gadget position.
4	$10	RIGHTBORDER	This makes sure that when borders are used that the page is adjusted to the size of the gadget so that it fits in the border.
5	$20	LEFTBORDER	
6	$40	TOPBORDER	
7	$80	BOTTOMBORDER	

8	$100	TOGGLESELECT	Allows the object's state to change every time it is clicked. If activated, it becomes deactivated and vice versa.
9	$200	STRINGCENTER	For a string gadget, these two bits determine whether the string should appear centered or right justified. If neither is set, the string is output left justified.
10	$400	STRINGRIGHT	
11	$800	LONGINT	Turns a string gadget into an Integer gadget (explanation later).
12	$1000	ALTKEYMAP	Causes another key board placement to be in effect for string gadget input.

That's it for the activation flags. Let's choose the TOGGLESELECT and GADGETIMMEDIATE flags for the example:

```
dc.w    $102    ;Activation
```

The next word of the gadget structure determines the gadget type. Here is the meaning of the individual bits:

Bit	Value	Name	Meaning (report what circumstances)
0	1	BOOLGADGET	This is a boolean gadget.
1	2	GADGET002	
2	4	STRGADGET	String order Integer gadget
0+1	3	PROPGADGET	Proportional gadget

System gadgets:

4	$10	SIZING	Size changing gadget
5	$20	WDRAGGING	Moving gadget for window
4+5	$30	SDRAGGING	Same for screen
6	$40	WUPFRONT	Gadget to move window forward
6+4	$50	SUPFRONT	Gadget to move screen forward
6+5	$60	WDOWNBACK	Move window back
6+5+4	$70	SDOWNBACK	Move screen back
7	$80	CLOSE	Window close gadget

Type definitions:

12	$1000	REQGADGET	Requester gadget
13	$2000	GZZGADGET	Border gadget in GIMMEZERO-ZERO window
14	$4000	SCRGADGET	Screen gadget when set
15	$8000	SYSGADGET	System gadget when set

You want to use a simple boolean gadget for your example, so enter:

```
dc.w    1       ;Gadget type: boolean
```

Next comes a pointer to the gadget structure. The first pointer contains the address of the Image or border structure which should be used to represent the gadget. If no representation is needed, put a zero here. You want to represent the gadget as an Image, so put a pointer to the Image structure that you produced in the chapter about Images:

```
dc.l    image   ;Gadget Image
```

The next pointer is only used if the GADGHIMAGE flag in the flag word of the structure is set. This is a pointer to another structure that should be put on the screen when the object is activated. If a border structure is used for the gadget representation, this must be a border structure as well. You won't use a second Image, so put a zero here:

```
dc.l    0       ;No new gadget displayed
```

The next pointer is to the text structure that should be output by the gadget. If no text is needed, just put a zero here. You want to use some text, however:

```
dc.l    ggtext  ;Gadget text
```

Next comes a long word that determines which gadgets are deactivated when this is activated. This function still doesn't work right so put a zero here:

```
dc.l    0       ;No exclude
```

You'll set the next pointer to zero as well, because it is only used for String and Proportional gadgets. For these gadgets, this is a special structure to describe the characteristics of the gadget. It's called SpecialInfo.

```
dc.l    0       ;No SpecialInfo
```

The next word contains the Gadget Identification (ID) number:

```
dc.w    1       ;Gadget ID
```

Finally there is a long word that doesn't have any function, so put a zero here:

```
dc.l    0       ;User data (ignored)
```

That's it. Here's a quick overview of the gadget structure:

```
gadget1:
        dc.l    0       ;No more gadgets
        dc.w    40      ;X- and
        dc.w    50      ;Y-position of the gadget
        dc.w    32      ;Width and
        dc.w    13      ;Height of the Hit box
        dc.w    4       ;Flags: Image, invert
        dc.w    $102    ;Activation flags
```

```
        dc.w    1        ;Gadget type: boolean
        dc.l    image    ;Gadget Image
        dc.l    0        ;No new gadget displayed
        dc.l    ggtext   ;Gadget text
        dc.l    0        ;No exclude
        dc.l    0        ;No SpecialInfo
        dc.w    1        ;Gadget ID
        dc.l    0        ;User data (ignored)
```

You've already prepared a structure that you can use for the Image. Now you need the text that appears under the gadget.

Since this gadget looks like a switch, label it "Switch". The text structure looks like this:

```
ggtext:
        dc.b 1,0        ;Colors
        dc.b 1          ;Mode
    align
        dc.w -8,14       ;X- and Y-position
        dc.l 0           ;Standard font
        dc.l swtext      ;Pointer to text
        dc.l 0           ;No more text
swtext:
        dc.b "Switch",0
    align
```

Once you've typed this in, save it, assemble it and start it. You can click the switch and cause it to be inverted. Click it again, and it appears normal.

Now you can experiment with the structure. If you change the flag from four to five, you can cause the gadget to be framed when it is activated. Set the RELVERIFY bit (Bit 0: +1) in the Activation Flag word. Then you can move the mouse pointer onto the object and press the button. It is activated. Keep the mouse button pressed down and move the mouse. Once you leave the Hit box, the activation disappears. This way, you can avoid accidently activating a gadget.

Now you want to display the switch in an on state. This is easy. All you need to do is produce another Image structure, one for the on state. You put this pointer in the long word right after the pointer to the normal Image structure. You change the flag word to six which causes a second Image to be displayed when the gadget is activated.

Here is the Image structure for the switch in the on state.

```
image2:
        dc.w 0,0            ;No offset
        dc.w 32,13          ;32x13 pixels
        dc.w 1             ;Mode 1
        dc.l imgdata2      ;Pointer to the data
        dc.b 2,1           ;Same colors as before
        dc.l 0             ;Nothing else
imgdata2:                   ;Data for switch in the ON state
        dc.l %00000000000000000000000000000000
        dc.l %00000000001110000000000000000000
        dc.l %00000000011111000001110100100000
        dc.l %00000000011111000001010110100000
        dc.l %00000000011111000001010101100000
        dc.l %00000000000011100001110100100000
        dc.l %00000000000001110000000000000000
        dc.l %00000000000001110000000000000000
        dc.l %00000000000011111111110000000000
        dc.l %00000000000111111111110000000000
        dc.l %00000000000111111111110000000000
        dc.l %00000000000110000011000000000000
        dc.l %00000000000000000000000000000000
```

Now the state of the object can be determined by looking at the picture. If the gadget is activated, the switch is on. If not, the switch is off.

That's it for Boolean gadgets. You can learn about the things you didn't touch with some experimentation. You want to get to the string gadgets that also do some interesting things.

7.9.2   String gadgets

Let's pretend you want a program to load data from the disk. To get the user to enter the filename, you need to output text telling the user to enter the name. Then you need to call an input routine to evaluate the keyboard input.

It's easier and more elegant to use a String gadget. This function allows for easy input and/or editing of short text. You have the option of having the text framed. The Undo function can be used by pressing the right <Amiga> key and a "Q", and the old contents of the gadget, the old text are restored.

You can also vary the size of the text and the input field. If the text is longer than the input field is wide, the text is moved back and forth through the visible area when you move the cursor keys or the normal input to the border.

You can also restrict input to just digits. This makes it possible to accept numeric input. Intuition even converts the digit string into a binary number. This saves the machine language programmer some work. A specialized String gadget of this sort is called an Integer gadget.

The structure is similar to the Boolean gadget's structure. There are only two major differences:

The type word of the structure must be a four to declare that this is a String gadget (STRGADGET).

The pointer to the SpecialInfo structure is needed. Put a pointer to the StringInfo structure that you are going to design later here.

The width and height entries in the gadget structure have a different meaning than they had previously. They do declare the area in which you can bring the mouse pointer to activate the String gadget. However, it is also used for the representation of text. These values determine the size of the box in which the text is output. You should surround the box with a border using the Border function, so that the user can see where it is.

If the text is longer than the box, only a portion of it is seen on the screen. You can move through the area by entering text or using the left/right cursor keys to move through the box. The characters that are entered are inserted at the cursor position, so the rest of the text is shifted by one character when you are on the right edge of the input area. The following functions can be used for editing this text:

Cursor key left/right
> Moves the cursor over the text that's already on hand. Moves the text through the Container.

Cursor keys with <Shift>
> Puts the cursor on the beginning or the end of the text.

<Del>   Deletes the character under the cursor.

<Backspace>
> Deletes the character to the left of the cursor.

<Return>
> Ends text input.

<Amiga> right + "Q"
> This is the Undo function. It replaces the text with the original contents.

The StringInfo structure only has a few entries:

First there's a pointer to the memory area that is used to store the text that is input. The memory buffer must be big enough to handle all the text entered.

```
strinfo:
        dc.l    strpuffer       ;Pointer to text buffer
```

Next comes a pointer to the Undo buffer. This pointer and this buffer are only needed if you want the Undo function. If you do, you must have a buffer that is at least as big as the text buffer. Every time the string gadget function is called, the text buffer's contents are copied into this buffer. To get the old contents back, just press the right <Amiga> key and the "Q" key. The contents of the Undo buffer are copied back to the text buffer. If you use several String gadgets in a program, you can use the same Undo buffer for all of them, since only one String gadget is used at a time.

```
        dc.l    undo    ;Pointer to Undo buffer
```

The following word contains the cursor position in the text. You should set this word to zero, so that the user can see the beginning of the text when the String gadget appears.

```
        dc.w    0       ;Cursor position
```

The next word contains the maximum number of characters that can be input. If you type one more than this number of characters, the screen blinks, to show that you can't enter a longer input string. The number of characters and the reserved space for the input field don't have to agree, since text can be scrolled by typing.

```
        dc.w    10      ;Maximum # of characters
```

The following word tells at which character of the text in the buffer, the output to the box should begin. You should put a zero here, so that the user can see the beginning of the text.

```
        dc.w    0       ;Output text from this character
```

The next five words are used by Intuition, so you don't have to initialize them. Just put zeros here. The words contain the following information:

```
        dc.w    0       ;Character position in Undo buffer
        dc.w    0       ;Number of chars in text buffer
        dc.w    0       ;Number of chars visible in box
        dc.w    0       ;Horizontal box offset
```

```
        dc.w    0        ;Vertical box offset
```

The next two long words are initialized by Intuition as well:

```
        dc.l    0        ;Pointer to RastPort
        dc.l    0        ;Long word with value of the input
;                        ;(for Integer gadgets)
```

The final entry is a pointer to the keyboard table that is used if the
ALTKEYMAP flag of the gadget is set.

```
        dc.l    0        ;Standard keyboard table
```

Here's a quick overview of the StringInfo structure:

```
strinfo:
        dc.l    strpuffer ;Pointer to text buffer
        dc.l    undo      ;Pointer to Undo buffer
        dc.w    0         ;Cursor position
        dc.w    10        ;Maximum # of characters
        dc.w    0         ;Output text from this character
        dc.w    0         ;Character position in Undo buffer
        dc.w    0         ;Number of chars in text buffer
        dc.w    0         ;Number of chars visible in box
        dc.w    0         ;Horizontal box offset
        dc.w    0         ;Vertical box offset
        dc.l    0         ;Pointer to RastPort
        dc.l    0         ;Long word with value of the input
;                         ;(for Integer gadgets)
        dc.l    0         ;Standard keyboard table
```

Here are the text and Undo buffers:

```
strpuffer:
        dc.b    "Hello !",0,0,0
undo:
        dc.l    0,0,0,0
    align
```

Once you've entered these lines, you can either alter the old gadget
structure or build a new one. We'd recommend building another gadget
structure so that you can have the switch and use it later. Change the first
pointer in the old structure from zero to "gadget1" and insert this new
structure. Here is an example structure for the String gadget. It has the
following entries:

```
gadget1:                 ;* Structure for String gadget
        dc.l    0        ;No more gadgets
        dc.w    20,80    ;Position
        dc.w    80,10    ;Width and height of box
        dc.w    0        ;Flags: normal
        dc.w    2        ;Activation ($802 for long int)
        dc.w    4        ;Type: String gadget
```

```
          dc.l     border     ;Pointer to border
          dc.l     0          ;No drawing selected
          dc.l     0          ;No text
          dc.l     0          ;No exclude
          dc.l     strinfo    ;Pointer to StringInfo structure
          dc.w     2          ;Gadget ID
          dc.l     0          ;No user data
border:                       ;* Border for box frame
          dc.w     0,0        ;No offset
          dc.b     3,3        ;Red color
          dc.b     0          ;Mode: JAM1
          dc.b     5          ;5 X,Y pairs
          dc.l     coord      ;Pointer to coordinates table
          dc.l     0          ;No more structures
coord:                        ;* Coordinates for frame
          dc.w     -2,-2      ;Start in upper left corner
          dc.w     80,-2      ;Upper right
          dc.w     80,9       ;Lower right
          dc.w     -2,9       ;Lower left
          dc.w     -2,-2      ;Back to beginning
```

This data causes a red rectangle, the Border, to appear around the "Hello !"
text. You can change the text by clicking in the field and editing once the
cursor appears. If you type something wrong, you can use the Undo
function (The right <Amiga> key and the Q key), to get "Hello !" back.

Once you've done some typing and deactivated the gadget by pressing
<Return> or by clicking outside the field (Cursor disappears), you can
terminate the program.

Change the Activation flag to $802 and the "strbuffer" to "dc.l 0,0,0,0",
assemble, and then start the program. You can type in the string gadget
once it has been activated, but you can only enter digits. The screen
blinks if you enter letters.

Enter a number, and then end the program after deactivating the gadget. If
you look at the StringInfo structure you can look at the value of the
number you input (in hex) in the eighth long word.

After looking at boolean, text and numeric input to gadgets, let's look at
Proportional gadgets which allow the user to enter analog values by moving a symbol.

7.9.3   Proportional gadgets

You've seen the advantages of slider devices over knobs that you turn, maybe on a Hi Fi, maybe on a toaster, but certainly someplace. It's easier to tell the state the item is in with a slider, especially if several such devices are next to each other (for example graphic equalizers). You can represent sliders on the Amiga's screen and work with them with the mouse. This offers a nice way to represent information graphically in your programs.

You can do this with gadgets. Using Proportional gadgets, you can put a symbol in a frame and move it horizontally and/or vertically. The size of the frame and the slider can be of variable size, so that the frame size is relative to the screen size so when the window changes size, it will also. The slider can be set up so that its size in the frame grows or shrinks.

These options are best seen via example and experimentation. (The possibilities mentioned do not form a complete list by any stretch of the imagination.) You want to set up a simple Proportional gadget that can be moved horizontally.

You need a gadget structure that has the same form as the others. To show the differences, here's a complete example structure for your gadget. You can connect this gadget to the other one, by changing the first long word in the last structure to "dc.l gadget2".

```
gadget2:                         ;* Structure for Proportional
                                 gadget
        dc.l    0                ;No more gadgets
        dc.w    150,30           ;Position
        dc.w    100,10           ;Width and height of frame
        dc.w    4                ;Flags: GADGIMAGE
        dc.w    2                ;Activation: GADGIMMEDIATE
        dc.w    3                ;Type: Proportional gadget
        dc.l    mover            ;Pointer to slider data
        dc.l    0                ;No select structure
        dc.l    0                ;No text
        dc.l    0                ;No exclude
        dc.l    propinfo         ;Pointer to PropInfo structure
        dc.w    3                ;Gadget ID
        dc.l    0                ;No user data
```

You see two special features. Use an Image structure for the mover and put a pointer to another structure in the spot for the SpecialInfo pointer.

First, let's look at the "mover" structure, the slider's Image structure. Here's an example of this structure:

```
mover:                          ;* Structure for slider image
        dc.w    0,0             ;No offset
        dc.w    16,7            ;16x7 pixels big
        dc.w    1               ;One bit plane
        dc.l    moverdata       ;Pointer to image data
        dc.b    1,0             ;Color: white
        dc.l    0               ;Don't continue
moverdata:                      ;* Image data for mover
        dc.w %0111111111111110
        dc.w %0101111111111010
        dc.w %0101011111101010
        dc.w %0101010110101010
        dc.w %0101011111101010
        dc.w %0101111111111010
        dc.w %0111111111111110
```

Up till now, there wasn't anything new. Now let's look at the PropInfo
structure that describes the properties of the Proportional gadget.

The structure starts with a flag word that contains the following flag bits:

Bit	Value	Name	Meaning
0	1	AUTOKNOB	Mover is set up automatically
1	2	FREEHORIZ	Allows horizontal movement
2	4	FREEVERT	Allows vertical movement
3	8	PROPBORDERLESS	Turns off automatic framing
8	$100	KNOBHIT	Set when the mover is touched

You can set the first four bits to get the representation that you want. Bit
8 is set by Intuition when the mover is clicked with the mouse pointer.

Bit 0, AUTOKNOB, allows for the simplest sort of Proportional gadget.
If this bit is set, no move data are used for the mover Image. Instead, a
white mover is generated that is adjusted to the size of the box and the
value to be represented. When you use this slider to represent the
displayed lines in a long text of a text program, the displayed lines are a
percentage of the total text. The relationship between the total number of
lines and the lines shown is represented by an AUTOKNOB as the
relationship between the frame and the slider. The bigger the percentage,
the bigger the slider is. You don't want to work with this though, even
though it is simple and interesting, because a simple white button isn't
particularly attractive. If you experiment with it, make sure that the
pointer to the Image data points to a four word long buffer that Intuition
can use to store values. The buffer is of the following form:

```
buffer:
        dc.w    0       ;X-position of the slider in the box
        dc.w    0       ;Y-position in the box
        dc.w    0       ;Width of slider
        dc.w    0       ;Height of slider
```

Let's look at the PropInfo structure. Since you're not using AUTOKNOB and wish to allow horizontal movement only, put two in as a flag:

```
propinfo:
        dc.w    2        ;Flags: FREEHORIZ
```

In the next two words of the structure, the horizontal (HorizPot) and vertical (VertPot) position of sliders are stored. A value of zero means left or upper, while the value $FFFF means right or lower. The value that results from movement is in this range. You set these values to zero at the start of the program. After moving the mouse, there is different values here.

```
        dc.w    0,0      ;X- and Y-position of slider
```

Next come two words which determine the size of the AUTOKNOB or the step size of the slider (this determines how far the slider moves when you click in the box next to the slider). These words are called HorizBody (horizontal movement) and VertBody (vertical movement).

```
        dc.w    $ffff/16        ;Horizontal step size: 1/16
        dc.w    0               ;No vertical movement
;The next six words are initialized by Intuition.
        dc.w    0       ;Box width
        dc.w    0       ;Box height
        dc.w    0       ;Absolute step size horizontal
        dc.w    0       ;And vertical
        dc.w    0       ;Left border of box
        dc.w    0       ;Upper border of box
```

That's it. Here's a quick overview of the PropInfo structure:

```
propinfo:
        dc.w    2               ;Flags: FREEHORIZ
        dc.w    0,0             ;X- and Y-position of slider
        dc.w    $ffff/16        ;Horizontal step size: 1/16
        dc.w    0               ;No vertical movement
        dc.w    0               ;Box width
        dc.w    0               ;Box height
        dc.w    0               ;Absolute step size horizontal
        dc.w    0               ;and vertical
        dc.w    0               ;Left border of box
        dc.w    0               ;Upper border of box
```

Once you've typed this in, you can start the program and try it out.

You can also try vertical movement by setting the flag word equal to six, the vertical step size to $FFFF/10, and the height of the gadget to 80, for example. To try out the AUTOKNOBs, change the flag value to seven.

218

7.10   Example program

Here is a complete example program using what you have learned in this chapter:

```
; 7_Intuition.asm
;** Demo-Program for working with Intuition **

movescreen       = -162
openscreen       = -198
closescreen      = -66
openwindow       = -204
closewindow      = -72
autorequest      = -348
SetMenuStrip     = -264
ClearMenuStrip   = -54
PrintIText       = -216
DrawImage        = -114
DrawBorder       = -108
DisplayBeep      = -96
closelibrary     = -414
openlib          = -408
execbase         = 4
GetMsg           = -372

joy2             = $dff0c
fire             = $bfe001

;!!! when > 500KB !!!
;org $40000
;load $40000
; or use AssemPro to place in CHIP RAM
;!!!!!!!!!!!!!!!!!!!!!!

run:
        bsr     openint
        bsr     scropen
        bsr     windopen
        bsr     setmenu
        bsr     print

        lea     border,a1
        move    #22,d0
        move    #30,d1
        bsr     borderdraw

        bsr     draw

        bsr     request
```

```
loop:
          move.l   execbase,a6
          move.l   windowhd,a0
          move.l   86(a0),a0          ;User-Port
          jsr      GetMsg(a6)
          tst.l    d0
          beq      loop              ;no event
          move.l   d0,a0
          move.l   $16(a0),msg        ;Event: LO=Item, HI=Event
          move.l   msg,d6             ;to test
          move.l   d6,d7
          lsr      #8,d7
          lsr      #3,d7             ;Sub menu point in D7
          clr.l    d5
          roxr     #1,d6
          roxl     #1,d5             ;Menu number in D5
          and.l    #$7f,d6
          cmp      #$7f,d6           ;no menu point ?
          beq      loop              ;no: continue
          lsr      #4,d6             ;Menu point in D6
          cmp      #1,d6             ;Point 2 ?
          bne      no1
          move.l   intbase,a6
          move.l   screenhd,a0
          jsr      DisplayBeep(a6)
no1:
          cmp      #0,d6
          bne      loop

ende:
          bsr      clearmenu
          bsr      windclose
          bsr      scrclose
          bsr      closeint
          rts

openint:
          move.l   execbase,a6
          lea      intname,a1
          jsr      openlib(a6)
          move.l   d0,intbase
          rts

closeint:
          move.l   execbase,a6
          move.l   intbase,a1
          jsr      closelibrary(a6)
          rts

scropen:
          move.l   intbase,a6
          lea      screen_defs,a0
          jsr      openscreen(a6)
          move.l   d0,screenhd
          rts
```

```
scrclose:
        move.l   intbase,a6
        move.l   screenhd,a0
        jsr      closescreen(a6)
        rts

scrmove:
        move.l   intbase,a6
        move.l   screenhd,a0
        jsr      movescreen(a6)
        rts

windopen:
        move.l   intbase,a6
        lea      windowdef,a0
        jsr      openwindow(a6)
        move.l   d0,windowhd
        rts

windclose:
        move.l   intbase,a6
        move.l   windowhd,a0
        jsr      closewindow(a6)
        rts

request:
        move.l   windowhd,a0
        lea      btext,a1
        lea      ltext,a2
        lea      rtext,a3
        move.l   #0,d0
        move.l   #0,d1
        move.l   #180,d2
        move.l   #80,d3
        move.l   intbase,a6
        jsr      autorequest(a6)
        rts

setmenu:
        lea      mentab,a0          ;Pointer to text pointer in A0
        lea      menu,a1            ;Pointer to Menu field in A1
        move     #10,d1             ;Menu position=10

menuloop:
        clr.l    d2                 ;Menu point-Y =0
        move.l   a1,a2              ;Save pointer
        tst.l    (a0)
        beq      setmenu1           ;End
        clr.l    (a1)+
        move     d1,(a1)+
        add.l    #70,d1
        move.l   #50,(a1)+
        move.l   #$a0001,(a1)+
        move.l   (a0)+,(a1)+        ;Menu title
        lea      12(a1),a3
        move.l   a3,(a1)+           ;Menu point
```

```
              clr.l    (a1)+
              clr.l    (a1)+

itemloop:
              tst.l    (a0)              ;last one ?
              beq      menuend           ;yes
              lea      54(a1),a3
              move.l   a3,(a1)+          ;Pointer to next Point
              move.l   d2,(a1)+          ;X/Y
              add      #10,d2
              move.l   #$5a000a,(a1)+    ;width/height
              move     #$52,(a1)+
              clr.l    (a1)+
              lea      16(a1),a3
              move.l   a3,(a1)+          ;Text structor-pointer
              clr.l    (a1)+
              clr.l    (a1)+
              clr.l    (a1)+

              move     #$1,(a1)+         ;Text-Structor set
              clr      (a1)+
              move.l   #$50003,(a1)+
              clr.l    (a1)+
              move.l   (a0)+,(a1)+       ;Text-pointer
              clr.l    (a1)+

              bra      itemloop          ;next Point...

menuend:
              clr.l    -54(a1)
              tst.l    (a0)+
              tst.l    (a0)              ;still in Menu ?
              beq      setmenu1          ;no: ready
              move.l   a1,(a2)           ;Pointer to next menu
              bra      menuloop          ;and continue

setmenu1:
              move.l   intbase,a6
              move.l   windowhd,a0
              lea      menu,a1
              jsr      SetMenuStrip(a6)
              rts

clearmenu:
              move.l   intbase,a6
              move.l   windowhd,a0
              jsr      ClearMenuStrip(a6)
              rts

print:
              move.l   intbase,a6
              move.l   windowhd,a0
              move.l   50(a0),a0
              lea      ggtext,a1
              move.l   #30,d0 ;X
              move.l   #16,d1 ;Y
```

```
        jsr     PrintIText(a6)
        rts

draw:
        move.l  intbase,a6
        move.l  windowhd,a0
        move.l  50(a0),a0
        lea     image,a1
        move.l  #200,d0
        move.l  #100,d1
        jsr     DrawImage(a6)
        rts

borderdraw:
        move.l  intbase,a6
        move.l  windowhd,a0
        move.l  50(a0),a0
        jsr     DrawBorder(a6)
        rts

screen_defs:
        dc.w    0,0
        dc.w    640,200
        dc.w    4
        dc.b    0
        dc.b    1
        dc.w    $800
        dc.w    15
        dc.l    0
        dc.l    titel
        dc.l    0
        dc.l    0

windowdef:
        dc.w    10,20
        dc.w    300,150
        dc.b    0,1
        dc.l    $300
        dc.l    $100f
        dc.l    gadget
        dc.l    0
        dc.l    windname
screenhd: dc.l 0
        dc.l    0
        dc.w    200,40,600,200
        dc.w    $f

btext:
        dc.b    3,3
        dc.b    0
        align   dc.w 10,10
        dc.l    0
        dc.l    bodytxt
        dc.l    0

bodytxt: dc.b    "Requester-Text",0
```

```
            align
ltext:
            dc.b      3,1
            dc.b      0
            align     dc.w 5,3
            dc.l      0
            dc.l      lefttext
            dc.l      0

lefttext: dc.b  "left",0
            align
rtext:
            dc.b      0,1
            dc.b      0
            align     dc.w 5,3
            dc.l      0
            dc.l      righttext
            dc.l      0

righttext: dc.b "right",0
            align
titel: dc.b       "User Screen",0
windname: dc.b    "Window-Title",0
            align   windowhd: dc.l 0
intbase: dc.l     0
intname: dc.b     "intuition.library",0
            align   msg: dc.l 0
mentab:
            dc.l      menu1
            dc.l      mp11,mp12,mp13,mp14,mp15,mp16,mp17,mp18,mp19,0
            dc.l      menu2
            dc.l      mp21,mp22,mp23,0
            dc.l      menu3
            dc.l      mp31,mp32,0
            dc.l      menu4,mp41,0
            dc.l      0

menu1:  dc.b      "Menu 1",0
mp11:   dc.b      "Point 11",0
mp12:   dc.b      "Point 12",0
mp13:   dc.b      "Point 13",0
mp14:   dc.b      "Point 14",0
mp15:   dc.b      "Point 15",0
mp16:   dc.b      "Point 16",0
mp17:   dc.b      "Point 17",0
mp18:   dc.b      "Point 18",0
mp19:   dc.b      "Point 19",0

menu2:  dc.b      "Menu 2",0
mp21:   dc.b      "End !",0
mp22:   dc.b      "Beep",0
mp23:   dc.b      "Point 23",0

menu3:  dc.b      "Menu 3",0
mp31:   dc.b      "Point 31",0
mp32:   dc.b      "Point 32",0
```

```
menu4:    dc.b      "Menu 4",0
mp41:     dc.b      "Point 41",0
          align
gadget:
          dc.l      gadget1
          dc.w      20,80,80,10
          dc.w      0
          dc.w      $2                ;Activation, $802 for LongInt
          dc.w      4
          dc.l      border
          dc.l      0
          dc.l      0
          dc.l      0
          dc.l      strinfo
          dc.w      2
          dc.l      0

border:
          dc.w      0,0
          dc.b      1,0,0
          dc.b      5                 ;XY-Pair
          dc.l      koord
          dc.l      0
koord:
          dc.w      -2,-2,80,-2,80,9,-2,9,-2,-2

strinfo:
          dc.l      strpuffer
          dc.l      undo
          dc.w      0                 ;Cursor-Position
          dc.w      10                ;max.Char
          dc.w      0
          dc.w      0,0,0,0,0
          dc.l      0,0,0
strpuffer: dc.b "Hello !",0,0,0
undo: dc.l      0,0,0
          align
gadget1:
          dc.l      gadget2           ;more Gadget
          dc.w      40,50,32,13
          dc.w      $6                ;Flags: invert
          dc.w      $103              ;Activate
          dc.w      1                 ;Gadget-Type
          dc.l      image             ;Gadget-Image
          dc.l      image2            ;Select-Gadget
          dc.l      ggtext            ;Gadget-Text
          dc.l      0                 ;no Exclude
          dc.l      0                 ;special Info
          dc.w      1                 ;ID
          dc.l      0                 ;UserData

ggtext:
          dc.b      1,0,1
          align     dc.w -8,14
          dc.l      0
```

```
            dc.l    swtext
            dc.l    0
swtext: dc.b    "Switch",0
        align
image:
            dc.w    0,0
            dc.w    32,13
            dc.w    1
            dc.l    imgdata
            dc.b    2,1
            dc.l    0


image2:
            dc.w    0,0
            dc.w    32,13
            dc.w    1
            dc.l    imgdata2
            dc.b    2,1
            dc.l    0


imgdata:
            dc.l 0
            dc.l %00000000011100000000000000000000
            dc.l %00000000111110000011101001000000
            dc.l %00000000111110000010101101000000
            dc.l %00000000111100000010101011000000
            dc.l %00000000000111000011101001000000
            dc.l %00000000000011100000000000000000
            dc.l %00000000000001110000000000000000
            dc.l %00000000000111111111100000000000
            dc.l %00000000000111111111110000000000
            dc.l %00000000000111111111110000000000
            dc.l %00000000000011000000110000000000
            dc.l 0
imgdata2:
            dc.l    0
            dc.l %00000000000000000000111000000000
            dc.l %00011101110111000001111100000000
            dc.l %00010101000100000001111100000000
            dc.l %00010101100110000001111000000000
            dc.l %00011101000100000011100000000000
            dc.l %00000000000000000111000000000000
            dc.l %00000000000000001110000000000000
            dc.l %00000000000111111111100000000000
            dc.l %00000000000111111111110000000000
            dc.l %00000000000111111111110000000000
            dc.l %00000000000011000000110000000000
            dc.l 0


gadget2:
            dc.l    0
            dc.w    150,30,100,50
            dc.w    5
            dc.w    2
            dc.w    3                   ;Prop. Gadget
            dc.l    mover               ;border
```

```
        dc.l    0,0,0
        dc.l    specinfo
        dc.w    3
        dc.l    0
specinfo:
        dc.w    6                       ;Flags: free horiz
        dc.w    0,0
        dc.w    $ffff/10,$ffff/5
        dc.w    0,0,0,0,0,0

mover:
        dc.w    0,0,16,7
        dc.w    1
        dc.l    moverdata
        dc.b    1,0
        dc.l    0
moverdata:
        dc.w %0111111111111110
        dc.w %0101111111111010
        dc.w %0101011111101010
        dc.w %0101010110101010
        dc.w %0101011111101010
        dc.w %0101111111111010
        dc.w %0111111111111110

menu: blk.w     500

        end
```

Chapter 8

Advanced Programming

8 Advanced Programming

You've learned a lot about machine language programming on the Amiga. What you need yet are a few routines that can be used as programming tools. We'll work on that right now. They'll be easy to use in your own program. The sky's the limit now!

8.1 Supervisor Mode

As mentioned in the chapter on the MC68000 processor, there are two operating modes: the User and the Supervisor mode. It is often necessary to move between the two modes. However, this isn't a simple process.

The reason you want to do this, is that in User mode, you can't access the Status registers. If you write to one of them, an Exception is executed which crashes the program.

How can you get into Supervisor mode?

No problem. The operating system of the Amiga contains a function in the EXEC library that lets you get into the Supervisor mode. It's called SuperState and it doesn't need any parameters. You can easily call this program by using the following lines:

```
ExecBase      = 4            ;EXEC base address
SuperState    = -150         ;Turn on function
      ...
      move.l  ExecBase,a6    ;EXEC base address in A6
      jsr     SuperState(a6) ;Turn on Supervisor mode
      move.l  d0,savesp      ;Save return value
      ...
savesp: blk.l  1             ;Space for SP value
```

You get the value of the Stack Pointer (SP) back in the D0 register. You'll also find it in register A7, but this register is changed regularly. The reason is that in Supervisor mode, the Amiga works with all the Interrupts and with the SP, and there are lots of Interrupts for this computer. We'll talk about Interrupts in a bit.

After this call, you'll use the User stack instead of the Supervisor stack. In this way, you can access the old User stack. You need to make sure that the User stack is large enough since the Interrupts must have enough room for their data on the stack.

You need to save the value returned in D0, because you'll need this value later. You need to return to User mode sometime. There's a function for this in the EXEC library as well. It is called the UserState function. It needs one parameter, the SP value that comes back from the SuperState function.

Since you've saved this value in the long word starting at "savesp", you can write the following:

```
UserState      =-156
    ...
    move.l  ExecBase,a6     ;EXEC base address in A6
    move.l  savesp,d0       ;Put old SP in D0
    jsr     UserState(a6)   ;Return to User mode
```

Now you are back in the User mode. The User Stack Pointer (USP) is the same as before. You can write functions that need to be run from the Supervisor mode as subroutines. First you call SuperState, save the return value, execute the desired function, call UserState, and end with a RTS command. If the USP was changed, the RTS command wouldn't work right, and the computer would jump who know's where and perhaps crash. Here it works though.

Now comes the question: how does the operating system get into Supervisor mode? That's not too difficult; it goes like this:

The SuperState function attempts to access a Status Register. This causes an Exception to occur and a routine is called whose address begins at the long word starting at $20. It is the Exception Vector for Privilege Violation. The routine that it branches to is called in Supervisor mode. Then it tests where this Exception came from. If the routine finds that the Exception comes from the SuperState routine whose address it knows, the matter is settled. It just branches to the routine without turning off the User mode. That's all there is to it.

8.2 Exception programming

The exceptions described in the processor chapter offer you a lot of opportunities to control the Amiga's functions. You can use them to specify how errors should be handled and even list a crashed program.

Here is a list of vectors that are used to jump to the Exception routines:

Number	Address	Use with
2	$008	Bus Error
3	$00C	Address Error
4	$010	Illegal command
5	$014	Division by zero
6	$018	CHK command
7	$01C	TRAPV command
8	$020	Privilege Violation
9	$024	Trace
10	$028	Axxx command emulation
11	$02C	Fxxx command emulation
	$030-$038	Reserved
15	$03C	Uninitialized Interrupt
	$040-$05F	Reserved
24	$060	Unauthorized Interrupt
25-31	$064-$083	Level 1-7 Interrupt
32-47	$080-$0BF	TRAP commands
	$0C0-$0FF	Reserved
64-255	$100-$3FF	User Interrupt vector

Let's look at the TRAP commands as an example. They aren't used in the Amiga operating system. A TRAP command and a number between zero and fifteen are used to call one of 16 possible TRAP routines. If the command TRAP #0 is executed, the processor (in Supervisor mode) branches to the routine whose address lies at $80 in memory. This routine must end with a RTE (ReTurn from Exception) command.

Some operating systems, for example, the ATARI ST's TOS operating systems, are completely callable via these TRAPs. Parameters are put on the stack, and then a TRAP command is executed. The advantage is that you don't have to know any of the operating system addresses. In the Amiga you must know the addresses (ExecBase = 4).

Let's write your own TRAP routine to demonstrate the use of the TRAP command. You'll need three program sections:

1. The initialization of the TRAP vector.
2. The TRAP routine itself. (It must end with RTE.)
3. A test routine that calls the TRAP command.

Initialization is very short:

```
init:
        move.l   #trap0,$80       ;Set vector for TRAP #0
        rts
```

Now you need to write the trap0 routine. Let's use the example from the hardware chapter that produced a beep.

Let's write this routine using as little effort as possible. Change the RTS to a RTE at the end, erase the line in which the loop counter D0 was loaded for the tone production, and change the loop so that it works with long words. Now you can load the register with an arbitrary value and have the TRAP #0 followed by a peep of arbitrary duration.

```
;**      Beep tone production after a TRAP #0 **
ctlw    = $dff096               ;DMA control
c0thi   = $dff0a0               ;HI table address
c0tlo   = c0thi+2               ;LO table address
c0tl    = c0thi+4               ;Table length
c0per   = c0thi+6               ;Read in rate
c0vol   = c0thi+8               ;Volume
trap0:                          ;* Produce a short peep
        move.l   #table,c0thi   ;Table beginning
        move     #4,c0tl        ;Table length
        move     #300,c0per     ;Read in rate
        move     #40,c0vol      ;Volume
        move     #$8201,ctlw    ;Start DMA (sound)
loop:
        subq.l   #1,d0          ;Counter-1
        bne      loop           ;Count down to zero
still:
        move     #1,ctlw        ;Turn on tone
        rte                     ;Exception end
table:                          ;Sound table
        dc.b     -40,-70,-40,0,40,70,40,0
```

You need to make sure that "table" is in Chip RAM ($00000-$7FFFF), otherwise the Sound Chip can't access the data!

After entering this, you can test it out using the following routine:

```
test:
        move.l   #$2ffff,d0     ;Pass tone length in D0
        trap     #0             ;Carry out Exception: peep
        rts
```

Now assemble both routines and start the initialization routine, init. Nothing happens.

Start the second routine, test. A beep that lasts about one second is output.

One thing you must keep in mind is that if you change the program and reassemble it, the address of the trap0 routine can change. Before you execute the TRAP command, you must repeat the initialization, so that the computer doesn't jump to the wrong location!

Appendices

Overview of Library Functions

The following table gives you an overview of the available libraries and their functions. Each sublist of functions is preceded by the name of the library it is found in.

These functions are listed with their negative offset in hex and decimal. Their name and their parameters are also specified. The parameter names are in parenthesis behind the function name. The second set of parenthesis includes a list of registers that correspond to the parameter names. If no parameters are needed, we put () to let you know.

clist.library

```
-$001E    -30     InitCLPool (cLPool, size) (A0,D0)
-$0024    -36     AllocCList (cLPool) (A1)
-$002A    -42     FreeCList (cList) (A0)
-$0030    -48     FlushCList (cList) (A0)
-$0036    -54     SizeCList (cList) (A0)
-$003C    -60     PutCLChar (cList,byte) (A0,D0)
-$0042    -66     GetCLChar (cList) (A0)
-$0048    -72     UnGetCLChar (cList,byte) (A0,D0)
-$004E    -78     UnPutCLChar (cList) (A0)
-$0054    -84     PutCLWord (cList,word) (A0,D0)
-$005A    -90     GetCLWord (cList) (A0)
-$0060    -96     UnGetCLWord (cList,word) (A0,D0)
-$0066    -102    UnPutCLWord (cList) (A0)
-$006C    -108    PutCLBuf (cList,buffer,length) (A0,A1,D1)
-$0072    -114    GetCLBuf (cList,buffer,maxLength) (A0,A1,D1)
-$0078    -120    MarkCList (cList,offset) (A0,D0)
-$007E    -126    IncrCLMark (cList) (A0)
-$0084    -132    PeekCLMark (cList) (A0)
-$008A    -138    SplitCList (cList) (A0)
-$0090    -144    CopyCList (cList) (A0)
-$0096    -150    SubCList (cList,index,length) (A0,D0,D1)
-$009C    -156    ConcatCList (sourceCList,destCList) (A0,A1)
```

console.library

```
-$002A    -42     CDInputHandler (events,device) (A0,A1)
-$0030    -48     RawKeyConvert (events,buffer,length,keyMap)
                  (A0,A1,D1,A2)
```

diskfont.library

```
-$001E    -30     OpenDiskFont (textAttr) (A0)
-$0024    -36     AvailFonts (buffer,bufBytes,flags) (A0,D0,D1)
```

dos.library

```
-$001E    -30     Open (name,accessMode) (D1,D2)
-$0024    -36     Close (file) (D1)
-$002A    -42     Read (file,buffer,length) (D1,D2,D3)
-$0030    -48     Write (file,buffer,length) (D1,D2,D3)
-$0036    -54     Input ()
-$003C    -60     Output ()
-$0042    -66     Seek (file,position,offset) (D1,D2,D3)
-$0048    -72     DeleteFile (name) (D1)
-$004E    -78     Rename (oldName,newName) (D1,D2)
-$0054    -84     Lock (name,type) (D1,D2)
-$005A    -90     UnLock (lock) (D1)
-$0060    -96     DupLock (lock) (D1)
-$0066   -102     Examine (lock,fileInfoBlock) (D1,D2)
-$006C   -108     ExNext (lock,fileInfoBlock) (D1,D2)
-$0072   -114     Info (lock,parameterBlock) (D1,D2)
-$0078   -120     CreateDir (name) (D1)
-$007E   -126     CurrentDir (lock) (D1)
-$0084   -132     IoErr ()
-$008A   -138     CreateProc (name,pri,segList,stackSize) (D1,D2,D3,D4)
-$0090   -144     Exit (returnCode) (D1)
-$0096   -150     LoadSeg (fileName) (D1)
-$009C   -156     UnLoadSeg (segment) (D1)
-$00A2   -162     GetPacket (wait) (D1)
-$00A8   -168     QueuePacket (packet) (D1)
-$00AE   -174     DeviceProc (name) (D1)
-$00B4   -180     SetComment (name,comment) (D1,D2)
-$00BA   -186     SetProtection (name,mask) (D1,D2)
-$00C0   -192     DateStamp (date) (D1)
-$00C6   -198     Delay (timeout) (D1)
-$00CC   -204     WaitForChar (file,timeout) (D1,D2)
-$00D2   -210     ParentDir (lock) (D1)
-$00D8   -216     IsInteractive (file) (D1)
-$00DE   -222     Execute (string,file,file) (D1,D2,D3)
```

exec.library

```
-$001E    -30     Supervisor ()
-$0024    -36     ExitIntr ()
-$002A    -42     Schedule ()
-$0030    -48     Reschedule ()
-$0036    -54     Switch ()
-$003C    -60     Dispatch ()
-$0042    -66     Exception ()
-$0048    -72     InitCode (startClass,version) (D0,D1)
-$004E    -78     InitStruct (initTable,memory,size) (A1,A2,D0)
-$0054    -84     MakeLibrary (funcInit,structInit,libInit,dataSize,
                    codeSize) (A0,A1,A2,D0,D1)
-$005A    -90     MakeFunctions (target,functionArray,funcDispBase)
                    (A0,A1,A2)
-$0060    -96     FindResident (name) (A1)
-$0066   -102     InitResident (resident,segList) (A1,D1)
-$006C   -108     Alert (alertNum,parameters) (D7,A5)
-$0072   -114     Debug ()
```

```
-$0078   -120    Disable ()
-$007E   -126    Enable ()
-$0084   -132    Forbid ()
-$008A   -138    Permit ()
-$0090   -144    SetSR (newSR,mask) (D0,D1)
-$0096   -150    SuperState ()
-$009C   -156    UserState (sysStack) (D0)
-$00A2   -162    SetIntVector (intNumber,interrupt) (D0,A1)
-$00A8   -168    AddIntServer (intNumber,interrupt) (D0,A1)
-$00AE   -174    RemIntServer (intNumber,interrupt) (D0,A1)
-$00B4   -180    Cause (interrupt) (A1)
-$00BA   -186    Allocate (freeList,byteSize) (A0,D0)
-$00C0   -192    Deallocate (freeList,memoryBlock,byteSize) (A0,A1,D0)
-$00C6   -198    AllocMem (byteSize,requirements) (D0,D1)
-$00CC   -204    AllocAbs (byteSize,location) (D0,A1)
-$00D2   -210    FreeMem (memoryBlock,byteSize) (A1,D0)
-$00D8   -216    AvailMem (requirements) (D1)
-$00DE   -222    AllocEntry (entry) (A0)
-$00E4   -228    FreeEntry (entry) (A0)
-$00EA   -234    Insert (list,node,pred) (A0,A1,A2)
-$00F0   -240    AddHead (list,node) (A0,A1)
-$00F6   -246    AddTail (list,node) (A0,A1)
-$00FC   -252    Remove (node) (A1)
-$0102   -258    RemHead (list) (A0)
-$0108   -264    RemTail (list) (A0)
-$010E   -270    Enqueue (list,node) (A0,A1)
-$0114   -276    FindName (list,name) (A0,A1)
-$011A   -282    AddTask (task,initPC,finalPC) (A1,A2,A3)
-$0120   -288    RemTask (task) (A1)
-$0126   -294    FindTask (name) (A1)
-$012C   -300    SetTaskPri (task,priority) (A1,D0)
-$0132   -306    SetSignal (newSignals,signalSet) (D0,D1)
-$0138   -312    SetExcept (newSignals,signalSet) (D0,D1)
-$013E   -318    Wait (signalSet) (D0)
-$0144   -324    Signal (task,signalSet) (A1,D0)
-$014A   -330    AllocSignal (signalNum) (D0)
-$0150   -336    FreeSignal (signalNum) (D0)
-$0156   -342    AllocTrap (trapNum) (D0)
-$015C   -348    FreeTrap (trapNum) (D0)
-$0162   -354    AddPort (port) (A1)
-$0168   -360    RemPort (port) (A1)
-$016E   -366    PutMsg (port,message) (A0,A1)
-$0174   -372    GetMsg (port) (A0)
-$017A   -378    ReplyMsg (message) (A1)
-$0180   -384    WaitPort (port) (A0)
-$0186   -390    FindPort (name) (A1)
-$018C   -396    AddLibrary (library) (A1)
-$0192   -402    RemLibrary (library) (A1)
-$0198   -408    OldOpenLibrary (libName) (A1)
-$019E   -414    CloseLibrary (library) (A1)
-$01A4   -420    SetFunction (library,funcOffset,funcEntry) (A1,A0,D0)
-$01AA   -426    SumLibrary (library) (A1)
-$01B0   -432    AddDevice (device) (A1)
-$01B6   -438    RemDevice (device) (A1)
-$01BC   -444    OpenDevice (devName,unit,ioRequest,flags) (A0,D0,A1,D1)
-$01C2   -450    CloseDevice (ioRequest) (A1)
```

```
     -$01C8      -456     DoIO (ioRequest)(A1)
     -$01CE      -462     SendIO (ioRequest)(A1)
     -$01D4      -468     CheckIO (ioRequest)(A1)
     -$01DA      -474     WaitIO (ioRequest)(A1)
     -$01E0      -480     AbortIO (ioRequest)(A1)
     -$01E6      -486     AddRescource (rescource)(A1)
     -$01EC      -492     RemRescource (rescource)(A1)
  \ -$01F2      -498     OpenRescource (resName,version)(A1,D0)
     -$01F8      -504     RawIOInit ()
     -$01FE      -510     RawMayGetChar ()
     -$0204      -516     RawPutChar (char)(D0)
     -$020A      -522     RawDoFmt ()(A0,A1,A2,A3)
     -$0210      -528     GetCC ()
     -$0216      -534     TypeOfMem (address)(A1)
     -$021C      -540     Procedure (semaport,bidMsg)(A0,A1)
     -$0222      -546     Vacate (semaport)(A0)
     -$0228      -552     OpenLibrary (libName,version)(A1,D0)
```

graphics.library

```
     -$001E       -30     BltBitMap (srcBitMap,srcX,srcY,destBitMap,destX,destY,
                          sizeX,sizeY,minterm,mask,tempA)
                          (A0,D0,D1,A1,D2,D3,D4,D5,D6,D7,A2)
     -$0024       -36     BltTemplate (source,srcX,srcMod,destRastPort,destX,
                          destY,sizeX,sizeY)(A0,D0,D1,A1,D2,D3,D4,D5)
     -$002A       -42     ClearEOL (rastPort)(A1)
     -$0030       -48     ClearScreen (rastPort)(A1)
     -$0036       -54     TextLength (RastPort,string,count)(A1,A0,D0)
     -$003C       -60     Text (RastPort,String,count)(A1,A0,D0)
     -$0042       -66     SetFont (RAstPortID,textFont)(A1,A0)
     -$0048       -72     OpenFont (textAttr)(A0)
     -$004E       -78     CloseFont (textFont)(A1)
     -$0054       -84     AskSoftStyle (rastPort)(A1)
     -$005A       -90     SetSoftStyle (rastPort,style,enable)(A1,D0,D1)
     -$0060       -96     AddBob (bob,rastPort)(A0,A1)
     -$0066      -102     AddVSprite (vSprite,rastPort)(A0,A1)
     -$006C      -108     DoCollision (rastPort)(A1)
     -$0072      -114     DrawGList (rastPort,viewPort)(A1,A0)
     -$0078      -120     InitGels (dummyHead,dummyTail,GelsInfo)(A0,A1,A2)
     -$007E      -126     InitMasks (vSprite)(A0)
     -$0084      -132     RemIBob (bob,rastPort,viewPort)(A0,A1,A2)
     -$008A      -138     RemVSprite (vSprite)(A0)
     -$0090      -144     SetCollision (type,routine,gelsInfo)(D0,A0,A1)
     -$0096      -150     SortGList (rastPort)(A1)
     -$009C      -156     AddAnimObj (obj,animationKey,rastPort)(A0,A1,A2)
     -$00A2      -162     Animate (animationKey,rastPort)(A0,A1)
     -$00A8      -168     etGBuffers (animationObj,rastPort,doubleBuffer)
                          (A0,A1,D0)
     -$00AE      -174     InitGMasks (animationObj)(A0)
     -$00B4      -180     GelsFuncE ()
     -$00BA      -186     GelsFuncF ()
     -$00C0      -192     LoadRGB4 (viewPort,colors,count)(A0,A1,D0)
     -$00C6      -198     InitRastPort (rastPort)(A1)
     -$00CC      -204     InitVPort (viewPort)(A0)
     -$00D2      -210     MrgCop (view)(A1)
```

```
-$00D8   -216    MakeVPort (view,viewPort)(A0,A1)
-$00DE   -222    LoadView (view)(A1)
-$00E4   -228    WaitBlit ()
-$00EA   -234    SetRast (rastPort,color)(A1,D0)
-$00F0   -240    Move (rastPort,x,y)(A1,D0,D1)
-$00F6   -246    Draw (rastPort,x,y)(A1,D0,D1)
-$00FC   -252    AreaMove (rastPort,x,y)(A1,D0,D1)
-$0102   -258    AreaDraw (rastPort,x,y)(A1,D0,D1)
-$0108   -264    AreaEnd (rastPort)(A1)
-$010E   -270    WaitTOF ()
-$0114   -276    QBlit (blit)(A1)
-$011A   -282    InitArea (areaInfo,vectorTable,vectorTableSize)
                 (A0,A1,D0)
-$0120   -288    SetRGB4 (viewPort,index,r,g,b)(A0,D0,D1,D2,D3)
-$0126   -294    QBSBlit (blit)(A1)
-$012C   -300    BltClear (memory,size,flags)(A1,D0,D1)
-$0132   -306    RectFill (rastPort,xl,yl,xu,yu)(A1,D0,D1,D2,D3)
-$0138   -312    BltPattern (rastPort,ras,xl,yl,maxX,maxY,fillBytes)
                 (A1,A0,D0,D1,D2,D3,D4)
-$013E   -318    ReadPixel (rastPort,x,y)(A1,D0,D1)
-$0144   -324    WritePixel (rastPort,x,y)(A1,D0,D1)
-$014A   -330    Flood (rastPort,mode,X,y)(A1,D2,D0,D1)
-$0150   -336    PolyDraw (rastPort,count,polyTable)(A1,D0,A0)
-$0156   -342    SetAPen (rastPort,pen)(A1,D0)
-$015C   -348    SetBPen (rastPort,pen)(A1,D0)
-$0162   -354    SetDrMd (rastPort,drawMode)(A1,D0)
-$0168   -360    InitView (view)(A1)
-$016E   -366    CBump (copperList)(A1)
-$0174   -372    CMove (copperList,destination,data)(A1,D0,D1)
-$017A   -378    CWait (copperList,x,y)(A1,D0,D1)
-$0180   -384    VBeamPos ()
-$0186   -390    InitBitMap (bitMap,depth,width,heigth)(A0,D0,D1,D2)
-$018C   -396    ScrollRaster (rastPort,dX,dY,minx,miny,maxx,maxy)
                 (A1,D0,D1,D2,D3,D4,D5)
-$0192   -402    WaitBOVP (viewPort)(A0)
-$0198   -408    GetSprite (simpleSprite,num)(A0,D0)
-$019E   -414    FreeSprite (num)(D0)
-$01A4   -420    ChangeSprite (vp,simpleSprite,data)(A0,A1,A2)
-$01AA   -426    MoveSprite (viewPort,simpleSprite,x,y)(A0,A1,D0,D1)
-$01B0   -432    LockLayerRom (layer)(A5)
-$01B6   -438    UnlockLayerRom (layer)(A5)
-$01BC   -444    SyncSBitMap (1)(A0)
-$01C2   -450    CopySBitMap (11,12)(A0,A1)
-$01C8   -456    OwnBlitter ()
-$01CE   -462    DisownBlitter ()
-$01D4   -468    InitTmpRas (tmpras,buff,size)(A0,A1,D0)
-$01DA   -474    AskFont (rastPort,textAttr)(A1,A0)
-$01E0   -480    AddFont (textFont)(A1)
-$01E6   -486    RemFont (textFont)(A1)
-$01EC   -492    AllocRaster (width,heigth)(D0,D1)
-$01F2   -498    FreeRaster (planeptr,width,heigth)(A0,D0,D1)
-$01F8   -504    AndRectRegion (rgn,rect)(A0,A1)
-$01FE   -510    OrRectRegion (rgn,rect)(A0,A1)
-$0204   -516    NewRegion ()
-$020A   -522    ** reserved **
-$0210   -528    ClearRegion (rgn)(A0)
```

```
  -$0216   -534   DisposeRegion (rgn)(A0)
  -$021C   -540   FreeVPortCopLists (viewPort)(A0)
  -$0222   -546   FreeCopList (coplist)(A0)
  -$0228   -552   ClipBlit (srcrp,srcX,srcY,destrp,destX,destY,sizeX,
                   sizeY,minterm)(A0,D0,D1,A1,D2,D3,D4,D5,D6)
  -$022E   -558   XorRectRegion (rgn,rect)(A0,A1)
  -$0234   -564   FreeCprList (cprlist)(A0)
  -$023A   -570   GetColorMap (entries)(D0)
  -$0240   -576   FreeColorMap (colormap)(A0)
  -$0246   -582   GetRGB4 (colormap,entry)(A0,D0)
  -$024C   -588   ScrollVPort (vp)(A0)
  -$0252   -594   UCopperListInit (copperlist,num)(A0,D0)
  -$0258   -600   FreeGBuffers (animationObj,rastPort,
                   doubleBuffer)(A0,A1,D0)
  -$025E   -606   BltBitMapRastPort (srcbm,srcx,srcy,destrp,destX,
                   destY,sizeX,sizeY,minter)(A0,D0,D1,A1,D2,D3,D4,D5,D6)
```

icon.library

```
  -$001E   -30    GetWBObject (name)(A0)
  -$0024   -36    PutWBObject (name,object)(A0,A1)
  -$002A   -42    GetIcon (name,icon,freelist)(A0,A1,A2)
  -$0030   -48    PutIcon (name,icon)(A0,A1)
  -$0036   -54    FreeFreeList (freelist)(A0)
  -$003C   -60    FreeWBObject (WBObject)(A0)
  -$0042   -66    AllocWBObject ()
  -$0048   -72    AddFreeList (freelist,mem,size)(A0,A1,A2)
  -$004E   -78    GetDiskObject (name)(A0)
  -$0054   -84    PutDiskObject (name,diskobj)(A0,A1)
  -$005A   -90    FreeDiskObj (diskobj)(A0)
  -$0060   -96    FindToolType (toolTypeArray,typeName)(A0,A1)
  -$0066   -102   MatchToolValue (typeString,value)(A0,A1)
  -$006C   -108   BumbRevision (newname,oldname)(A0,A1)
```

intuition.library

```
  -$001E   -30    OpenIntuition ()
  -$0024   -36    Intuition (ievent)(A0)
  -$002A   -42    AddGadget (AddPtr,Gadget,Position)(A0,A1,D0)
  -$0030   -48    ClearDMRequest (Window)(A0)
  -$0036   -54    ClearMenuStrip (Window)(A0)
  -$003C   -60    ClearPointer (Window)(A0)
  -$0042   -66    CloseScreen (Screen)(A0)
  -$0048   -72    CloseWindow (Window)(A0)
  -$004E   -78    CloseWorkBench ()
  -$0054   -84    CurrentTime (Seconds,Micros)(A0,A1)
  -$005A   -90    DisplayAlert (AlertNumber,String,Height)(D0,A0,D1)
  -$0060   -96    DisplayBeep (Screen)(A0)
  -$0066   -102   DoubleClick (sseconds,smicros,cseconds,cmicros)
                   (D0,D1,D2,D3)
  -$006C   -108   DrawBorder (Rport,Border,LeftOffset,TopOffset)
                   (A0,A1,D0,D1)
  -$0072   -114   DrawImage (RPort,Image,LeftOffset,TopOffset)
                   (A0,A1,D0,D1)
  -$0078   -120   EndRequest (requester,window)(A0,A1)
```

```
-$007E    -126    GetDefPrefs (preferences,size) (A0,D0)
-$0084    -132    GetPrefs (preferences,size) (A0,D0)
-$008A    -138    InitRequester (req) (A0)
-$0090    -144    ItemAddress (MenuStrip,MenuNumber) (A0,D0)
-$0096    -150    ModifyIDCMP (Window,Flags) (A0,D0)
-$009C    -156    ModifyProp (Gadget,Ptr,Reg,Flags,HPos,VPos,HBody,
                      VBody) (A0,A1,A2,D0,D1,D2,D3,D4)
-$00A2    -162    MoveScreen (Screen,dx,dy) (A0,D0,D1)
-$00A8    -168    MoveWindow (Window,dx,dy) (A0,D0,D1)
-$00AE    -174    OffGadget (Gadget,Ptr,Req) (A0,A1,A2)
-$00B4    -180    OffMenu (Window,MenuNumber) (A0,D0)
-$00BA    -186    OnGadget (Gadget,Ptr,Req) (A0,A1,A2)
-$00C0    -192    OnMenu (Window,MenuNumber) (A0,D0)
-$00C6    -198    OpenScreen (OSArgs) (A0)
-$00CC    -204    OpenWindow (OWArgs) (A0)
-$00D2    -210    OpenWorkBench ()
-$00D8    -216    PrintIText (rp,itext,left,top) (A0,A1,D0,D1)
-$00DE    -222    RefreshGadgets (Gadgets,Ptr,Req) (A0,A1,A2)
-$00E4    -228    RemoveGadgets (RemPtr,Gadget) (A0,A1)
-$00EA    -234    ReportMouse (Window,Boolean) (A0,D0)
-$00F0    -240    Request (Requester,Window) (A0,A1)
-$00F6    -246    ScreenToBack (Screen) (A0)
-$00FC    -252    SCreenToFront (Screen) (A0)
-$0102    -258    SetDMRequest (Window,req) (A0,A1)
-$0108    -264    SetMenuStrip (Window,Menu) (A0,A1)
-$010E    -270    SetPointer (Window,Pointer,Height,Width,XOffset,
                      YOffset) (A0,A1,D0,D1,D2,D3)
-$0114    -276    SetWindowTitles (Window,windowTitle,screenTitle)
                      (A0,A1,A2)
-$011A    -282    ShowTitle (Screen,ShowIt) (A0,D0)
-$0120    -288    SizeWindow (Window,dx,dy) (A0,D0,D1)
-$0126    -294    ViewAddress ()
-$012C    -300    ViewPortAddress (Window) (A0)
-$0132    -306    WindowToBack (Window) (A0)
-$0138    -312    WindowToFront (Window) (A0)
-$013E    -318    WindowLimits (Window,minwidth,minheight,maxwidth,
                      maxheight) (A0,D0,D1,D2,D3)
-$0144    -324    SetPrefs (preferences,size,flag) (A0,D0,D1)
-$014A    -330    IntuiTextLength (itext) (A0)
-$0150    -336    WBenchToBack ()
-$0156    -342    WBenchToFront ()
-$015C    -348    AutoRequest (WIndow,Body,PText,NText,PFlag,NFlag,W,H)
                      (A0,A1,A2,A3,D0,D1,D2,D3)
-$0162    -354    BeginRefresh (Window) (A0)
-$0168    -360    BuildSysRequest (Window,Body,PosText,NegText,Flags,
                      W,H)  (A0,A1,A2,A3,D0,D1,D2)
-$016E    -366    EndRefresh (Window,Complete) (A0,D0)
-$0174    -372    FreeSysRequest (Window) (A0)
-$017A    -378    MakeScreen (Screen) (A0)
-$0180    -384    RemakeDisplay ()
-$0186    -390    RethinkDisplay ()
-$018C    -396    AllocRemember (RememberKey,Size,Flags) (A0,D0,D1)
-$0192    -402    AlohaWorkbench (wbport) (A0)
-$0198    -408    FreeRemember (RememberKey,ReallyForget) (A0,D0)
-$019E    -414    LockIBase (dontknow) (D0)
-$01A4    -420    UnlockIBase (IBLock) (A0)
```

layers.library

```
-$001E    -30    InitLayers (li)(A0)
-$0024    -36    CreateUpfrontLayer (li,bm,x0,y0,x1,y1,flags,bm2)
                 (A0,A1,D0,D1,D2,D3,D4,A2)
-$002A    -42    CreateBehindLayer (li,bm,x0,y0,x1,y1,flags,bm2)
                 (A0,A1,D0,D1,D2,D3,D4,A2)
-$0030    -48    UpfrontLayer (li,layer)(A0,A1)
-$0036    -54    BehindLayer (li,layer)(A0,A1)
-$003C    -60    MoveLayer (li,layer,dx,dy)(A0,A1,D0,D1)
-$0042    -66    SizeLayer (li,layer,dx,dy)(A0,A1,D0,D1)
-$0048    -72    ScrollLayer (li,layer,dx,dy)(A0,A1,D0,D1)
-$004E    -78    BeginUpdate (layer)(A0)
-$0054    -84    EndUpdate (layer)(A0)
-$005A    -90    DeleteLayer (li,layer)(A0,A1)
-$0060    -96    LockLayer (li,layer)(A0,A1)
-$0066    -102   UnlockLayer (li,layer)(A0,A1)
-$006C    -108   LockLayers (li)(A0)
-$0072    -114   UnlockLayers (li)(A0)
-$0078    -120   LockLayerInfo (li)(A0)
-$007E    -126   SwapBitsRastPortClipRect (rp,cr)(A0,A1)
-$0084    -132   WhichLayer (li,x,y)(A0,D0,D1)
-$008A    -138   UnlockLayerInfo (li)(A0)
-$0090    -144   NewLayerInfo ()
-$0096    -150   DisposeLayerInfo (li)(A0)
-$009C    -156   FattenLayerInfo (li)(A0)
-$00A2    -162   ThinLayerInfo (li)(A0)
-$00A8    -168   MoveLayerInFrontOf (layer_to_move,
                 layer_to_be_in_front_of)(A0,A1)
```

mathffp.library

```
-$001E    -30    SPFix (float)(D0)
-$0024    -36    SPFlt (integer)(D0)
-$002A    -42    SPCmp (leftFloat,rightFloat)(D1,D0)
-$0030    -48    SPTst (float)(D1)
-$0036    -54    SPAbs (float)(D0)
-$003C    -60    SPNeg (float)(D0)
-$0042    -66    SPAdd (leftFloat,rightFloat)(D1,D0)
-$0048    -72    SPSub (leftFloat,rightFloat)(D1,D0)
-$004E    -78    SPMul (leftFloat,rightFloat)(D1,D0)
-$0054    -84    SPDiv (leftFloat,rightFloat)(D1,D0)
```

mathieeedoubbas.library

```
-$001E    -30    IEEEDPFix (integer,integer)(D0,D1)
-$0024    -36    IEEEDPFlt (integer)(D0)
-$002A    -42    IEEEDPCmp (integer,integer,integer,integer)
                 (D0,D1,D2,D3)
-$0030    -48    IEEEDPTst (integer,integer)(D0,D1)
-$0036    -54    IEEEDPAbs (integer,integer)(D0,D1)
-$003C    -60    IEEEDPNeg (integer,integer)(D0,D1)
```

```
-$0042    -66     IEEEDPAdd (integer,integer,integer,integer)
                  (D0,D1,D2,D3)
-$0048    -72     IEEEDPSub (integer,integer,integer,integer)
                  (D0,D1,D2,D3)
-$004E    -78     IEEEDPMul (integer,integer,integer,integer)
                  (D0,D1,D2,D3)
-$0054    -84     IEEEDPDiv (integer,integer,integer,integer)
                  (D0,D1,D2,D3)
```

mathtrans.library

```
-$001E    -30     SPAtan (float)(D0)
-$0024    -36     SPSin (float)(D0)
-$002A    -42     SPCos (float)(D0)
-$0030    -48     SPTan (float)(D0)
-$0036    -54     SPSincos (leftFloat,rightFloat)(D1,D0)
-$003C    -60     SPSinh (float)(D0)
-$0042    -66     SPCosh (float)(D0)
-$0048    -72     SPTanh (float)(D0)
-$004E    -78     SPExp (float)(D0)
-$0054    -84     SPLog (float)(D0)
-$005A    -90     SPPow (leftFloat,rightFloat)(D1,D0)
-$0060    -96     SPSqrt (float)(D0)
-$0066    -102    SPTieee (float)(D0)
-$006C    -108    SPFieee (float)(D0)
-$0072    -114    SPAsin (float)(D0)
-$0078    -120    SPAcos (float)(D0)
-$007E    -126    SPLog10 (float)(D0)
```

potgo.library

```
-$0006    -6      AllocPotBits (bits)(D0)
-$000C    -12     FreePotBits (bits)(D0)
-$0012    -18     WritePotgo (word,mask)(D0,D1)
```

timer.library

```
-$002A    -42     AddTime (dest,src)(A0,A1)
-$0030    -48     SubTime (dest,src)(A0,A1)
-$0036    -54     CmpTime (dest,src)(A0,A1)
```

translator.library

```
-$001E    -30     Translate (inputString,inputLength,outputBuffer,
                  bufferSize)(A0,D0,A1,D1)
```

Overview of MC68000 instructions

Abbreviations (Symbols) used

Label	A label (address)
Reg	Register
An	Address register n
Dn	Data register n
Source	Source operand
Dest	Destination operand
<ea>	Address or Register
#n	Direct value

Mnemonic		Meaning
ABCD	Source,Dest	Addition of two BCD numbers
ADD	Source,Dest	Binary addition
ADDA	Source,An	Binary addition to an address register
ADDI	#n,<ea>	Addition with a constant
ADDQ	#n,<ea>	Fast addition of a constant which only needs bits 0 to 7
ADDX	Source,Dest	Addition with transfer to X flag
AND	Source,Dest	Logical AND
ANDI	#n,<ea>	Logical AND with a constant
ASL	n,<ea>	Arithmetic shift left ($*2^n$)
ASR	n,<ea>	Arithmetic shift right ($/2^n$)
Bcc	Label	Branch depending on the condition
BCHG	#n,<ea>	Change bit n (0 becomes 1 and vice versa)
BCLR	#n,<ea>	Erase bit n
BRA	Label	Unconditional branch (similar to JMP)
BSET	#n,<ea>	Set bit n
BSR	Label	Branch to a subroutine. The return address is put on the stack just like for the JSR command. You return with a RTS command.
BTST	#n,<ea>	Test bit n, the result goes in the Z flag
CHK	<ea>,Dx	Check a data register
CLR	<ea>	Erase an operand
CMP	Source,Dest	Compare two operands
CMPA	<ea>,An	Compare with an address register
CMPI	#n,<ea>	Compare with a constant
CMPM	Source,Dest	Compare two operands in memory
DBcc	Reg,Label	Check condition, decrement and branch. This command is used with loops a lot.
DIVS	Source,Dest	Sign correct division of a 32 bit destination operand by a 16 bit source operand. The result goes in the LO word of the destination long word. The remainder goes in the HI word.
DIVU	Source,Dest	Division without sign, similar to DIVS

Mnemonic		Meaning
EOR	Source,Dest	Exclusive OR
EORI	#n,<ea>	Exclusive OR with a constant
EXG	Rn,Rn	Exchange the contents of two registers (don't mix this up with SWAP).
EXT	Dn	Sign correct extension to double width
JMP	Label	Jump to an address (similar to BRA)
JSR	Label	Jump to a subroutine. The return address is put on the stack. A RTS returns to the command after this one.
LEA	<ea>,An	Load an effective address into An
LINK	An,#n	Build stack area
LSL	n,<ea>	Logical shift left
LSR	n,<ea>	Logical shift right
MOVE	Source,Dest	Transfer a value from Source to Dest.
MOVE	SR,<ea>	Transfer the Status register contents
MOVE	<ea>,SR	Transfer the Status register contents
MOVE	<ea>,CCR	Load flags
MOVE	USP,<ea>	Transfer the User Stackpointer
MOVE	<ea>,USP	Transfer the User Stackpointer
MOVEA	<ea>,An	Transfer a value to address register An
MOVEM	Regs,<ea>	Transfer several registers at the same time
MOVEM	<ea>,Regs	Transfer several registers at the same time
MOVEP	Source,Dest	Transfer data to peripheral devices
MOVEQ	#n,Dn	Transfer a 8 bit constant to data register Dn quickly
MULS	Source,Dest	Sign correct multiplications of two words to a long word
MULU	Source,Dest	Multiplication without sign, similar to MULS
NBCD	Source,Dest	Negate a BCD number (Nine's complement)
NEG	<ea>	Negate an operator (Two's complement)
NEGX	<ea>	Negates an operator with transfer
NOP		No Operation
NOT	<ea>	Inverts an operand (0s become 1s and vice versa)
OR	Source,Dest	Logical OR
ORI	#n,<ea>	Logical OR with a constant
PEA	<ea>	Put an address on the stack
RESET		Reset peripheral device (carefull!)
ROL	n,<ea>	Rotate left
ROR	n,<ea>	Rotate right
ROXL	n,<ea>	Rotate left with transfer to X flag
ROXR	n,<ea>	Rotate right with transfer to X flag
RTE		Return from an Exception
RTR		Return and load flags
RTS		Return from a subroutine (after a BSR or JSR command)
SBCD	Source,Dest	Subtract two BCD coded numbers
Scc	<ea>	Set a byte to -1 if the condition is fulfilled
STOP		Stop work. (careful!) Leads to a TRAPV Exception.

Mnemonic		Meaning
SUB	Source,Dest	Binary subtraction.
SUBA	<ea>,An	Binary subtraction from an address register
SUBI	#n,<ea>	Subtract a constant.
SUBQ	#n,<ea>	Fast subtraction of a three bit constant.
SUBX	Source,Dest	Subtraction with transfer to X flag
SWAP	Dn	Exchange the two halves of the register (the upper and lower 16 bits)
TAS	<ea>	Test a bit and set bit 7
TRAP	#n	Jump to an Exception
TRAPV		Check if overflow flag set, then TST <ea>. Test an operand and set the N and Z flag
UNLK	An	Un-link stack area

Index

Companion Diskette

For your convenience, the program listings contained in this book are available on an Amiga formatted floppy diskette. You should order the diskette if you want to use the programs, but don't want to type them in from the listings in the book.

All programs on the diskette have been fully tested. You can change the programs for your particular needs. The diskette is available for $14.95 plus $2.00 ($5.00 foreign) for postage and handling.

When ordering, please give your name and shipping address. Enclose a check, money order or credit card information. Mail your order to:

Abacus Software
5370 52nd Street SE
Grand Rapids, MI 49512

Or for fast service, call **616/698-0330**.
Credit Card orders only **1-800-451-4319**.

Abacus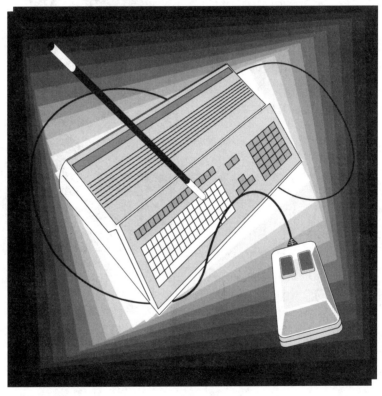
Amiga Catalog

Order Toll Free 1-800-451-4319

Amiga for Beginners

A perfect introductory book if you're a new or prospective Amiga owner. **Amiga for Beginners** introduces you to Intuition (the Amiga's graphic interface), the mouse, windows and the versatile CLI. This first volume in our Amiga series explains every practical aspect of the Amiga in plain English. Clear, step-by-step instructions for common Amiga tasks. **Amiga for Beginners** is all the info you need to get up and running.

Topics include:

- Unpacking and connecting the Amiga components
- Starting up your Amiga
- Exploring the Extras disk
- Taking your first step in AmigaBASIC programming language
- AmigaDOS functions
- Customizing the Workbench
- Using the CLI to perform "housekeeping" chores
- First Aid, Keyword, Technical appendixes
- Glossary

Item #B021 ISBN 1-55755-021-2. Suggested retail price: $16.95

Companion Diskette not available for this book.

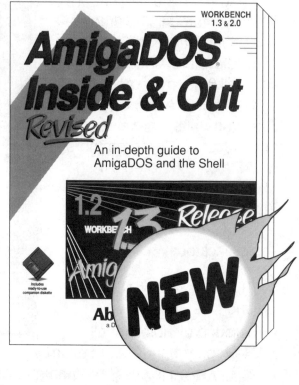

The Best Amiga Tricks & Tips

The Best Amiga Tricks & Tips is a great collection of Workbench, CLI and BASIC programming "quick-hitters", hints and application programs. You'll be able to make your programs more user-friendly with pull-down menus, sliders and tables. BASIC programmers will learn all about gadgets, windows, graphic fades, HAM mode, 3D graphics and more.

The Best Amiga Tricks & Tips includes a complete list of BASIC tokens and multitasking input and a fast and easy print routine. If you're an advanced programmer, you'll discover the hidden powers of your Amiga.

- Using the new AmigaDOS, Workbench and Preferences 1.3 and Release 2.0
- Tips on using the new utilities on Extras 1.3
- Customizing Kickstart for Amiga 1000 users
- Enhancing BASIC using ColorCycle and mouse sleeper
- Disabling FastRAM and disk drives
- Using the mount command
- Writing an Amiga virus killer program
- Disk drive operations and disk commands
- Learn machine language calls.

Includes companion diskette

Item # B107 ISBN 1-55755-107-3.
Suggested retail price $29.95